THE WHAT WORKS CENTRES

Lessons and Insights from an
Evidence Movement

Edited by
Michael Sanders and Jonathan Breckon

With a foreword by
David Halpern

D1612449

First published in Great Britain in 2023 by

Policy Press, an imprint of
Bristol University Press
University of Bristol
1–9 Old Park Hill
Bristol
BS2 8BB
UK
t: +44 (0)117 374 6645
e: bup-info@bristol.ac.uk

Details of international sales and distribution partners are available at
policy.bristoluniversitypress.co.uk

British Library Cataloguing in Publication Data
A catalogue record for this book is available from the British Library

ISBN 978-1-4473-6509-9 paperback
ISBN 978-1-4473-6510-5 ePub
ISBN 978-1-4473-6511-2 ePdf

Cover design: Nicky Borowiec
Front cover image: Adobe Stock/dule964
Bristol University Press and Policy Press use environmentally
responsible print partners.
Printed and bound in Great Britain by CPI Group (UK) Ltd,
Croydon, CR0 4YY

FSC
www.fsc.org
MIX
Paper | Supporting
responsible forestry
FSC® C013604

Contents

List of figures and tables

Figures

Tables

List of abbreviations

ANPR   Automatic Number Plate Recognition
CHI   Centre for Homelessness Impact
COM-B   Capability Opportunity Motivation – Behaviour
DWP   Department for Work and Pensions
EAB   Employer Advisory Board
EBIs   evidence-based interventions
EBP   evidence-based policing
EEF   Education Endowment Foundation
EIF   Early Intervention Foundation
EPPI-Centre   Evidence for Policy and Practice Information and
              Co-ordinating Centre
ESRC   Economic and Social Research Council
ETF   Evaluation Task Force
ISF   Interactive Systems Framework
KCPO   Knife Crime Prevention Order
MetREC   Metropolitan Police Research Ethics Committee
NEET   not in education, employment or training
NELI   Nuffield Early Language Intervention
NHS   National Health Service
NICE   National Institute for Clinical Excellence (renamed
              National Institute for Health and Care Excellence)
OfS   Office for Students
PEEL   Police Effectiveness, Efficiency, and Legitimacy
PPIW   Public Policy Institute for Wales
QALY   Quality Adjusted Life Year
REA   Rapid Evidence Assessment
RCT   randomised controlled trial
RJC   Restorative Justice Conference
SEBP   Society of Evidence Based Policing
TASO   Centre for Transforming Access and Student Outcomes
              in Higher Education

WCPP	Wales Centre for Public Policy
WWCCR	What Works Centre for Crime Reduction
WWCSC	What Works for Children's Social Care

Notes on contributors

Annette Boaz is Professor in Health and Social Care Policy at the London School of Hygiene and Tropical Medicine. She is a leading expert on the impact of research on policy and practice and was one of the founding editors of the journal *Evidence & Policy*.

Jonathan Breckon is an independent research consultant specialising in evidence-based policy making and practice. He was previously the founding director of the Alliance for Useful Evidence at Nesta. He is studying for a PhD at St George's University of London and Kingston University.

Jo Casebourne is Chief Executive of the Early Intervention Foundation. Previously, Jo served as director of development at the Institute for Government, leading the institute's work on public services and English devolution, after earlier stints as director of public and social innovation at Nesta and director of research at the Centre for Economic and Social Inclusion. Jo has spent the last 20 years conducting research on public services, social innovation, disadvantaged groups in the labour market, welfare-to-work, employment and skills, work–life balance and child care. Jo's PhD examined the impact of welfare reform in the US and the UK on work and poverty for lone-parent families.

Jane Colechin is Head of Evidence and Evaluation at the Youth Futures Foundation. She is a social researcher with a decade of experience working on high-profile labour market, education and welfare reform evaluations and studies. Jane has particular expertise in theory-led evaluations and ensuring co-design is part of evaluation and programme delivery and ensures that rigorous and youth-informed principles are used in all of the Youth Futures Foundation's evaluation and evidence processes.

Catherine Fitzgerald is Senior Research Manager at the Youth Futures Foundation.

Becky Francis is Chief Executive of the Education Endowment Foundation. Becky was previously director of the UCL Institute of Education, which is ranked number 1 in the world for education in the international QS rankings. Her prior roles include Professor of Education and Social Justice at King's College London, Director of Education at the RSA and Standing Advisor to the Parliamentary Education Select Committee. Throughout her career, Becky has sought to maximise the impact of academic research by working closely with teachers and policy makers. She has spearheaded high-profile research programmes assessing the impact of major reforms in the English school system on educational inequalities, and is sought out internationally as an advisor to governments on education policy.

David Gough is Professor of Evidence Informed Policy and Practice and the Director of the Evidence for Policy and Practice Information and Co-ordinating Centre in University College London's Social Research Institute. He previously worked at the University of Glasgow and Japan Women's University. Until around 1998 he worked predominantly on research on child protection and abuse, but since then has spent most of his time on the study of methods for research synthesis and the study of research use.

Chris Goulden leads the Impact and Evidence at the Youth Futures Foundation. Previously he was Deputy Director of Evidence and Impact at the Joseph Rowntree Foundation, where he has worked as Head and Deputy Director of Policy and Research, since joining the organisation as Poverty Programme Manager in 2003. He previously served as a policy analyst with the Prime Minister's Strategy Unit and Senior Research Officer at the Home Office.

David Halpern is Chief Executive of the Behavioural Insights Team. David has led the team since its inception in 2010. Prior to that, David was the first Research Director of the Institute for

Government and between 2001 and 2007 was the Chief Analyst at the Prime Minister's Strategy Unit. David was also appointed as the What Works National Advisor in July 2013. He supports the What Works Network and leads efforts to improve the use of evidence across government. Before entering government, David held tenure at Cambridge and posts at Oxford and Harvard. He has written several books and papers on areas relating to behavioural insights and wellbeing, including *Social capital* (2005), the *Hidden wealth of nations* (2010), *Online harms and manipulation* (2019) and is co-author of the MINDSPACE report. In 2015, David wrote a book about the team entitled *Inside the nudge unit: How small changes can make a big difference.*

Nancy Hey is Executive Director of the What Works Centre for Wellbeing. Nancy Hey is a global leader in the field of wellbeing. Prior to setting up the What Works Centre for Wellbeing, she worked in the UK civil service in nine departments as a policy professional and coach, delivering cross-UK government policies including on constitutional reform. She has worked with the UK's top civil servants to introduce wellbeing into public policy and to establish the professional policy community in the UK. She has degrees in law and in coaching and development, specialising in emotions, and is a passionate advocate for learning systems.

Ryan Howsham is Strategy Advisor at the Youth Futures Foundation. Ryan supports the development and delivery of the Youth Futures Foundation's organisational strategy to transform youth employment and is responsible for turning complex information into meaningful options to achieve systemic change. Ryan previously worked in local government, most recently focusing on developing approaches to deliver sustainable economic growth in Greater Cambridge, including responding to the impacts of the COVID-19 pandemic.

Jonathan Kay is Head of Evidence Synthesis at the Education Endowment Foundation (EEF). He works to promote the use of evidence in schools and policy making. Jon also leads on the EEF's evidence synthesis work through the Teaching and Learning Toolkit. Jon has been at the EEF since 2014 and previously led the publication of EEF's evaluation reports. Prior to joining the EEF, he worked at the National Education Trust and on a research project on using text messages to increase parental engagement.

Omar Khan is Director of the Centre for Transforming Access and Student Outcomes in Higher Education (TASO). Omar has led TASO's transition into an independent charity, developing its team and strategy to widen participation in higher education and eliminate equality gaps between students. His research and professional background has focused on equality and social mobility, particularly in education and the labour market, and he regularly speaks on these topics in the UK and globally. Omar joined TASO from race equality think tank the Runnymede Trust, where he had been director since 2014, growing the organisation and increasing its profile. He completed a doctorate in political science from the University of Oxford in 2008.

Eliza Kozman is Deputy Director of the Centre for Transforming Access and Student Outcomes in Higher Education (TASO). Before joining TASO Eliza worked for the Behavioural Insights Team where she designed and implemented research projects with a focus on reducing inequality in education. Eliza holds a PhD from University College London. In her academic work she uses experimental methods to test ways of improving education outcomes for disadvantaged students. Eliza has a strong interest in social mobility and a background in higher education policy.

Jane Lewis is Managing Director of the Centre for Evidence and Implementation, a global evidence intermediary, where she leads evaluation, evidence synthesis, implementation support and capacity-building projects to embed evidence in policy and services for children and families. She has a long career in developing evidence and supporting its use in policy-making and in practice. She was previously Head of UK Programme Development and Quality with Save The Children UK (SCUK), leading on innovation, implementation, evaluation and scale-up strategies for SCUK's UK programmes, and before that she was Director of Research in Practice, supporting evidence-informed practice in children's services in local government and non-governmental organisations.

Ben Linton is Chief Inspector in the Metropolitan Police Service where he works in the Strategic Insight Unit. He is the London Coordinator of the Society of Evidence Based Policing.

Harry Madgwick is Research and Policy Manager at the Education Endowment Foundation. He works with the Department for Education and other policy makers to ensure evidence underpins decision making, as well as the content of statutory and non-statutory teacher development programmes. Harry joined the Education Endowment Foundation in September 2019, while completing a master's degree in social justice and education. Previous to this Harry taught English at a comprehensive secondary school in Islington, North London.

Steve Martin is Director of the Wales Centre for Public Policy and Professor of Public Policy and Management in the Cardiff Business School. Steve leads the Wales Centre for Public Policy (www. wcpp.org.uk). Funded by the Economic and Social Research Council and Welsh Government, the Centre is a member of the What Works Network. It collaborates with researchers from across the UK and internationally to bridge the gap between academia and policy makers in order to provide ministers, civil servants and public service leaders with the best available evidence on key policy challenges. In 2019 the Centre was a finalist in the prestigious Economic and Social Research Council's Impact on Public Policy awards and alongside its work with policy makers it is conducting a programme of leading edge research to advance understanding of evidence use in policy making.

Danielle Mason is Head of Policy, What Works Centre for Local Economic Growth. Danielle has spent 15 years working to improve the use of high-quality evidence in policy making, as an academic, researcher and civil servant. She joined the team from the RSA where she was the Education Director. Prior to that she spent four years as Head of Research at the Education Endowment Foundation, where she oversaw the development of their evidence toolkit as a global resource, creating versions for use in Australia, South America and Europe.

Robyn Mildon, PhD, is an internationally recognised figure in the field of implementation science, evidence synthesis and knowledge translation, and programme and policy evaluations in health, education and human services. She is Founding Executive Director of the Centre for Evidence and Implementation (www. ceiglobal.org), a global social purpose organisation whose work now spans across eight countries. She is also Adjunct Associate Professor at Monash University, Visiting Associate Professor at the Yong Loo Lin School of Medicine, National University of Singapore, and Co-Director of the recently established Behavioural and Implementation Science Interventions, National University of Singapore.

Max Nathan is Associate Professor in Applied Urban Sciences at CASA, University College London and in the Urban Programme at the Centre for Economic Performance. He is an economic geographer with a background in public policy. His work looks at urban economic development, especially innovation systems and clusters, immigration and diversity and urban public policy. Max co-founded the Centre for Cities and the What Works Centre for Local Economic Growth, and has over 15 years' experience in think tanks, consultancy and government.

Sandy Oliver is Professor of Public Policy at University College London's Social Research Institute and Distinguished Visiting Professor in the Faculty of the Humanities at the University of Johannesburg. She is a founding member of the Evidence for Policy and Practice Information and Coordinating Centre and developed a stream of work addressing Perspectives, Participation and Research. She directed the work of the Social Science Research Unit from 2015 to 2021. She is a member of the Board of the Campbell Collaboration, a Cochrane editor with two review groups – Consumers and Communication, and Infectious Diseases – and a co-convenor of the Cochrane Agenda and Priority Setting Methods Group. She is a founder member of the Partnership for Evidence and Equity in Responsive Social Systems and co-edits *Research for All*, an open-access, peer-reviewed journal focusing on research that involves universities and communities, services or industries working together.

Eleanor Ott is Senior Advisor at the Centre for Evidence and Implementation. She has led research to improve the lives of children and families facing adversity across academia, government and non-profit organisations. She is also a research methodologist focused on evidence synthesis and systematic reviews, mixed-methods research, and impact evaluations. Previously, Eleanor managed research, knowledge exchange, impact evaluations and systematic reviews around children's social care at the Rees Centre at the University of Oxford and led the Humanitarian Evidence Programme at Oxfam. She has a doctorate from the Centre for Evidence-Based Intervention at the University of Oxford, where she studied as a Rhodes Scholar. Dr Ott also holds an MSc in Refugee and Forced Migration Studies from the University of Oxford. Eleanor has been a consultant to the UN Refugee Agency and previously worked as a research analyst and Truman-Albright Fellow in the US Department of Health and Human Services, improving research on children and families.

Henry G. Overman is Professor of Economic Geography in the Department of Geography and Environment at the London School of Economics and Director of the What Works Centre for Local Economic Growth. He is Research Director of the Centre for Economics Performance, and was formerly director of the Spatial Economics Research Centre.

Anna Round is Head of Research and Impact at the Youth Futures Foundation. Her research experience includes extensive work on education and skills, regional labour markets and economies, and young people's issues. Before joining the Youth Futures Foundation she worked at the Institute for Public Policy North, after over a decade as a researcher in higher education and in government.

Michael Sanders is Professor of Public Policy in the Policy Institute at King's College London. He has spent much of his career working in and around the UK's What Works Network. He is Associate at the Centre for Homelessness Impact, Academic Lead at the Centre for Transforming Access and Student Outcomes and Head of Evidence at the What Work Centre for Wellbeing, and was previously Chief Executive of What Works for Children's Social Care.

Lígia Teixeira is the founding Chief Executive of the Centre for Homelessness Impact, a member of the What Works Network. She set up the centre in 2018 and led the feasibility study which preceded its creation while at Crisis UK. Lígia is bringing 'what works' methodology to homelessness: the use of reliable evidence and reason to improve outcomes with existing resources. In 2019 Lígia was conferred the Award of Fellow of the Academy of Social Sciences for her contribution to social science. Lígia was previously at Crisis UK, where over a period of nine years she led the organisation's evidence and data programme. Lígia was awarded a PhD from the Government Department of the London School of Economics in 2007.

Nick Timmins is the author of *The five giants: a biography of the welfare state*, of *Glaziers and window breakers: The role of the Secretary of State for Health, in their own words*, and co-authored *A short history of NICE*. He is a senior fellow at the Institute for Government, a senior associate of the Nuffield Trust, and a visiting professor in social policy at the London School of Economics. He was president of the Social Policy Association between 2008 and 2011 and is an honorary fellow of the Royal College of Physicians.

Rachel Tuffin is Executive Director at the College of Policing responsible for creating and sharing knowledge and good practice in policing in England and Wales. She led the development of the College's What Works Centre and its authoritative toolkit. Her published studies cover issues ranging from neighbourhood policing and what works in crime reduction to police/researcher partnerships, and from tackling race hate and the recruitment and career progression of minority ethnic police officers, to leadership and flexible working. Rachel previously led research and knowledge teams in the Home Office and National

Policing Improvement Agency, has been seconded to several independent and UK government police reviews and has advised governments internationally.

Ella Whelan is passionate about improving children's social care and spent 4 years working in a North London children's home. She has previously published on inequalities and the what works network, lesbian, gay, bisexual, transgender, queer and other people and care leavers' experiences of homelessness. Ella has an MA in Child's studies from King's College London and currently is a Research Association Research Associate at What Works for Children's Social Care where leads on the implementation and process evaluation for the Safeguarding Families, Protecting Children programme.

Acknowledgements

The work of creating this book has, like the creation of evidence-based policy itself, only been possible because of the work of a great many people. As well as our excellent chapter contributors, we are grateful to everyone who has produced the evidence about which we are able to talk, and who has driven forward the What Works agenda in the UK and further afield. Notable thanks are due to Sir Kevan Collins and the late Lord Jeremy Heywood for their roles in changing the way we think about policy-relevant research forever and for the better. We are also very grateful for the challenge and interest from fellow travellers in Australia, France, the US and Canada, and from the support of What Works champions in the UK such as Jen Gold, David Gough, Sir Geoff Mulgan, Ruth Puttick, Phil Sooben, Jonathan Shepherd, Howard White, Greg Wilkinson and the indefatigable David Halpern who showed the value of this agenda to so many across Whitehall, and beyond. For their role in coordinating this agenda, thanks are also due to the various incarnations of the Cabinet Office What Works Team and latterly Evaluation Taskforce, particularly its leaders Danielle Mason, Laura Bainton, Jen Gold and Catherine Hutchinson. Finally, thank you to Ella Whelan for her amazing work in making this book happen.

Foreword

David Halpern
What Works National Advisor and Chief Executive
of the Behavioural Insights Team

'What Works Centres' are becoming an increasingly familiar part of the policy and professional landscape. In addition to the existing centres – covering more than a £250 billion expenditure – there is now a steady stream of interest in creating more.

Yet when the National Institute for Clinical Excellence (NICE) – in many ways the blueprint for later What Works Centres – was created in 1999, many doubted that it would survive to the next election. It was intended to get politicians, and the Department of Health, out of judgements about which treatments worked and for what. Yet senior figures feared that as soon as the young institution dared to say 'no' – that a given drug was not cost-effective – all hell would break loose.

Sure enough, it didn't take long for angry calls to be received in Whitehall from a major pharmaceutical company demanding that NICE guidance against its product be revoked. Against the expectations of many, the line was held, and the first of today's What Work Centres went on to help shape and guide the clinical practices of a generation.

At the time NICE was created, there was talk about creating a 'social policy NICE'. Archie Cochrane himself nodded towards the need to extend such evidence-based approaches to other fields in an epilogue to his famous 1972 book *Effectiveness and efficiency* (Cochrane, 1972).

Yet it was not until after the 2010 election that serious work began into the wider application of the What Works approach and centres. A number of factors helped spark the decade of institution-building that followed.

First, the fiscal context sharpened minds. The UK faced a structural deficit of 8 per cent. Against this background, tough questions were being asked about what programmes and activities merited protecting – what worked and at what cost? Second, a weird part of No 10 – the Behavioural Insights Team – starting running randomised controlled trials.[1] The rapid and practical conclusions these gave rise to helped to popularise experimental methods. Third, senior figures in the administration, including the new Cabinet Secretary Jeremy Heywood, the Cabinet Office Minister Oliver Letwin and the Chief Secretary to the Treasury Danny Alexander, came to support the idea – not least with Jeremy's decision to major on the idea at his first speech in 2012.

Alongside NICE, we borrowed heavily from the model and experience of Washington State Institute for Public Policy, and spent long sessions with its inspirational head, Steve Aos.[2] Indeed, it was an example from Washington State that persuaded UK Treasury ministers to first back the What Works approach – that Washington State legislature was persuaded against spending US$2 billion on a supermax prison on the basis that other youth interventions were much more cost-effective at reducing crime (just the kind of evidence the Treasury was looking for ...).

By 2013, the first clutch of new What Works Centres had been founded. These covered education (the Education Endowment Foundation), early intervention (the Early Intervention Foundation), crime and policing (What Works Centre for Crime Reduction) and local economic growth (the What Works Centre for Local Economic Growth). Against the tough fiscal background, and the politics and fragmentation of Whitehall, the centres were very different in their funding and form, but they had a common purpose and 'theory of change'. It was an evidence-based project built around a simple trilogy: 'generate–translate–adopt'.

At the core of the project was 'translation' – to get useful evidence into the hands of frontline practitioners. Answers to the questions and decisions they had to make every day – and on the basis of the best evidence that could be assembled. As Steve Aos had put it, centres needed to produce 'Consumer

Reports' – the US equivalent of 'Which?' – for busy public service professionals.

A decade on, there are now 14 officially recognised What Works Centres, many of which have written for this book.[3] As I write, there are active discussions about creating new What Works Centres – or extending existing ones – into further areas such as climate change; food systems; gender and race equality; and other public service areas not currently covered (such as probation, prisons and other parts of the Criminal Justice System). There are also new challenges, such as addressing the overlap between the What Work Centres that touch on different aspects of youth, and of course squaring up to the weaknesses of the evidence base laid bare in many areas by the scrutiny of the What Works Centres.

Over the decade from 2011 to 2021, the What Works approach has moved from 'guerrilla action' to mainstream (or close to it). There have been many milestones along this journey. These include both breakthrough results by the What Works Centres, and procedural changes such as the progressive revision of the Treasury's famous 'Green Book' to put more weight on the need for establishing 'what works'.

One of the most important developments of recent years was, appropriately enough, rooted in an analysis of how much government was itself evaluating what works. An analysis conducted by Treasury, Cabinet Office and the Behavioural Insights Team found that only 8 per cent of more than £400 billion of new spending was subject to any meaningful or robust impact evaluation. It was a statistic that shocked ministers, and was highlighted publicly by Michael Gove in his Ditchley speech.[4] It also helped catalyse growing Treasury interest, and was later picked up by the National Audit Office to add extra pressure.

As a consequence, in 2021, the Treasury funded the creation of the new Evaluation Task Force (ETF; jointly between the Cabinet Office and His Majesty's Treasury). This incorporated and enlarged the original 'What Works' team in the Cabinet Office, but also added a substantial 'Accelerator Fund' for new evaluations; leverage over a renewed £200 million joint outcomes fund; and more muscular pressure on departments through the Spending Review to genuinely find out 'what works'.

It is still early days to know the scale of impact that the ETF will have, but its influence can already be seen in the renewal of funding to existing What Works Centres and in the increased profile given to evaluation across government. In one of its earliest activities, the ETF organised a four-day event in Spring 2022 for public servants on evaluation, with speeches from Cabinet Office and Treasury ministers, sessions led by Permanent Secretaries from multiple departments; and of course a heavy presence from the What Works Centres.

We have come a long way from the uncertain early days of NICE more than 20 years ago. It is something to be celebrated. Yet we are still just scratching the surface. The UK spends around £1 trillion a year – itself a fraction of the global expenditure of governments. We have shocking little knowledge about which of this expenditure does good or harm, nor what alternatives might work better.

In the spirit of this book – as its authors seek to learn what works from 'What Works' – let me finally share my own suggestions on ten things we will need to do over the coming decade.[5]

1. *Map the gaps.* What don't we know? This should directly guide our research programmes and funders, including through the updating of department 'Areas of Research Interest', as well as likely spark a next generation of 'What Works Programmes' and where necessary the creation of new What Works Centres. At its core, we need to have the bravery and humility to be open about questions we don't have the answers to.
2. *Build the skills.* We need public servants – and a policy profession – that can tell the difference between a good and a bad piece of evidence, and has the skills and methods to build evaluation into programmes and systems. In a near future, it should be hard to get into the Senior Civil Service without demonstrating competency in evaluation and other methods that make it possible to answer the question: 'What works?'
3. *Expand the pipeline.* We need to increase the volume, as well as quality, of the What Works evidence base. This means innovation funds with robust evaluation; evaluation by default; and protocol publication (a early key performance indicator!).
4. *Build the data architecture.* It's currently just too hard to link and securely collate data on outcomes, intermediaries and

interventions. In particular, we need to build up the capacity to rapid ability to assess multiple group or aggregate outcomes, with a data architecture or/or Application Programme Interfaces to make this possible.[6]

5. *Mine the variance.* One paradoxical advantage of a long history of *not* identifying what works, is that our public (and private) services are awash with semi-random variations in practice. This creates a massive opportunity to 'mine this variance' in public services – through regression, machine learning and deep dives – to identify promising interventions. This variance is the 'tropical rainforest' of public service innovation – amazing discoveries of things that do, or don't, work better, including for who, when and where.

6. *Reproduce.* It's hard enough to get things evaluated once, let alone going back and repeating the process. But it's what we need to do, not only to increase our confidence intervals, but also to check on implementation – and to test further variations and improvements. We should borrow the adage of the skilled craftsperson: 'measure twice, cut once'. We need to replicate, iterate, improve … and both check on implementation, but not fossilise practice.

7. *Increase the hit rate.* Alongside increasing the pipeline of new interventions and evaluations, we can seek to increase our 'hit rate'. Currently, typically fewer than one in four new interventions in social policy are found to be better than 'business as usual'. It can be possible to increase this hit rate though careful prototyping (for example, to iron out issues pre-randomised controlled trial) and by identifying transferable solutions, techniques or insights.

8. *Translate and adopt+.* Increasing the pipeline of evidence will have little impact unless matched by corollary increases in the volume and sophistication of our translational activities, and the absorptive capacity of those who the evidence is 'aimed at'. So hand-in-hand with our plugging the gaps in the What Works landscape, we need to nurture evidence-curious professionals.

9. *Bring the public with us.* Although public service professionals have been the prime early focus of the What Works Centres and movement, the public matter too. They are the patients, parents, consumers and voters whom are actually impacted. We

should seek to nurture a nation of 'bullshit detectors' – who ask 'Why do you think that's the best thing to do?' They are the ones in the room (Nsangi et al, 2017).[7]

10. *Go global.* The UK, and a small clutch of other countries, are pressing ahead with building the What Works evidence. But the objects of education, public safety, economic growth and so on across countries overlap substantially. We should turn What Works into a global public good – through shared commissioning of systematic reviews, comparing contrasting approaches, and coordinating our research and development spend and institutional development through G20 and other international platforms.[8]

Imagine what's possible if we deliver on even a clutch of these challenges or tasks. It would be transformative. A second enlightenment even.

The What Works Centres have already had considerable impact. But in many ways, what they've really done is shine a light on the depth of our ignorance. There are so many choices we face, from the billions spent on one (unevaluated) programme or another, to the decision as to what is the right or wrong thing to say to, or do for, a troubled youth that might set them on a better path.

I think, and hope, we will look back one day and puzzle on how we ever managed without them.

Notes

[1] Disclosure! The Behavioural Insights Team was my team in No 10 at that time. The experimentation aspect wasn't something we made a fuss about. It certainly wasn't something Steve Hilton was very interested in, but he didn't block it. And it didn't even have the political backing of other agendas I was also covering at the time, such as Big Society or the prime minister's interest in wellbeing. But having hard, experimental results greatly helped us persuade Permanent Secretaries (and ourselves) that this was an agenda worth pursuing, and the team worth keeping. History may yet prove that the biggest value of the Behavioural Insights Team was acting as a Trojan horse for experimentation, rather than the behavioural science per se.

[2] www.wsipp.wa.gov/

[3] The 'What Works' brand is owned and awarded by the UK Cabinet Office. Members of the network also sit on the national What Works Council.

[4] www.gov.uk/government/speeches/the-privilege-of-public-service-given-as-the-ditchley-annual-lecture

5   This list is based on a keynote speech at the evaluation week organised by the ETF in late February 2022.
6   Including building on the important groundwork of the Economic and Social Research Council's ADRUK programme, the Office National Statistics, and 10DS activity.
7   I was very struck by a remark made by Ben Goldacre years ago over lunch in the Treasury, where he argued that a key change in medicine was when patients started to differentiate between claims based on the quality of evidence – such as medical treatment versus homeopathy. More recently, the fantastic Uganda trial showing that kids, parents and teachers can all be taught to be better 'bullshit detectors' is a profoundly encouraging result – for methodologists and for humanity in general.
8   The recent Global Commission on Evidence (2022) may prove to be an important stepping stone. www.mcmasterforum.org/networks/evidence-commission.

References

Cochrane, A.L. (1972) *Effectiveness and efficiency: Random reflections on health services*. Nuffield Provincial Hospitals Trust.

Nsangi, A., Semakula, D., Oxman, A.D., Austvoll-Dahlgren, A., Oxman, M., Rosenbaum, S. et al (2017) Effects of the Informed Health Choices primary school intervention on the ability of children in Uganda to assess the reliability of claims about treatment effects: A cluster-randomised controlled trial. *The Lancet*, 390(10092): 374–388.

PART I

1

The scene is set

Michael Sanders and Jonathan Breckon

Almost nobody is against evidence-informed policy and practice. Like motherhood and apple pie, there's not a lot there to object to. After all, who wants to take to a stage and argue in favour of evidence-free policy?

Yet, despite this near universal support, the use of evidence has been far from inexorably rising. Zombie policies – those that we believe had been killed off by evidence – rise again and again, while the truly evidence based struggle to gain traction.

Why is this?

First, in our experience, it is because our definition of evidence is too general. Research methodologies that are ill-suited to answer questions about the impact of a particular intervention are too often used to prove that the intervention is 'evidence based'. Far too little evidence and research is concerned with a question of central fixation to policy makers and practitioners: 'If I do X, what will happen to Y?' An analysis by the National Audit Office between 2006 and 2012 found only half of the departments looked at had 'evaluations [that] were of a sufficient standard to give confidence in the effects attributed to policy because they had a robust counterfactual' (National Audit Office, 2013, p 7).

Second, in many, many fields of social policy, saying you want to base your decisions on evidence is like saying you want to

3

commute by flying car – the evidence simply does not exist to base your policy on it. For example, out of the UK government's 108 most complex and strategically significant projects – the so-called Government Major Projects Portfolio, costing £432 billion of taxpayers' money – only nine are evaluated robustly (National Audit Office, 2021, p 6). The majority – 77 major projects – have no evaluation arrangements at all. And these are major projects. There is no data kept on how many of the 'business as usual' activities in the rest of government are evaluated.

Third, even when there is evidence, it is not explained clearly, or in the right way, to the right people, at the right time. Too much evidence exists behind academic paywalls, or, where it is not, behind academic language, spoken between academics and researchers. Where it is communicated to policy makers and practitioners, there are many barriers blocking the evidence (Innvaer et al, 2002; Orton et al, 2011; Oliver et al, 2014; Oliver and Cairney, 2019).

A particular challenge is reaching frontline professionals, such as teachers, police officers or nurses – a key target audience for many of the What Works Centres. An appetite for evidence is still rare among many professionals. The hope for evidence-based practice in policing, teaching, health and social care has not yet been realised and many remain sceptical about the whole idea of evidence-based practice in areas like social work (for example, Gray et al, 2009; Parrish, 2018), policing (for example, Moore, 2006; Brown et al, 2018) or schools (for example, Howe, 2009; Nelson and Campbell, 2017).

With these three factors arrayed against it, it is no wonder that evidence-informed policy and practice continues to be a distant goal. Producing rigorous evidence that answers the question 'If I do X, what will happen to Y?' is time-consuming, expensive and not guaranteed to lead to policy change. But, if we are serious about evidence-informed policy and practice, then we must, to paraphrase President Kennedy, 'do this, not because it is easy, but because it is hard'. The desire to bring about evidence-based change may be more pedestrian than putting a man on the moon but we will not be done with it this decade or even the next.

'If I do X, what will happen to Y?' is the central question that researchers and policy makers interested in evidence-informed

4

policy and practice should ask of any new policy or intervention. If we line up lots of questions like this – for lots of different 'Xs', then we get to a meta question, of which are the best Xs or, put differently, 'What works?'.

In fits and starts, answering this question has preoccupied governments of all stripes in the UK over the last 25 years (see Chapter 2, this volume). The establishment of the National Institute for Health and Care Excellence (NICE), in 1999, followed (after a 12-year gap) with the Education Endowment Foundation and, so far, a further 12 centres,[1] is an attempt to overcome the three failings that we identified earlier.

The main official launch of the What Works Centres was in 2013, at an event hosted by Nesta – the UK's innovation charity – with ministers from the coalition government of Conservative and Liberal Democrat parties, alongside some key funders such as the Economic and Social Research Council and the National Lottery Fund. At the launch, one of the Conservative ministers, Oliver Letwin, was struck that it should be "blindingly obvious" that such centres are needed, and that it was "a remarkable thing that we have not created such centres hundreds of years ago".

However, there had been much work behind the scenes before this public launch. A year earlier, the then head of the civil service, Jeremy Heywood, called for an equivalent to NICE for social policy in an interview that was splashed on the front page of a national newspaper (*The Guardian*, 2012) – a rare thing for a Cabinet Secretary who tend to shun the limelight. That same year, the 2012 Civil Service Reform Plan committed the UK government to setting up a 'What Works' institution that could 'test and trial approaches and assess what works in major social policy areas, so that commissioners in central or local government do not waste time and money on programmes that are unlikely to offer value for money' (HM Government, 2012, p 17).

Some of these centres were wholly funded by government (for example, NICE), others were part-funded by government in partnership with others (for example, What Works Wellbeing) and one was independently funded by the Lottery Fund (the Centre of Ageing Better). Although most receive funding from the government, all are described as being independent: some are established as charities, while others are based in universities

5

or non-departmental bodies. Although operating as independent bodies, the Cabinet Office has a cross-centre coordinating role. (For a more detailed overview of these centres see What Works Network, 2018).

And what exactly are these organisations that we ended up with? Many of these What Works Centres share, to a greater or lesser extent, a belief that it is possible to identify, estimate and synthesise the causal impacts of an intervention or policy statistically – mostly through the use of randomised controlled trials and, to a lesser extent, quasi-experimental evaluations, which seek to simulate the properties of random assignment where it is not present.

The way in which this belief manifests itself varies dramatically from centre to centre. Some, such as the Education Endowment Foundation, fund a huge number of randomised controlled trials. Others, like NICE, do not fund trials, but instead specialise in the synthesis of large numbers of individual studies in a particular area, and arrive at guidance based on this drawing together of research. Others, such as the Centre for Ageing Better, have not attempted to fill the evidence gaps, and have gone down a different route of delivering programmes or partnerships. Or they have found important evidential niches, such as the Wales Centre for Public Policy, which delivers rapid policy-relevant summaries of evidence to ministers. Smaller centres may often find themselves in the same space as NICE, but struggle to synthesise evidence that does not yet exist. For some, this means making a priority of advocating and capacity-building for more evidence to be produced.

Centres differ too by the firmness with which they take the line of positivist or post-positivist thinking. Some centres do not fund any research; others fund large-scale trials; others take a more 'realist' approach to evaluation. Some centres, like What Works for Children's Social Care, where one of us was chief executive, have been at pains to embrace a pluralistic approach to research, funding and conducting purely qualitative and mixed methods research alongside the purely quantitative. Others make more explicit in their standards of evidence that they view causal evidence as more advanced and superior. For some centres, their reliance on this positivist view varies from project to project – with some taking a view that some issues – such as matters of race – warrant a less strict adherence to quantitative or causal methodologies.

Alongside differences in activity and epistemological standpoints, centres differ radically in their funding and structures. Some, such as the Education Endowment Foundation, Youth Endowment Fund and Youth Futures Foundation, benefit from large endowments from government, yielding substantial long-term independence. Others, like the Early Intervention Foundation and What Works for Children's' Social Care, are funded by direct grants from government, which has thus far proven a reliable source of funding, albeit one that compromises the ability to fund long-term projects and necessitates foregoing some level of independence. Other centres, such as What Works Local Economic Growth and What Works Wellbeing, are funded through a mix of approaches including research councils, and one, the Centre for Homelessness Impact, stands apart in terms of being funded exclusively through philanthropic means.

Legally, NICE and What Works for Crime Reduction are (part of) non-departmental public bodies, while most are charities or non-profit businesses, or based in universities (What Works for Local Economic Growth, Wales Centre for Public Policy).

This description of the individual What Works Centres brings to mind the popular podcast, hosted by researchers from the UK television programme *QI*, 'No such thing as a fish'. The podcast draws its name from a fact the researchers found for the television show, a quote by the biologist Stephen Jay Gould, that because fish are so diverse in terms of their biology, there is no defining characteristic or set of characteristics which can be said to be true of all fish, but unique to fish. Hence – there is no such thing as 'a fish'.

In the same way, What Works Centres are so diverse in the work that they do, their structures, funding, philosophies and staffing, that we could say, with equal justification, that there is 'no such thing as a What Works Centre'.

Helpfully, the world of public policy research is more straightforward than the world of biology (described by the biologist Adam Rutherford as a "science of exceptions"?!). The thing that truly unites What Works Centres is that they are recognised as such by the UK government's Cabinet Office, whose Evaluation Taskforce (and formerly What Works Team), convene the What Works Council, quarterly meetings of the centres' chief executives. Since 2019, new centres must meet certain criteria, and then be subjected to a vote of this council before membership is allowed.

While this bureaucratic approach might be helpful in avoiding identity crises among centres, it doesn't assist anyone with an interest in evidence-informed policy and practice with their own journey. Instead, this diversity points to a major challenge for would-be finders of 'what works'. If there's 'no such thing' as a What Works Centre, what is the aspirant to do? From whom can they learn? A common approach, much loved of policy professionals, of creating a single 'framework' is appealing, but unlikely to yield much helpful insight. From an analytic perspective, we have more unknowns than equations, and so, in the words of Randall Munro, the creator of the webcomic *XKCD*, 'my usual approach is useless here'.[2]

The establishment of What Works Centres, and their characteristics, are in part arbitrary – they depend on the political whims and funding circumstances in which they are set up. Although there is clearly a mind at work in the establishment of each, there is little cohesive thought across the establishment of the network itself. Arbitrariness, unlike its sister, randomness, is not useful for analysis.

Not all elements of each centre are arbitrary, however. In fact, after arbitrary starts, there is substantial endogeneity in the paths chosen by each What Works Centre. That is, the paths emerging from those disparate origins may be different from each other, but are guided by the differences in circumstances. These circumstances are not merely financial – they are also a product of the context in which they work.

Some centres work in areas with well-established evidence bases. Others, in spaces where interventions are typically delivered by large numbers of very small charitable or non-governmental organisations. Others still work alongside huge state delivery partners – making research and evaluation much easier. For some, academics and practitioners working in their sector are receptive to randomised trials and impact evaluations, while, perhaps more commonly, some experience hostility and resistance from established players. Chief myriad stakeholders, has meant that audience needs to be at the core of their thinking.

The Youth Futures Foundation, which provides the authors for Chapter 7, faces a different situation – the youth labour market. This centre has an endowment, like the Education Endowment Foundation, but many (and often small) stakeholders, like the Early Intervention Foundation. As a newer centre, while it enjoys the benefits of being able to learn from what came before, it also face challenges of its own.

In Chapter 8 we hear from Steve Martin from What Works Wales. Unlike the other centres we hear from, this centre isn't focused on one outcome but on all outcomes within a devolved government – a different and even more varied feat than any of the centres. Finally in Part I, Chapter 9 tells the story of the What Works Centre for Local Economic Growth – one of the few centres to be based primarily inside a university, and to look at a policy area that many would argue is especially tricky for randomised controlled trials.

Part II of the book, which we introduce in Chapter 10, covers shared criticisms and challenges to the networks, the story of new, insurgent centres, and a forward look at grassroots evidence movements and what works for equality – an issue that cuts across most others.

Notes

[1]   As of March 2022 there are ten What Works Centres, two affiliates and one associate. What Works Scotland did not have its funding renewed and no longer exists.

[2]   https://xkcd.com/55/

References

Brown, J., Belur, J., Tompson, L., McDowall, A., Hunter, G. and May, T. (2018) Extending the remit of evidence-based policing. *International Journal of Police Science & Management*, 20(1): 38–51.

Gray, M., Plath, D. and Webb, S. (2009) *Evidence-based social work: A critical stance.* Routledge.

HM Government. (2012). *Civil Service reform plan.* www.gov.uk/government/publications/civil-service-reform-plan

Howe, K.R. (2009) Positivist dogmas, rhetoric, and the education science question. *Educational Researcher*, 38(6): 428–440.

Innvaer, S., Vist, G., Trommald, M. and Oxman, A. (2002) Health policy-makers' perceptions of their use of evidence: A systematic review. *Journal of Health Services Research & Policy*, 7(4): 239–244.

Moore, M.H. (2006) Improving police through expertise, experience, and experiments. In D. Weisburd and A. Braga (eds) *Police innovation: Contrasting perspectives*. Cambridge University Press, pp 322–338.

National Audit Office (2013) Evaluation in Government - National Audit Office insight .www.nao.org.uk/wp-cont ent/uploads/2013/12/10331-001-Evaluation-in-governm ent_NEW.pdf

National Audit Office. (2021). *Evaluating government spending*. National Audit Office.

Nelson, J. and Campbell, C. (2017) Evidence-informed practice in education: Meanings and applications. *Educational Research*, 59(2): 127–135.

Oliver, K. and Cairney, P. (2019) The dos and don'ts of influencing policy: A systematic review of advice to academics. *Palgrave Communications*, 5(1): 1–11.

Oliver, K., Innvar, S., Lorenc, T., Woodman, J. and Thomas, J. (2014) A systematic review of barriers to and facilitators of the use of evidence by policymakers. *BMC Health Services Research*, 14(1): 1–12.

Orton, L., Lloyd-Williams, F., Taylor-Robinson, D., O'Flaherty, M. and Capewell, S. (2011) The use of research evidence in public health decision making processes: Systematic review. *PLoS One*, 6(7): e21704.

Parrish, D.E. (2018) Evidence-based practice: A common definition matters. *Journal of Social Work Education*, 54(3): 407–411.

The Guardian (2012) 'Cabinet secretary calls for social policy 'kitemark' to highlight quality initiatives'. *The Guardian*, 10 January. www.theguardian.com/politics/2012/jan/10/cabinet-secretary-social-policy-kitemark

What Works Network (2018) 'The What Works Network: Five years on'. Cabinet Office. www.gov.uk/government/publicati ons/the-what-works-network-five-years-on

2

How did we get here? What Works in the UK? A personal journey

Jonathan Breckon and Annette Boaz

Although initiatives to promote evidence in policy are not a recent invention, we have seen a rapid blossoming of activity in recent years. A study mapped the activities of 346 organisations running nearly 2,000 research-policy engagement initiatives – such as the UK's Department of Health Policy Research Units, the US Bipartisan Policy Centre's Evidence Project or the African Evidence Network – spanning 31 countries (Hopkins et al, 2021). Although the very oldest organisations identified in the study began over 500 years ago, the majority date from 1945 onwards with a more rapid expansion from 2010 onwards.

In this chapter we reflect on the acceleration in activity in the UK and the emergence of the What Works Network, a flagship initiative attracting attention around the world. We tell the story from the personal perspective of two 'eyewitnesses' who worked in organisations tasked with putting evidence use more firmly on the policy agenda: Jonathan Breckon as the director of the Alliance for Useful Evidence, and Annette Boaz as a fellow in the Centre for Evidence Based Policy and Practice, and founding editor of the journal *Evidence & Policy*.

What a difference leadership makes

Arguably, what transformed the fate of those working to promote evidence use in the UK was the 1997 general election. The new prime minister, Tony Blair, swept into office with a mantra of 'what counts is what works' (Labour Party, 1997, p 1). Government documents were awash with references to the role of evidence (Nutley et al, 2002, p 10).

In addition to political leadership, there was also leadership from within the heart of Whitehall. Two newly created posts were crucial: a Chief Social Scientist and a Chief Social Researcher.

The former government-wide post of Chief Social Scientist included the disciplines of statistics and economics, and sat with the wider group of Government Chief Scientific Advisers. Based in the Home Office, criminologist Professor Paul Wiles was the first – and last – to hold this post, between 1999 and 2010. Wiles was then the only social scientist who was a member of the influential group of Chief Scientific Advisers.

The other important new role was that of Chief Government Social Researcher, based at the centre of government, a post held by Sue Duncan between 2003 and 2008. Duncan was also the Head of Government Social Research – covering over 2,000 social researchers working in government (Burnett and Duncan, 2008). Before Duncan's arrival, there was no full-time leadership or support for this work. But with her arrival a small unit was able to develop a proper infrastructure to support Government Social Research, including a competency, skills and knowledge framework; professional training including a master's course; a logo; recruitment and publication protocols; and guidance on professional issues such as research ethics.

Duncan and Wiles both played crucial roles in championing social research across Whitehall. But so too did others within government. There was a medley of Cabinet Office and government teams grappling with evidence use as part of an agenda of evidence-based policy and modernising government (Wells, 2007). This included groups such as the Strategic Policy Making Team, Performance and Innovation Unit, the Social Exclusion Unit and the Centre for Policy and Management Studies (Davies et al, 2000).

Some of the individuals from those teams continued to play a leadership role a decade later. Three leaders from the Prime Minister's Strategy Unit – during Tony Blair's and Gordon Brown's premierships – went on to be key protagonists in the What Works Network. Geoff Mulgan ran the Performance and Innovation Unit and the government's Strategy Unit, went on to set up the Alliance for Useful Evidence in 2011, and supported the set-up of a number of What Works Centres, including incubating What Works for Children's Social Care.

Another former director of the Prime Minister's Strategy Unit, Stephen Aldridge, has been a member of the What Works Council, and helped back the What Works for Local Economic Growth, while Chief Analyst since 2011 at the Department for Levelling Up, Housing and Communities.

And David Halpern, formerly Chief Analyst in the Prime Minister's Strategy Unit, was appointed as What Works National Adviser in 2013, and has provided leadership through the coordination and promotion of the What Works Network.

At the same time academics engaged with ideas around 'what works', providing thought-leadership and much needed empirical and conceptual work to stimulate the field. Academics including Sandra Nutley and Huw Davies at St Andrews University; Jonathan Shepherd at Cardiff University; and Ann Oakley and colleagues at University College London, to name but a few, developed research methods and insights on how to make What Works a reality (see, for example, Oakley, 1999; Nutley and Davies, 2000; Shepherd, 2014). While a significant drive for promoting evidence use has come from within the academic community, the support from within government was critical to establishing evidence use as a core priority area, worthy of investment and effort.

Investment and infrastructure (uneasy collaboration and competition)

The flagship evidence-to-practice initiative was the National Institute for Clinical Excellence (NICE) established in 1999 (later renamed as the National Institute for Health and Care Excellence to reflect its wider social care remit). NICE worked with stakeholders to produce national guidelines for health-care practitioners based on the latest research evidence (see Chapter 3). In the same year, the Economic and Social Research Council (ESRC), under the leadership of their then chief executive Professor Ron Amman, set up the Centre for Evidence Based Policy and Practice, based at Queen Mary University of London. The centre had a series of topic-based nodes based in universities around the UK – also called the Evidence Network – intended to foster the exchange of social science research between policy, researchers and practitioners (Solesbury, 2001). Much of the work of this programme centred on promoting the production of systematic reviews of evidence – seeking to build a narrative that policy and practice should be built on bodies of evidence rather than single studies.

For example, one of the multi-university 'nodes' on Evidence-Based Public Health Policy looked for effective policy interventions based on an informed understanding of 'what works' via systematic reviews (Petticrew et al, 2006). Visiting Fellow Ray Pawson joined the main ESRC centre to conduct work on 'realist' syntheses – which looked at potential causal mechanisms and tried to answer the question 'What works for whom under what circumstances?' rather than purely 'What works?' (Pawson et al, 2005). The centre also launched the journal *Evidence & Policy* in 2005, which remains a key journal for the evidence use community. The centre ran ESRC summer postgraduate training schools that developed several cohorts of PhD students in the relationship between evidence, policy and practice.

Alongside this programme of work, other initiatives pre-dated and developed alongside the centre in the late 1990s and early 2000s. We touch on five evidence initiatives that we believe are most relevant to UK What Works Centres.

First, the Evidence for Policy and Practice Information and Coordinating Centre (now simply called the EPPI-Centre) developed from a project set up by Ann Oakley in 1992 at the Institute of Education, University of London. It was started with a modest grant from the ESRC of £25,000 to create a 'a social science database of controlled interventions in education and social welfare' which would 'parallel similar databases established for medical intervention' (Oakley et al, 2005, p 9). However, the ESRC initially rejected the grant application for what it called the

15

'database project' because the grant reviewers doubted there would be enough evidence to review, and questioned the soundness of focusing on experimental and quasi-experimental studies (Oakley et al, 2005, p 9). But after some negotiations, the ESRC grant was finally awarded. EPPI has gone on to conduct hundreds of reviews for government departments, charities and others, and has provided systematic reviews for five of the current What Works Centres (as of October 2021).

A second initiative was the Research Unit for Research Utilisation, which was established in 2001 through initial funding from the ESRC. Based at the School of Management, St Andrews University in Scotland, the unit conducted influential research on the use of evidence across a number of policy domains (for example, Walter et al, 2003) and produced a key text covering a range of public services entitled *What works* (Davies et al, 2000).

In the same year as the launch of the Research Unit for Research Utilisation, the ESRC co-funded What Works for Children? – a collaboration between the UK's City and York universities, and the large UK children's charity Barnardo's (Roberts, 2006). This initiative built on a previous Barnardo's What Works initiative that began in the early 1990s – which had created a series of research-informed plain English reports for frontline workers and 'end-point users' on what seemed likely to result in better outcomes for children. Much of what underpinned the Barnardo's initiative came from the health sector and, in particular, the Cochrane Collaboration (Roberts, 2006, p 52).

Cochrane, as it is now known, was a fourth key development in this period. Founded in 1993 by 70 international researchers and the health-care academic Sir Iain Chalmers, it aimed to disseminate their particular brand of systematic reviews of randomised controlled trials (RCTs) in health. However, the reports of the Barnardo's What Works project did not create full-blown systematic reviews as advocated by Cochrane, but produced more sweeping literature reviews that used a variety of evidence, including qualitative research, to answer questions such as 'Does it matter? Does it work? How does it work? What do children make of it?' (Roberts, 2006, p 54). The Barnardo's work was informed by an ethos of 'horses for courses' – matching appropriate research methodologies to the questions in hand (Petticrew and Roberts,

2003) and thus had less focus on causal impact questions, as characterised by most of the What Works Network.

A fifth initiative during this period was the Campbell Collaboration, which aimed to be the social policy equivalent of Cochrane. After an exploratory meeting organised by Sir Iain Chalmers at University College London in 1999, the Campbell Collaboration was launched at an inaugural meeting Philadelphia the following year, with researchers from 13 countries. The name of the organisation was suggested by Chalmers after the American sociologist Donald Campbell who called for an 'experimenting society' comprised of a 'disputatious community of truth seekers devoted to improving social policy through evaluation and research' (Dunn, 1997, p 35).[1] The Campbell Collaboration would focus on systematic reviews – mostly of RCTs or quasi-experimental designs – in the fields of education, criminology, international development and social welfare (Davies and Boruch, 2001; Littell and White, 2017).

However, this period was characterised as much by competition as by collaboration. The bidding process for the ESRC Centre for Evidence Based Policy and Practice had been divisive and had a detrimental effect on the efforts to collaborate across the programme. Scant opportunities for further funding in particular hampered progress as did the very different visions as to the task in hand. While some felt the funding was largely designed to promote a transfer of a medical model of evidence-based medicine to other areas of policy, others felt that there was a need to develop a new vision for evidence use for policy and practice, drawing more on social science.

It was perhaps the arrival of the UK What Works Network that put the work on evidence use in the UK securely on the international map. The significant investment, such as £200 million from the Home Office for the Youth Endowment Fund, or £125 million from the Department for Education for the Education Endowment Foundation, and, consequently, the scale of the activity and the range of topics made quite an impression both within the UK and externally. Parallels were drawn with the US Institute of Education Sciences' What Works Clearinghouse model. Established in 2002, the US What Works Clearinghouse was created with a remit to provide educators with evidence of the effectiveness of programmes and practices. Other international models also had an informal influence on the UK What Works Centres, such as the Washington State Institute for Public Policy and the Dutch Centraal Planbureau for Economic Policy Analysis (Rutter, 2012; Lenihan, 2013; Puttick and Mulgan, 2013).

The elephant in the room: what was meant by evidence?

While this period was characterised by a substantial increase in both interest and activity, much of the debate about evidence glossed over the very different views the various centres and initiatives have about what counted as evidence. Within government the narrative about evidence use often included different sources of evidence, such as administrative data. The Cabinet Office Strategic Policymaking Team listed an eclectic range of evidence:

> This Government's declaration that 'what counts is what works' is the basis for the present heightened interest in the part played by evidence in policy making. ... The raw ingredient of evidence is information. Good quality policy making depends on high-quality information, derived from a variety of sources—expert knowledge; existing domestic and international research; existing statistics; stakeholder consultation; evaluation of previous policies; new research, if appropriate; or secondary sources, including the internet. (Cabinet Office, 1999, Section 7.1)

Some initiatives included a vision to promote more 'top of the pyramid' hierarchies of evidence such as RCTs and systematic reviews of trial evidence (Nutley et al, 2013). Annette can still remember the anxious faces at the more quantitatively focused Campbell Collaboration inaugural meeting in Philadelphia when some qualitative researchers found their way into a discussion about evidence. Debates about what should or should not be included as evidence have been a recurring theme over the last two decades. In contrast to the hierarchical approach taken in health care, particularly the adaption of Grading of Recommendations Assessment Development and Evaluation (GRADE) standards of evidence implemented by NICE for their clinical guidelines in 2009 (Breckon and Ruiz, 2014), other sectors such as education, criminal justice and social care have been 'riven with disputes as to what constitutes appropriate evidence ... and divisions between qualitative and quantitative paradigms run deep' (Nutley et al, 2002, p 3).

Our experience is that these epistemological and methodological disputes have become less heated but still exist. But we have certainly not seen any unanimity around a single set of evidence standards. Indeed, evidence frameworks have continued to multiply year on year. A recent analysis found 18 frameworks used by 16 UK organisations for judging evidence used in UK domestic social policy – covering government, charities and public service providers (Puttick, 2018), growing at roughly two per year. There is thus much potential for confusion about what evidence standards means (Gough et al, 2021).

The arrival of the What Works Centres Network was underpinned with a more explicit claim with regards to evidence. The network was set up with the idea of promoting a particular vision of quality evidence – involving impact evaluations and research synthesis such as systematic reviews. The centres sign up to a Concordat which includes a commitment to being 'methodologically rigorous' and giving primacy to findings from impact evaluations with a 'robust system for ranking evidence' and 'using a common currency for rating quality' including using, where possible, cost information and cost–benefit analysis where possible (Cabinet Office, 2018, p 4).

The focus on evidence of the effectiveness of programmes and policy has not been without its critics. Educational researchers, for example, have expressed concerns about a diversion of educational research spending into what they see as expensive experimental study designs that may not be that informative for schools' policy and practice (Lortie-Forgues and Inglis, 2019). Several projects at the Education Endowment Foundation have fallen through because the developers would not agree to the design proposed by the independent academic or consultant evaluator (Edovald and Nevill, 2021). Some of the What Works Centres see advocating for RCTs as part of their remit. More recently, in the context of the Black Lives Matter movement, there has been a renewed debate about the neutrality and diversity of evidence brokers and intermediaries (Doucet, 2021; University Policy Engagement Network, 2021). The ways in which we decide what to research, how to research it and who will conduct the research are not neutral processes. This debate echoes a more long-standing concern, particularly in Australia, New Zealand and Canada, about the extent to which indigenous knowledge is valued alongside research evidence (Boaz et al, 2019). In our efforts to promote the use of research evidence it is ever more clear that we need to also recognise its limitations and to consider how it can be done better in future.

Research impact carrots and sticks

Throughout the last two decades, the government has been assessing the impact of research with a series of university-based evaluation exercises through the Research Excellence Framework. In 2014, this created some funding 'carrots' to incentivise academics to be policy-relevant (Williams and Grant, 2018). An advantage of the evolving debate around assessing impact for accountability purposes has been a general increase in impact literacy in the research community, reflected in the hundreds of case studies written by universities on their pathways to influencing policy influence (Bastow et al, 2014). There has also been a development of a cadre of UK university staff tasked with thinking about and promoting impact. What has been less helpful has been the focus on the impact of individual pieces of research, individual researchers and the construction of impact narratives that may overclaim their influence in policy.

Devolution

We have seen interesting developments in the individual countries of the UK following the devolution of various functions of government in 1998. The smaller countries have the potential for closer working relationships between academic and non-academic stakeholders because people are more likely to know each other and not get lost in the relative vastness and anonymity of Whitehall in London. The Public Policy Institute for Wales

(PPIW), based at Cardiff University, has developed a more demand-focused approach, providing rapid reviews of evidence combined with expert roundtables and briefings for the Welsh Government and public services. Established in 2014 with core funding from the Welsh Government, and additional project funding from the ESRC, the PPIW has tailored its output to each Welsh Government Minister's needs (Bristow et al, 2015). The PPIW was invited to join the What Works Centres in 2014, along with What Works Scotland, as an 'associate' member. 'Affiliate' members are those seeking full What Works membership. Three years later, after this 'proof of concept' stage as PPIW, it evolved into the Wales Centre for Public Policy and it has continued to be an active player and collaborator alongside the UK What Works Centres (see Chapter 8, this volume).

What Works Scotland took a very different approach to the London-based centres, shunning RCTs and systematic reviews, and instead focusing on much more collaborative ways of working, such as co-production, participatory budgeting, place-based and collaborative action research (Geyer, 2019). This initiative was more like a time-limited research project than a centre, working on a short timescale (2014–2018) as a partnership across Scottish Government, Edinburgh and Glasgow universities, and the ESRC. What Works Scotland was an object lesson in the challenges of managing multi-partner consortia and recognised at the end how hard it was to grow meaningful collaborations and handle multiple partnerships in a short period of time (Geyer, 2019, p 3). As interest in more time-limited initiatives grows in the Cabinet Office's Evaluation Taskforce, it is important to heed these lessons. In another devolved UK jurisdiction, attempts were made to set up a What Works Northern Ireland. Although funding from the ESRC was on the table, no government department in Belfast came forward to match this funding – a crucial criteria for the ESRC – despite a commitment by one of the main political parties (DUP, 2016, p 28).

Learning by doing

Perhaps what is most notable about the evidence landscape in the UK today is how much the different initiatives have matured over time. As groups build relationships with their policy and practice communities this has shaped their vision of what is useful and usable evidence for policy and practice. This learning culture has been supported by the What Works Network activities, which have supported cross-network learning and information sharing. Other forums have grown to share the best ways to share evidence. For example, the Evidence Quarter has become a physical home to a small but growing number of evidence-minded organisations, including half of the current What Works Centres. The UK Knowledge Mobilisation Forum has provided a space for people engaged in knowledge mobilising roles within What Works Centres and other initiatives to come together to learn. The Universities Policy Engagement Network has been successful in bringing together universities to learn together about how best universities and their research can be used in policy making. Our own initiative, Transforming Evidence, seeks to bring together different communities of scholars, policy makers and practitioners in different geographies and policy domains to help us learn from each other.

Conclusion

An advantage of writing this together has been the opportunity to question and discuss our different memories of the journey we have been on. There were so many steps along the way that we had forgotten. This area of work has suffered more than most from the 'Groundhog Day' effect where we discover time and time again the important topic of supporting evidence use in policy and practice and begin anew to develop interventions and methods to evaluate them. Evidence-based policy itself paraded under the guise of a novel framing, rarely connecting with previous relevant bodies of relevant thinking (such as knowledge mobilisation, policy implementation and utilisation focused evaluation).

We may be hopeless optimists, but it feels like we have reached a point where there is a diverse range of activity and actors committed to promoting the use of evidence from within government, practice organisations and the academy. In addition to the What Works Centres, we have, for example, a Knowledge Exchange Unit supporting evidence use in Westminster parliament, a Government Office for Science specifically focused on supporting the use of research in policy, an Open Innovation Team in Whitehall bridging academia and policy makers, and voluntary organisations such as Sense about Science championing public engagement in science. It will be up to us all to ensure that we make the best use of this opportunity as we move forwards. The resources available to support this work are rarely plentiful, making it all the more important that we work together to ensure complementarity rather than duplication of effort. As Bev Holmes and Allan Best suggested over a decade ago, the next step forward is to build systems that make best use of evidence (Best and Holmes, 2010). We have the building blocks but there is still work to do in joining together all our evidence initiatives be stronger together.

Note
[1] The 'disputatious' community remains a permanent fixture of the evidence movement, although the debates and 'paradigm wars' (Oakley, 1999) can feel narrowly methodological and epistemological, cut off from the wider policy and public realm.

References
Bastow, S., Dunleavy, P. and Tinkler, J. (2014) *The impact of the social sciences: How academics and their research make a difference*. SAGE.

Best, A. and Holmes, B. (2010) Systems thinking, knowledge and action: Towards better models and methods. *Evidence & Policy: A Journal of Research, Debate and Practice*, 6(2): 145–159.

Boaz, A., Davies, H.T.O., Fraser, A. and Nutley, S.M. (2019) *What works now? Evidence-informed policy and practice*. Policy Press.

Breckon, J. and Ruiz, F. (2014) *The NICE way: Lessons for social policy and practices from the National Institute for Health and Care Excellence*. The Alliance for Useful Evidence. www.alliance 4usefulevidence.org/publication/the-nice-way-lessons-for-soc ial-policy-and-practices-from-the-national-institute-for-hea lth-and-care-excellence/

Bristow, D., Carter, L. and Martin, S. (2015) Using evidence to improve policy and practice: The UK What Works Centres. *Contemporary Social Science*, 10(2): 126–137.

Burnett, J. and Duncan, S. (2008) Reflections and observations: An interview with the UK's first Chief Government Social Researcher. *Critical Social Policy*, 28(3): 283–298.

Cabinet Office (1999) *Professional policy making in the twenty-first century*. https://gsdrc.org/document-library/professional-pol icy-making-in-the-twenty-first-century/

Cabinet Office (2018) *The What Works Network: Five years on*. GOV.UK. www.gov.uk/government/publications/the-what-works-network-five-years-on

Davies, H.T.O., Nutley, S. and Smith, P. (2000) *What works? Evidence-based policy and practice in public services*. Policy Press.

Davies, P. and Boruch, R. (2001) The Campbell collaboration. *BMJ: British Medical Journal*, 323(7308): 294–295.

Doucet, F. (2021) Why not honest issue advocates? The honest broker: More than meets the eye. *Transforming Evidence* [blog], 21 September. https://transforming-evidence.org/blog/why-not-honest-issue-advocates

Dunn, W.N. (ed) (1997) *The experimenting society: Essays in honor of Donald T. Campbell*. Routledge.

DUP (Democratic Unionist Party) (2016) *2016 Northern Ireland Assembly election manifesto: 'Our plan for Northern Ireland'*. Democratic Unionist Party.

Edovald, T. and Nevill, C. (2021) Working out what works: The case of the Education Endowment Foundation in England. *ECNU Review of Education*, 4(1): 46–64.

Flanagan, K., Clarke, S., Agar, J., Edgerton, D. and Craig, C. (2019) *Lessons from the history of UK science policy*. The British Academy.

Geyer, J. (2019) *Reflections on the What Works Scotland initiative*. Scottish Government. http://whatworksscotland.ac.uk/publicati ons/reflections-on-the-what-works-scotland-initiative/

Gough, D., Maidment, C. and Sharples, J. (2021) Enabling knowledge brokerage intermediaries to be evidence-informed. *Evidence & Policy*, 1(aop): 1–15.

Hopkins, A., Oliver, K., Boaz, A., Guillot-Wright, S. and Cairney, P. (2021) Are research-policy engagement activities informed by policy theory and evidence? 7 challenges to the UK impact agenda. *Policy Design and Practice*, 4(3): 341–356.

Labour Party (1997) *New Labour, new life for Britain*. Labour Party.

Lenihan, A.T. (2013) *Lessons from abroad: Intl. approaches to promoting evidence-based policy.* Alliance for Useful Evidence, Nesta. www.academia.edu/4052947/Lessons_from_Abroad_Intl_Approaches_to_Promoting_Evidence_Based_Policy

Littell, J.H. and White, H. (2017) The Campbell collaboration: Providing better evidence for a better world. *Research on Social Work Practice*, 28(1): 6–12.

Lortie-Forgues, H. and Inglis, M. (2019) Rigorous large-scale educational RCTs are often uninformative: Should we be concerned? *Educational Researcher*, 48(3): 158–166.

Nutley, S. and Davies, H. (2000) Making a reality of evidence-based practice: Some lessons from the diffusion of innovations. *Public Money & Management*, 20(4).

Nutley, S., Davies, H. and Walter, I. (2002) Evidence based policy and practice: Cross sector lessons from the UK. *Social Policy Journal of New Zealand.*

Nutley, S.M., Powell, A.E. and Davies, H.T.O. (2013) 'What counts as good evidence'. Nesta: Alliance for Useful Evidence. https://research-repository.st-andrews.ac.uk/handle/10023/3518

Oakley, A. (1999) Paradigm wars: Some thoughts on a personal and public trajectory. *International Journal of Social Research Methodology*, 2(3): 247–254.

Oakley, A., Gough, D., Oliver, S. and Thomas, J. (2005) The politics of evidence and methodology: Lessons from the EPPI-Centre. *Evidence & Policy: A Journal of Research, Debate and Practice*, 1(1): 5–32.

Parker, M. (2016) The Rothschild report (1971) and the purpose of government-funded R&D: A personal account. *Palgrave Communications*, 2(1): 1–9.

Pawson, R., Greenhalgh, T., Harvey, G. and Walshe, K. (2005) Realist review: A new method of systematic review designed for complex policy interventions. *Journal of Health Services Research & Policy*, 10(1): 21–34.

Petticrew, M. and Roberts, H. (2003) Evidence, hierarchies, and typologies: Horses for courses. *Journal of Epidemiology and Community Health*, 57(7): 527–529.

executives, directors and boards of trustees must chart their own course through the challenges that their organisation faces.

If quantitative analysis is not useful here, instead, we must rely on the narrative and argument of individuals. This is the focus of this book. We will hear from leaders and fellow travellers of most of the extant centres; hearing from them about their triumphs, their challenges, and how they would do things differently if they had their time again. In the absence of an overarching framework, we instead offer an oral history of the What Works Network, that we hope can act as a guide to the future of effective evidence-informed policy and practice.

As well as learning about why the centres are so different, and their journeys, we can learn from the common challenges that are faced across the network. If the missions of the centres differ, the challenges are more similar – and this is something that will be drawn out in the coming chapters.

In Chapter 2, Jonathan Breckon and Annette Boaz, who have worked in and around the What Works movement, provide an overarching history of the movement. The rest of Part I consists of a series of chapters written by What Works Centres with quite different histories and mandates.

In Chapter 3, Nick Timmins gives an account of the founding and growth of NICE, the oldest and largest centre, which also benefits from both its heightened status as a non-departmental government body, but also from the vast evidence-producing conventions of medicine. In Chapter 4, Rachel Tuffin talks about the What Works Centre for Crime Reduction, which is located within the College of Policing and hence has a role in the training received by all police officers.

Further removed from the direct levers of power is the Education Endowment Foundation, the topic of Chapter 5. The Education Endowment Foundation's initial endowment from the Department for Education, and its focus on producing high quality randomised trials, has allowed it to be at the forefront of producing an evidence base and feeding it into England's 20,000 schools. This is a very different reality than that faced by the Early Intervention Foundation discussed in Chapter 6. As Jo Casebourne, the organisation's chief executive officer, makes clear, tackling a diverse topic area like early intervention, with

Petticrew, M., Whitehead, M., Bambra, C., Egan, M., Graham, H., Macintyre, S. and McDermott, E. (2006) The Centre for Evidence-based Public Health Policy: Part of the ESRC Evidence Network. In A. Killoran, C. Swann and M.P. Kelly (eds) *Public health evidence: Tackling health inequalities*. Oxford University Press, pp 141–154.

Puttick, R. (2018) *Mapping the standards of evidence used in UK social policy*. Nesta, Alliance for Useful Evidence. www.nesta.org. uk/report/mapping-standards-evidence-used-uk-social-policy/

Puttick, R. and Mulgan, G. (2013) *What should the 'What Works Network' do?* Nesta. www.nesta.org.uk/report/what-should-the-what-works-network-do/

Roberts, H. (2006) What works for children? Reflections on building research and development in a children's charity. *Journal of Children's Services*, 1(2): 51–60.

Rutter, J. (2012) *Evidence and evaluation in policy making*. Institute for Government. www.instituteforgovernment.org.uk/publicati ons/evidence-and-evaluation-policy-making

Shepherd, J.P. (2014) *How to achieve more effective services: The evidence ecosystem*. What Works Network/Cardiff University. www.scie-socialcareonline.org.uk/how-to-achieve-more-effect ive-services-the-evidence-ecosystem/r/a11G0000006z7vXIAQ

Solesbury, W. (2001) Evidence based policy: Whence it came and where it's going. *ESRC Evidence Based Policy and Practice Centre, Working Paper*.

University Policy Engagement Network (2021) *Surfacing equity, diversity and inclusion within academic-policy engagement*. www.upen. ac.uk/news/latest_news/?action=story&id=251

Walker, D. (2015) *Exaggerated claims? The ESRC, 50 years on*. SAGE.

Walter, I., Nutley, S. and Davies, H. (2003) *Research impact: A cross sector literature review*. Research Unit for Research Utilisation, University of St Andrews.

Wells, P. (2007) New Labour and evidence based policy making: 1997–2007. *People, Place and Policy*, 1(1): 22–29.

Williams, K. and Grant, J. (2018) A comparative review of how the policy and procedures to assess research impact evolved in Australia and the UK. *Research Evaluation*, 27(2): 93–105.

3

The role of NICE in the evidence-based health system

Nick Timmins

In early October 1999, Sir Richard Sykes, the chairman of Glaxo Wellcome, then Britain's biggest pharmaceutical company, stormed into 10 Downing Street. He was incandescent.

A body that most people had not heard of – the National Institute for Clinical Excellence (NICE) – in its very first decision had just recommended that the National Health Service (NHS) in England should not prescribe what the company had expected to be its next big money-spinner. A treatment for influenza, known as Relenza.

Given by inhaler, if used within 48 hours of symptoms, it reduced the duration of the symptoms from six to five days. But of the 6,000 patients in the clinical trial, just 70 had been elderly and there was no evidence that it reduced complications in those most at risk from flu: the elderly and asthmatics, for example. Furthermore, it cost £24 for a five-day course and NICE had calculated that in an epidemic year – and when the initial symptoms of flu differ little from a bad cold – Relenza could cost the NHS £100 million. At a time when the entire drug budget outside hospitals was under £4 billion. NICE judged that Relenza was not cost-effective and should not be prescribed.

Sir Richard branded the decision 'ludicrous'. Proof of efficacy in high risk patients would come as the drug was used, he said, otherwise clinical trials to prove that would run on for years. He threatened to withdraw Glaxo Wellcome from the UK, saying that the decision called into question whether the UK was a suitable base for a multinational pharmaceutical company. However Tony Blair, still a relatively new prime minister, and Frank Dobson, his health secretary, stood by their new baby's recommendation. Relenza was not prescribed – other than by one defiant practice in Devon – and the threat of the company withdrawing from the UK evaporated. NICE had been launched. It was there to provide not just recommendations on whether new pharmaceuticals and other technologies are sufficiently cost-effective for the NHS to adopt them, but also guidelines for clinicians on best practice.

Of all of the many new arm's-length bodies created by the 1997 Labour government, NICE is one of the few to have survived with its essential remit unchanged, celebrating its 20th anniversary in 2019. So, how did NICE come about? What has led to its longevity? How does its history offer lessons for other areas of public policy where evidence might be best applied?

NICE's origins are complex. They stretch back at least to the 1970s and arguably even earlier. The post-war explosion of medical advances – new drugs, new technologies, new treatments from kidney dialysis to transplants – had made it impossible for any individual doctor to keep up. Back in the 1950s, the *Index Medicus*, the index of all medical research, had been two thin volumes. By the late 1990s it came four times a year on computer discs that were each the equivalent of 30–40 volumes.

In 1972, Dr Archie Cochrane – after whom the Cochrane Collaboration is named (see Chapter 2, this volume) – published a seminal work on the importance of evidence-based medicine. He argued that treatments needed to be based not just on custom, tradition and hunch or 'on the opinion of senior consultants', but on 'hard evidence' of the gain to be expected for the patient, and on their cost. And in the face of the explosion in the research literature, medical specialists attempted to draw up guidelines on best practice. These varied enormously, however, in their quality and their evidence base – it being said that at one point there were 167 different guidelines for the treatment of asthma.[1] Health also began for the first time to attract the serious interest of economists, some of whom, in both the US and the UK, began to develop the Quality Adjusted Life Year (QALY). That allowed not just the year or extra years of life that a treatment might provide to be assessed, but also the quality of that life in terms of freedom from or reduction of pain, and the ability to carry on the normal activities of daily living. A monetary value could be put on that, producing a measure that allowed the value of new treatments of very different types to be compared. Thus, for example, a cheap and effective polio vaccine has a very low cost per QALY, despite millions of doses being needed, while a cancer drug that costs tens of thousands of pounds but which may have distressing side effects and extend life for only a few months, and in only a portion of those treated, will have a very high cost per QALY.

In 1985 and 1986 the English Department of Health commissioned its first economic evaluations – of heart transplants and breast cancer screening, judging both to be cost-effective, and in the early 1990s it created centres to synthesise the results of clinical trials to provide the best available evidence on the effectiveness of treatments and then disseminate them out into the NHS. It also began investing in health technology assessment centres at a number of universities, while working with British drug companies to produce guidance on the economic evaluation of new pharmaceuticals. And, by now, in academic circles at least, the idea had taken root that in order to get a licence, new drugs should not just have to pass the three established hurdles of safety, quality of manufacture and efficacy, but a 'fourth hurdle' – cost-effectiveness.

These are just a few of the many tributaries that fed the stream that eventually became NICE. Others included the decision from 1991 to create a 'purchaser/provider split' in the English NHS with the then health authorities and some general practitioners 'purchasing' health care from competing public – and occasionally private – hospitals. That led to the purchasers wanting to know which were the most cost-effective treatments to buy in order to make their budgets go furthest. And that in turn led to the creation of regional 'development and evaluation committees' to provide just such advice, particularly for new treatments. The fact that local purchasers could – and did – make different decisions from each other, however, led to charges that there was a 'postcode lottery' in health care – patients in some areas getting treatments that were denied to others.

Then along came Beta-interferon. The latest, and at the time the most expensive, of a list of increasingly costly new drugs. It was a treatment for multiple sclerosis that appeared to have some limited benefits, but one that, on the worst estimates, threatened to consume around 10 per cent of the drugs bill for uncertain long-term impact.

The health minister at the time was the Conservative Gerry Malone who was faced with the decision of whether the NHS should fund that. As he pointed out himself, in highly colourful language, he was probably the least qualified person in a room full of advisers to make that decision. A compromise was reached. But when it was done, Malone told his civil servants in 1995 to 'go away and devise some scheme where ministers do not have to take these decisions. This is not something that in my view should ever again land on a minister's desk' (Timmins et al, 2017).

This still was not NICE. But when an energetic new Labour government was elected in 1997 and wanted to do something about the quality of care – amid mounting concerns about the 'postcode lottery' and that the ever-rising cost of treatments was leading to the rationing of health care – NICE, after much tortured debate, was created. Both to assess whether new treatments were in fact cost-effective – and the QALY had provided the tool for that – and to provide a single authoritative source of clinical guidelines.

But if that is a highly truncated account of the origins of NICE, it alone does not explain its success. There were powerful forces aligned against it.

As Tony Culyer, the health economist who was NICE's first deputy chair, has put it:

> NICE constituted a threat to a lot of people – to politicians for whom this was a major piece of delegated decision making which some could reasonably argue should be for them or for a committee of the House of Commons. To the pharmaceutical industry – manifestly – who would not like some of what we were going to do. To clinicians who did not want to be told what to do – 'clinical freedom' and all of that. To patients and patient groups who had an obviously

vested interest in their own condition or disease.
(Timmins et al, 2017)

As Sykes's reaction showed, many of the pharmaceutical
companies baulked, at least initially, at the additional research
needed to demonstrate cost-effectiveness, while patient groups
could react with fury – descending on parliament and occasionally
into NICE's own offices – when the organisation judged a new
treatment to be insufficiently cost-effective for adoption. NICE
found itself accused by cancer sufferers and others of 'barbarism'
and of 'condemning us to death'. In the US, NICE found itself
characterised by some as being 'a death panel' because there were
treatments it refused to recommend.

Despite all that, NICE worked, with the pharmaceutical
industry coming to recognise that the cost-effectiveness of
treatments did have to be taken into account.

The guidelines

The recommendations on the cost-effectiveness of new treatments
have always been the part of NICE's work that attracted the big
headlines. But there are those – including Professor Sir Michael
Rawlins, NICE's chair for its first 14 years – who believe that the
best practice guidelines may have been NICE's most important
work: raising the quality of care. Even those on occasion
cause controversy.[2]

Why did it work?

There are many reasons that NICE has succeeded; particularly for
its work around cost-effectiveness. Among them are that it created
an independently managed Citizens' Council that, particularly in
the early days, helped it tackle some of the ethical issues that it
faced. For example, should it favour the young over the elderly?
Should it pay a premium for very expensive drugs to treat very
rare diseases? Or pay more for treatments for those in imminent
danger of dying – a version of 'the rule of rescue'?

NICE developed a far from simple but nonetheless fairly
transparent process for reaching its decisions. It publishes

preliminary rulings, allowing appeals. Its most common judgements are nuanced. Not a simple 'yes' or 'no', but often that a new drug is cost-effective for some sub-groups of patients but not for others, pending further evidence. And, absolutely critically, when the evidence changes, it changes its mind. Relenza being an early example of that. A year after the original decision, evidence emerged suggesting that Relenza did indeed reduce hospitalisation among the most vulnerable, so the institute recommended limited use in high-risk patients in years with a significant flu outbreak. Many years later, when a global epidemic of swine flu threatened in 2009, the NHS was to stockpile £136 million worth of the drug.

Most crucially, however, this part of NICE's remit worked because ministers allowed it to. At any one time, the NHS has a fixed budget. Thus, over the years, NICE has helped provide better value for money by reducing the risk that new, cost-ineffective treatments will drive out existing, cost-effective ones. Ministers have grasped this, while at the same time recognising that NICE has sheltered them from having to take deeply controversial decisions over what the NHS should and should not provide. It is to the credit of Department of Health (latterly the Department of Health and Social Care) civil servants that they have succeeded in repeatedly explaining this to successive ministers – that while overruling NICE to force the NHS to provide something the institute has rejected might win them short-term popularity, over time it would lead to every controversial decision landing back on their desks.

There have been some policy changes. In 2009, following a government-instituted review, NICE gave more value to 'end of life' treatments – often cancer drugs – so that the threshold at which it tended to approve such treatments moved to around £50,000 per QALY against the £20,000 to £30,000 range that it usually applied. This was, in essence, a political decision, as indeed was the 2010 decision when David Cameron, as prime minister, insisted on the introduction of a Cancer Drugs Fund through which the NHS would pay higher prices for such treatments. Mike Rawlins, the chair of NICE, Bruce Keogh, the NHS's medical director, and even Mike Richards, the so-called 'cancer czar', all urged ministers not to do it. Richards, despite oncology being his field, asking 'Why just cancer? There are a lot of other rotten diseases out there.' However, the Cancer Drugs Fund went ahead, the fund repeatedly over-spending as it largely turned the NHS into a price taker for whatever the companies wanted to charge. By 2016, the fund had largely been re-absorbed into something closer to NICE's more standard approach.

An expanded role

The success of NICE, despite it living a life that seemed at times to be one of permanent controversy, saw its role expanded. It was first asked to advise ministers on public health measures in 2005, producing a change of name to the National Institute for Health and Care Excellence – while retaining the acronym NICE – and in 2013 guidance on social care best practice was added. Public health is a bit of a crowded field, with Public Health England and its predecessors already existing (with Public Health England itself now split into two new bodies). And while there were and are levers that encourage clinicians to follow the medical guidelines, the levers to ensure that social care guidelines are adopted are weaker.[3]

Challenges

When it comes to health technology assessment, NICE's life has not become any easier. Gene therapies are becoming available that can fix the once incurable. Regulatory changes and in some cases subsidies are seeing more 'orphan drugs' come to market – treatments for diseases which have been too rare to create a viable market for pharmaceutical companies. The cost of many of these, even by the high prices that have been seen in the past, can be eye-watering, and the once pretty much standard way of assessing cost-effectiveness – using double-blind trials – can no longer be used because the numbers are too small for statistical rigour. Hybrid products that blur the lines between pharmaceuticals, medical devices and diagnostics are emerging, while the growing power of data and artificial intelligence will also change the landscape in which NICE operates.

Many of these changes 'will challenge normal health technology assessment methods and will require innovative regulation, access and reimbursement models to support their managed entry into the market', as NICE itself noted in a recently launched five-year strategy.[4]

The desire to achieve better integration between health and social care is likely to lead to guidelines that cross those traditional boundaries, while the impact of environmental concerns play into medicine as well as the rest of the world. The challenges are growing, not diminishing.

How far is NICE a model for others?

The UK – via NICE – was not the first country to get into the evaluation of the cost-effectiveness of treatments. Australia and New Zealand were ahead. NICE has, however, probably been the most influential globally, with many other countries learning at least something from it in terms of health technology assessment (Culyer et al, 2017). It has an international division which charges overseas agencies and governments for assistance on a not-for-profit basis.

Serious attempts have been made to understand how NICE's approach can be adapted for other areas of social policy. But it cannot be a case of 'copy and paste'. The point has already been made that NICE itself can no longer rely as heavily as it once did on what was once seen as the 'gold standard' of double-blind trials. But these are often harder to do in other areas, and they may be more ethically challenging than in medicine where there are standardised methods of ethical approval. Certainly when it comes to health technology assessment, much of NICE's work is underpinned by a huge volume of numbers – statistical analysis of trials and other evidence. It should be stressed that these statistical analyses are an aid to the judgements that NICE makes – its decisions are not merely the product of a desiccated calculating machine. (For example, on occasion, it recommends treatments that have a higher cost per QALY than the thresholds it normally uses.) But the fact remains that the quality of numerical evidence that is available to NICE may be harder to acquire in other fields.

For all that, there are clearly lessons that can be learnt from the experience of NICE, not least the way it tackled some of the pretty profound ethical issues it faced.

Notes

[1] www.publications.parliament.uk/pa/cm199899/cmselect/cmhealth/222/9020402.htm

[2] See, for example, www.theguardian.com/society/2021/aug/17/uk-health-watchdog-nice-delays-new-me-guidance-therapy-row-chronic-fatigue

[3] For example, doctors have to undergo a five-yearly re-validation of their fitness to practice and failure to adhere to NICE guidance can play a part in that. Social care is a local government responsibility and how far local government insists in its contracts with providers that NICE guidance on social care is followed is a matter for individual councils. Against that, the quality of care in both the NHS and social care is assessed by the inspectorate the Care Quality Commission.

[4] *NICE strategy 2021 to 2026*, https://static.nice.org.uk/NICE%20strategy%202021%20to%202026%20-%20Dynamic,%20Collaborative,%20Excellent.pdf

References

Culyer, A., Podhisita, C. and Santatiwongchai, B. (2017) A star in the east: History of HITAP. *F1000Research*. https://f1000research.com/documents/6-487

Timmins, N., Rawlins, M. and Appleby, J. (2017) A terrible beauty: A short history of NICE the National Institute for Health and Care Excellence. *F1000Research*, 6: 915.

4

What works in crime and policing: getting closer to the frontline

Rachel Tuffin

The model of the National Institute for Clinical Excellence (NICE) inspired other What Works Centres in domains outside of health – including policing and crime reduction. But how was this model adapted and adopted in policing? The College of Policing, which was created as the Professional Body for Policing, and a precursor body, the National Policing Improvement Agency, have for many years promoted a 'professionalisation agenda' in policing through various methods, including embedding evidence-based practice into police standards and policies (Hunter et al, 2017). As part of this evidence agenda, the College established a What Works Centre for Crime Reduction (WWCCR) in 2013 and created a standard system to rate and rank interventions in terms of their effectiveness and cost-savings (Effect, Mechanism, Moderators, Implementation and Economic Cost [EMMIE]) and an online Crime Reduction Toolkit. The centre has worked closely with the police on evidence-based standards, national policies and learning.

How successful has this close engagement with the police and stakeholders been? Other What Works Centres have been set up with greater independence – as stand-alone charities, or within universities. But the WWCCR is part of the College of Policing, which is an operationally independent arm's-length body of government. I led on setting up the WWCCR and will discuss how the close relationship with the police has evolved and its practical lessons for other areas of policy and practice.

Why What Works in a crime and policing context

There were two obvious and long-standing evidence challenges in the crime and policing context in the 2010s. The first is fairly standard in government: with limited resources, where should investment be targeted? Or, to put it another way – which activities would impact most on crime? The second was a related practice problem: a significant amount of crime prevention and policing practice lacked a clear evidence base. Even where we had the evidence, decisions were sometimes taken with potential or known harmful effects for the public – such as introducing initiatives taking young people to visit prisons, in line with the well-known Scared Straight example, found to increase offending (Petrosino et al, 2013).

These questions were still pertinent despite the pursuit of evidence-based policy since the Blair government (Chapter 2, this volume), hence the Cabinet Office carried out an assessment of the need for a greater What Works effort, looking for the following components of a healthy system:

- a pipeline of research;
- robust and easy to access synthesis of the findings; and
- a willingness and capability to use the evidence.

In terms of the pipeline, there was very limited funding going into new evaluation research in crime and policing, and while syntheses of the existing research existed, they were not easily accessible for practitioners and policy makers – either in terms of being comprehensible, or being locked behind the paywalls common to academic publishing. Finally, there were gaps in willingness and capacity to use evidence. The Cabinet Office proposed that a new What Works Centre, using the model drawn from medicine, be established to fill the perceived gap in supporting evidence-based crime policy (Cabinet Office, 2013). In responding to these identified gaps, while there was a reluctance to create a new organisation at a time when existing 'quangos' were being abolished, the Home Office was willing to agree to the College of Policing taking on a what works in crime reduction role.

The College of Policing was created in 2012 with an overt evidence-based and professionalising mission. The 'what works' function seemed to the new leadership of the College to be a natural fit in terms of the recommendations of previous policy reviews (Neyroud, 2011) and the focus of its research team. The team had moved from the Home Office to a precursor body, the National Policing Improvement Agency, seeking a closer relationship to practice, building on the experience of the Home Office's Crime Reduction Programme and Police Research Group with Professors Gloria Laycock, Ken Pease and Nick Tilley.

In terms of where to focus effort, in addition to the pipeline, access, capacity and willingness, we identified the lack of a strong system feeding research into decision-making processes. Our initial assessment was that the decision makers who would be most likely to affect adoption of evidence-based approaches, based on accountabilities, on who tended to chair crime reduction partnership working and be active locally as part of neighbourhood policing, were police officers. We therefore needed evidence-based decision-making and understanding of what works to be of interest and valued in policing.

Reflecting on our previous work, prior to the What Works Centre role, we recognised our tacit theory of change had been that if we encouraged and supported innovators and early adopters, they would 'pull' the rest of policing towards an evidence-based approach (Rogers, 2003). We tended to provide small-scale, targeted offerings, such as evidence review workshops or evidence-based policing master classes, following Sherman's insights (Sherman, 1998), which created awareness and a network for the innovators, but did not affect the wider system sufficiently. The policing culture seemed too strongly rooted for this to be enough on its own. People could attend motivating courses and opportunities but would then return to an environment where what they had learned was considered irrelevant. We needed evidence-based approaches to be far more generalised and we needed to find other points in the system which could support its adoption.

As an example, the College had inherited what is known as Authorised Professional Practice for policing. This library of documents varied considerably in their scope and were created largely from professional consensus building and selective use of evidence. There was limited explicit standard-setting, the cost of implementation was rarely described, and possibly as a consequence only monitored and assured in high-risk areas, such as the use of firearms. The content varied from awareness raising and 'calls to arms' to detailed procedures and protocols. Amidst this variety of formats and evidence standards was a real opportunity to introduce a transparent process including formal evidence reviews and multi-disciplinary committee processes in line with the NICE model (NICE, 2014).

Positive academic/practitioner partnerships, allowing rapid sharing of ideas from new research, did occur, but were an activity pursued by a minority. The view of the College team was that there was still too wide a gap between academia and policing, a sense that the two sectors were shouting at each other from adjacent hilltops (Bradley and Nixon, 2009), rather than working collaboratively. Unless this could be changed, the mere production of evidence could not be sufficient.

The new college was not set up with an endowment to allow major investment in commissioning new evaluations for the research pipeline – the model for the Education Endowment Foundation and Youth Endowment Fund. While we continued to identify research funding sources we needed to find an approach which could tap into the policing context specifically.

A final factor in our context was to appreciate that while the influence of leaders mattered hugely in policing, the level of independent discretion and decision-making in the hands of officers on the ground, day-to-day, mattered just as much.

There was evidence to suggest that, despite some senior views to the contrary, it mattered whether or not officers knew why they were asked to carry out a specific action. In the case of 'hotspots', where officers patrol very specific 'micro' locations for short periods, it was reported that officers didn't see why they should patrol where 'nothing was happening' because the preventive approach had not been explained and this was despite geographical tracking being possible (Fielding and Jones, 2012a, 2012b). Once officers were carefully briefed, compliance with the approach increased (Jones, personal communication, circa 2015).

What success would look like and how would it be delivered

We selected basic indicators of the conditions that needed to be met in order for crime and harm to be reduced as a result of our effort. The number of primary studies available for synthesis would grow, and there would be clear evidence of this information being used to inform decision making. On this last point, our summary of what the police could do to reduce crime pointed to the need for problem-solving preventive approaches rather than relying on enforcement (Quinton and Tuffin, 2012), so an increase in commitment to prevention activity, measured, for example, through inspection, public plans and tracking of the implementation of guidelines seemed a good proxy for the use of evidence-based approaches in decision making.

Increased access: toolkit and standards

One of our earliest decisions was to follow the approach of other What Works Centres (Higgins et al, 2013) to make the evidence easily available with a toolkit, in partnership with an academic consortium (Hunter et al, 2017) co-funded by the Economic and Social Research Council. We also set out to tackle one of the key previous challenges with the so-called black box of randomised trials, where minimal information was available about the context and mechanisms of the initiative, which made it hard to explain results, and hard to replicate effective practice (Tilley and Sidebottom, 2021).

To embed the evidence in standard setting, bringing it closer to use, our research and practice team designed and implemented new guidelines, directly informed by the NICE approach (Chapter 3, this volume), including as well as evidence review, a committee stage involving a range of individuals, not only specialists from policing, but academics, and other frontline or generalist practitioners able to challenge specialists, particularly in terms of how realistic the content would be in practice for a busy response officer.

Getting the evidence used in the policing context

The College team carried out a careful analysis of the requirements of a What Works system to develop the plan for evidence use. The research team had already carried out a review of the evidence on training and guidance, and behaviour change (Wheller and Morris, 2010), which had highlighted that these levers on their own would not be sufficient to resolve the problem, they needed to be part of a wider system approach. We used evidence from the reviews, including implementation science (see Wheller and Morris, 2010), to develop theories of change which analysed the problem we were trying to solve and articulated the end outcomes.

Shepherd's (2014) report on the evidence ecosystem highlighted the vital importance of the 'pull' factor. More than just being relatively willing recipients of findings, we needed key decision makers to be actively seeking it out, encouraging its creation and use. We recognised that a key difference compared to the NICE context was that practitioners lacked basic training in evidence-based approaches – something taken for granted in medicine, and which gives them a framework they can use for risky decisions.

At the same time, one of the College's research team, Julia Morris, had been exploring the findings of Lum and Palmer on police receptivity to research (Lum et al, 2012; Palmer et al, 2019). She noticed that the surveys found that the more officers knew about research, the less they believed the police alone had enough information about crime and how to address it, and at the same time the more they were exposed to research the more willing they were to do experiments. She hypothesised that if research become part of officers' professional experience, they would be much more likely to use it in their decision making.

Morris's insight gave us a clear direction in our efforts to overcome police officers' sense that academics were trying to tell them what to do, and that academic research was of limited practical value. If policing felt a sense of ownership of its evidence base, and could be confident in challenging and adding to it, there should be an eventual seismic shift in the value of evidence within policing. We used this insight as a guiding principle of our programmes of work from that point, including founding a policing bursary programme (Hunter et al, 2017), despite some initial scepticism and resistance to the idea that officers and staff beyond a minority had, or could develop, the capability.

Pulling all the levers

Moving beyond standard-setting, where evidence was more explicit, our approach to whole system change started with the elements the College of Policing oversee in our role as the professional body, specifically setting learning standards and the curriculum (Shepherd, 2014) – something that makes the WWCCR unique among What Works Centres. We instituted a review which led to the inclusion of an evidence-based policing module as a requirement for people to achieve the rank of chief officer. We also added it to earlier ranks/grades of leadership development, to address the feedback of officers at senior ranks who recognised they would have benefited from such input earlier in their careers (Neyroud, 2011).

At the same time, the learning programme for new police constables needed to be overhauled. Over ten years old, it lacked coverage of vulnerability, digital and cyber issues, mental health, as well as problem-solving and evidence-based policing. The curriculum was set at what can be understood as preparing people to follow orders known as 'level 3' (QAA, 2014, cited in College of Policing, 2016) when in reality they needed to make rapid, life-changing decisions with insufficient information in ambiguous settings with minimal supervision – pretty much a textbook definition of a need for 'level 6' education – the equivalent of a university degree (QAA, 2014, cited in College of Policing, 2016).

Police officers needed development in risk-based decision making – something which could also be foundational for an evidence-based policing system (Smith, 2021). At the time of writing, the changes required are gradually being rolled out across police forces, meaning, for example, that all officers on the initial apprenticeship scheme carry out a formal problem-solving or research project, an example of evidence-based policing (College of Policing, 2020). This approach can have a profound effect, as the acknowledgements of a final submission sent to the College suggest: '[My lecturer] has helped unlock my passion for research and academia and see potential in myself

I did not know I had' (Scott, 2021). At the same time, we have paid attention to profiles for all policing roles, our selection processes, the wider curriculum, and the syllabus for specific learning and training programmes. We have incorporated evidence-based approaches across our work from recruitment and selection (for example, College of Policing, 2015), to continuing professional development events, our design of national programmes, and direct support to forces on particular topics (Gough et al, 2018).

In order that these activities were reflected in the wider system, we seconded a member of staff into the policing inspectorate (Her Majesty's Inspectorate of Constabulary, now also Fire and Rescue Services) as it designed its force-by-force PEEL[1] inspection process, to help embed the evidence, so prevention and problem-solving activity was monitored (HMIC, 2016). We provided evidence-based inputs to the Cabinet Office commissioning academy, through which Police and Crime Commissioners, their offices and local government partners were supported to get value for money from their spending (Cabinet Office, 2016). We have fed in the appropriate what works evidence in briefings and presentations to the Home Office and central government meetings, roundtable events to inform the development of strategies and plans, such as the Home Office's Serious Violence Strategy (for example, Home Office, 2018).

How far have we got and what lessons have we learned?

As highlighted earlier, the College has tried to take a what works approach to our own work, being clear about the theories of change and impact. With that in mind, we included an independent evaluation requirement in our specification for the Economic and Social Research Council-funded academic consortium (Hunter et al, 2017). The evaluation findings, after three years, noted a shift in perceptions of senior officers of support for evidence-based practice, greater use of research and importance attached to its use. Five years later, there are further signs of it becoming standardised which are set out in this section.

Getting it shared: easily accessible evidence which is timely

Our toolkit, which now has 65 entries, is accessible to all and each entry pays careful attention to context, mechanism and implementation detail.[2] More evidence is still needed, both overall and to tackle the specific elements of interventions (Tompson et al, 2021). There is a particularly acute need for cost-benefit analysis to determine not just whether interventions are effective, but to weigh up their value relative to each other and inform investment choices. The number of people accessing our toolkit increased gradually at first and then more steeply recently, possibly thanks to incorporating problem-solving into the new officer curriculum (see Figure 4.1).[3]

Some commentators assumed that the focus of the What Works Centre would be on generating randomised trials, perhaps understandably because they are reliable for inclusion in systematic reviews. Our approach, however, has always been to use the best available evidence to fit the question, following the definition on the College website (College of Policing, 2012). When we publish evidence reviews on issues such as knife crime (Wheller and McNeil, 2019), we draw on the published evidence base – including trials and systematic reviews. But we also complement this with information about force activity which

Figure 4.1: Number of hits on the What Works Centre for Crime Reduction toolkit over time

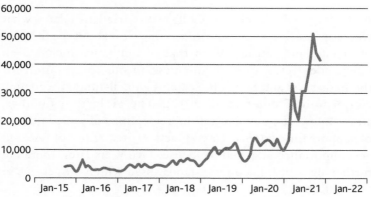

aims to tackle knife crime, has an explicit theory of change or a mechanism which aligns to the existing evidence base, but is not yet evaluated. We also share examples of new and emerging practice (for example, during the COVID-19 pandemic) through online events and briefing packs to be sure we remain as relevant as possible.

The evidence-based guidelines that have been delivered have benefited from the strong support of the National Police Chiefs' Council (the operational and employer coordination body) leads who collaborate by chairing the committees and input from forces. A call for practice goes out at the same time as the guidelines are developed, so the evidence-based principles are also accompanied by practical examples. Chief Constable Gavin Stephens, chairing the first committee on neighbourhood policing, has acted as a role model in terms of his focus on implementation, with repeated assessments of progress across forces following the publication of the guidelines (see Sharples et al, 2019, in the education context).

Improving the pipeline: getting more evidence

Of the 14 academic/police force partnerships founded from the Knowledge Fund we ran in the mid-2010s (Teers et al, 2018), eight continue to operate several years after their initial two-year funding period (for example, ExPERT), partly owing to the heavy emphasis we placed on sustainability in the application and award process. As well as finding increased access to evidence-based approaches for frontline officers and staff, the review of the fund found unexpected and valued impact for academics in terms of better understanding of the policing context and the value officers and staff could bring to research design, delivery and application (Tompson et al, 2017; Teers et al, 2018).

Along with some other specific programmes funded by the Home Office and others (for example, the Equality and Human Rights Commission), we have designed a number of programmes to increase access to funding for evaluation in partnership, including with public health and youth violence reduction funders. There has been feedback from funders that the intervention and evaluation design in policing are not yet strong enough, so we need more support for forces and partners to develop good theories of change and carefully designed interventions and evaluations (see Ghate, 2018).

Police forces such as Avon and Somerset, Devon and Cornwall, Durham, Hampshire, Kent, the Met and West Midlands have all taken steps to embed analytical approaches or evidence-based teams which are generating new research, using in-house officers and staff or partnerships with academia. The Society of Evidence-Based Policing, supported at its inception by Cambridge and Cardiff universities (Chapter 17, this volume), is also supporting individuals to carry out and share research, and has fostered the establishment of similar societies internationally.

Getting the evidence used at all levels

We mentioned earlier how evidence of preventive rather than enforcement approaches can be used as an indicator of success, and there are signs of this at all levels. Home Office programmes are increasingly driven by and creating new prevention evidence in line with their strategies and plans (Home Office, 2016, 2018, 2021).

Our toolkit was used to tie applications for the Safer Streets fund (College of Policing, 2020; Home Office, 2022) tightly to the prevention evidence base, with evaluations of the initiatives due to add to the evidence base. The Home Office has also funded a national programme of problem-solving and preventive policing, designed by the College and South Yorkshire Police, which has led to the creation of a new cross-cutting Prevention Committee of National Police Chiefs' Council. In terms of political oversight, in a recent review of Police and Crime Commissioners' Police and Crime plans, nearly all explicitly mention prevention.

Finally, at the frontline, evidence from the evaluation of the new 'level 6' police officer curriculum has been positive, with officers rating it on average around 15 percentage points higher than the previous curriculum in terms of how well it prepares them for their role (Price and Middleton, forthcoming). New curriculum officers also reported slightly higher levels of awareness of evidence-based policing and problem-solving, although there was room for improvement in their views on the extent of use of these techniques and how their university learning is received and linked to experience on the ground.

Widening the network of innovators and early adopters

Research delivered as part of officer and staff continuing professional development is increasing, with the Cambridge Evidence Based Policing Masters being particularly productive. Police forces have regularly funded students on these programmes, in addition to the Knowledge Fund and college bursary programme. Rothwell et al (2018), a recent graduate of the Cambridge course, and member of Kent Police's innovation taskforce, was supported by her force and successfully accessed Home Office funding to design and implement a randomised controlled trial of video response for domestic abuse, which is now being rolled out in her home force and considered for national adoption. Similarly, we have growing evidence of the impact of the College bursary on individuals, and beyond, as officers/staff commit to sharing their findings and getting their research evidence used where possible. An email received in 2021 highlights how this can reinvigorate officers:

> It's truly done wonders for my confidence and for my self-belief: a little over two years ago, I was a lowly DC [Detective Constable] looking for something to distract my brain. Currently, I'm considering an offer of a part-time PhD and being considered (by some poor souls!) as an expert in my field. ... Without the funding I received from the CoP [College of Policing], I would never have done it.

While we still want to appeal to the innovators and the early adopters in evidence-based practice, we have tried to appeal to those who would never consider themselves to be academic, remembering the earlier quote. Anyone can write or be a peer reviewer for *Going Equipped*, the College's magazine written by and for police officers and staff, which includes short idea and case study pieces as well as journal-type articles (see, for example, Holton, 2021), or be part of an evidence-based guideline committee. By making people part of the network of those sharing practice and reviewing each other's work, we hope to draw more people from the mainstream into the other opportunities to develop as evidence-based practitioners.

Where next?

We need everyone in crime and policing to be alert for the opportunities to evaluate that come with innovative ideas, projects and programmes. Where there is existing data of the right quality, evaluations can be designed and put in place without slowing down initiatives to any serious extent, the key is to be able to influence the implementation approach (Chapter 10). Furthermore, our assessment is that taking the few days or weeks needed to pay careful attention to mechanism and implementation does not only provide a stronger evaluation, but also a better chance of delivering impact.

We have found through analysis of the patterns from inspection, review and inquiries that areas for improvement in policing are repeated across time (Morris and Sims, nd). The need for officer and staff supervision to improve, for example, has recurred in topic silos (domestic abuse, stop and search, mental health), meaning a concerted effort to improve supervision overall has never happened. We are now using the ten issues we identified via this route to inform our business planning (which includes taking a preventive approach), with University College London's Capability Opportunity Motivation – Behaviour (COM-B)[4] model set alongside them (West and Michie, 2020) to guide the detailed development of initiatives to tackle these 'sticky' problems.

While we have made some progress in policing and it remains a core focus, there is a significant amount of further work required to encourage use of the relevant findings with all relevant crime and justice stakeholders, 'pulling' all the available levers. We are still only funded to provide the detailed supporting implementation work in a policing context, although we have managed to extend it in partnership, for example with public health, and to a limited extent with local authorities and community safety partnerships (Surrey County Council, 2017; College of Policing, 2021).

Finally, we need better mechanisms to collaborate, and share studies, findings and approaches across What Works Centres. There are cross-cutting issues in crime and justice where the sector that needs to implement a solution isn't funded to do so and doesn't benefit from its impact. An example would be a peer resistance intervention 'life skills training' with well-evidenced positive outcomes for risky health and crime behaviours

(Dartington Social Research Unit, 2013). Relatively cheap when delivered in a school environment, the initiative doesn't appear to have educational attainment outcomes, so would not be obviously attractive to governing bodies and headteachers. Incentives for the system to operate more collaboratively need to be introduced and tested, with the new Evaluation Accelerator Fund offering opportunities in this regard (Cabinet Office, 2022).

Acknowledgements

Thanks to Nerys Thomas and Michael Sanders for helpful comments on a draft of this chapter and to Angel Egbuji, Chris Price, Karin Rogers and Jo Wilkinson for answering my data and referencing queries rapidly and with good humour.

Notes

[1]   The acronym stands for Police Effectiveness, Efficiency and Legitimacy, spelling out the name of the person credited with the founding of the modern police service – Sir Robert Peel.
[2]   The toolkit can be found online at www.college.police.uk/research/crime-reduction-toolkit
[3]   There is some possibility of contamination by automated 'bots'.
[4]   The COM-B model takes an approach that behaviour change is brought about as a result of a person having the capability, opportunity and motivation to change.

References

Bradley, D. and Nixon, C. (2009) Ending the 'dialogue of the deaf': Evidence and policing policies and practices. An Australian case study. *Police Practice and Research*, 10(5–6): 423–435.
Cabinet Office (2013) *What works: Evidence centres for social policy*. Cabinet Office. https://assets.publishing.service.gov.uk/gov ernment/uploads/system/uploads/attachment_data/file/136 227/What_Works_publication.pdf
Cabinet Office (2016) *The Commissioning Academy*. Cabinet Office. www.gov.uk/guidance/the-commissioning-academy-information
Cabinet Office (2022) *Evaluation Accelerator Fund: Guidance*. Cabinet Office. www.gov.uk/government/publications/eva luation-accelerator-fund/evaluation-accelerator-fund-guidance

College of Policing (2012) *Evidence-based policing*. College of Policing. www.college.police.uk/research/evidence-based-polic ing-EBP

College of Policing (2015) *Tackling unconscious bias in recruitment, selection and promotion processes. A rapid evidence assessment: Executive summary*. College of Policing. https://library.college.police. uk/docs/college-of-policing/Unconscious_bias_REA_e xec_sum.pdf

College of Policing (2016) *Policing education qualifications framework consultation*. College of Policing. https://library.college.police.uk/ docs/college-of-policing/PEQF_consultation_final_290116.pdf

College of Policing (2020) *Policing education qualifications framework*. College of Policing. www.college.police.uk/guidance/policing-education-qualifications-framework-peqf

College of Policing (2021) *Policing and health collaboration: Landscape review*. College of Policing. https://assets.college.police.uk/ s3fs-public/2021-09/policing-and-health-collaboration-landsc ape-review-2021.pdf

Dartington Social Research Unit (2013) *Life skills training*. Investing in Children Database. www.investinginchildren. org.uk/

Fielding, M. and Jones, V. (2012a) 'Disrupting the optimal forager': Predictive risk mapping and domestic burglary reduction in Trafford, Greater Manchester. *International Journal of Police Science & Management*, 14(1): 30–41.

Fielding, M. and Jones, V. (2012b) *Repeat victimisation – road to reduction: Disrupting the optimal forager. Predictive mapping and super – cocooning in Trafford*. Submission to Goldstein Award. https://popcen ter.asu.edu/sites/default/files/12-08f_manchester_trafford.pdf

Ghate, D. (2018) Developing theories of change for social programmes: Co-producing evidence-supported quality improvement. *Palgrave Communication*, 4(1): 1–13.

Gough, D., Maidment, C. and Sharples, J. (2018) *UK What Works Centres: Aims, methods and context*. EPPI-Centre Social Science Research Unit UCL Institute of Education University College London. https://eppi.ioe.ac.uk/cms/Portals/0/PDF%20revi ews%20and%20summaries/UK%20what%20works%20cent res%20study%20final%20report%20july%202018.pdf?ver=2018-07-03-155057-243

Higgins, S., Katsipataki, M., Kokotsaki, D., Coleman, R., Major, L.E. and Coe, R. (2013) *The Sutton Trust: Education Endowment Foundation teaching and learning toolkit*. Education Endowment Foundation. https://educationendowmentfoundation.org.uk/education-evidence/teaching-learning-toolkit

HMIC (Her Majesty's Inspectorate of Constabulary) (2016) *PEEL: Police effectiveness 2016: A national overview*. HMIC. www.justiceinspectorates.gov.uk/hmicfrs/wp-content/uploads/peel-police-effectiveness-2016.pdf

Holton, J. (2021) Do frontline practitioners recognise the signs of honour-based abuse? *Going Equipped*, 3: 9–17. https://library.college.police.uk/docs/college-of-policing/Going-equipped-issue-3-2021.pdf

Home Office (2016) *Modern crime prevention strategy*. Home Office. https://assets.publishing.service.gov.uk/government/uploads/system/uploads/attachment_data/file/509831/6.1770_Modern_Crime_Prevention_Strategy_final_WEB_version.pdf

Home Office (2018) *Serious violence strategy*. Home Office. https://assets.publishing.service.gov.uk/government/uploads/system/uploads/attachment_data/file/698009/serious-violence-strategy.pdf

Home Office (2021) *From harm to hope: A 10-year drugs plan to cut crime and save lives*. Home Office. https://assets.publishing.service.gov.uk/government/uploads/system/uploads/attachment_data/file/1043484/From_harm_to_hope_PDF.pdf

Home Office (2022) *Safer Streets Fund: 2021 to 2022 prospectus*. Home Office. www.gov.uk/government/publications/safer-streets-fund-application-process/safer-streets-fund-2021-to-2022-prospectus-accessible-version

Hunter, G., May, T. and Hough, M. (2017) *An evaluation of the What Works Centre for Crime Reduction: Final report*. Birkbeck. https://library.college.police.uk/docs/what-works/ICPR_Final_Evaluation_WWCCR.pdf

Lum, C., Telep, C., Koper, C. and Grieco, J. (2012) Receptivity to research in policing. *Justice Research and Policy*, 14(1): 61–95.

Morris, J. and Sims, G. (nd) *Perennial issues in policing*. Unpublished. Available on request from whatworks@college.policing.uk

Neyroud, P. (2011) *Review of police leadership and training*. Home Office. www.gov.uk/government/publications/police-leaders hip-and-training-report-review

NICE (National Institute for Health and Care Excellence) (2014) *Developing NICE guidelines: The manual. Process and methods*. www.nice.org.uk/process/pmg20/resources/developing-nice-guidelines-the-manual-pdf-72286708700869

Palmer, I., Kirby, S. and Phythian, R. (2019) Assessing the appetite for evidence based policing: A UK based study. *International Journal of Police Science and Management*, 21(1): 91–100.

Petrosino, A., Turpin-Petrosino, C., Hollis-Peel, M.E. and Lavenberg, J.G. (2013) 'Scared Straight' and other juvenile awareness programs for preventing juvenile delinquency. *Cochrane Database of Systematic Reviews*, 4.

Price, C. and Middleton, E. (forthcoming) *Evaluation of the new entry routes into policing: Second interim report*. College of Policing.

Quinton, P. and Tuffin, R. (2012) *What works in policing to reduce crime*. College of Policing. www.college.police.uk/research/what-works-policing-reduce-crime

Rogers, E.M. (2003) *Diffusion of innovations*. Free Press.

Scott, N. (2021) *Towards Nottinghamshire Police's Mental Health and Wellbeing Services: A study to assess the services provided by Nottinghamshire Police that aim to support the mental health and wellbeing of their police officers*. Dissertation submission. Available on request from www.whatworks@college.police.uk

Sharples, J., Albers, B. and Fraser, S. (2019) *Putting evidence to work: A school's guide to implementation*, second edition. Education Endowment Foundation. https://d2tic4wvo1iusb.cloudfront.net/eef-guidance-reports/implementation/EEF_Implementati on_Guidance_Report_2019.pdf?v=1635355218

Shepherd, J. (2014) *How to achieve more effective services: The evidence ecosystem*. What Works Network/Cardiff University. https://library.college.police.uk/docs/what-works/Shepherd-effect ive-services-2014.pdf

Sherman, L. (1998) *Evidence-based policing*. Police Foundation. www.policefoundation.org/wp-content/uploads/2015/06/Sher man-1998-Evidence-Based-Policing.pdf

Smith, R. (2021) From practitioner to policymaker: Developing influence and expertise to deliver police reform. In E. Piza and B. Welsh (eds) *The globalization of evidence-based policing innovations in bridging the research-practice divide*. Routledge.

Surrey County Council (2017) *Joint strategic needs assessment: Community safety*. Surrey County Council. www.surreyi.gov.uk/jsna/community-safety/

Teers, R., Miller, N. and Braddock, R. (2018) *Knowledge fund review*. College of Policing. https://library.college.police.uk/docs/college-of-policing/Police-knowledge-fund-review-final-2018.pdf

Tilley, N. and Sidebottom, A. (2021) EMMIE and the What Works Centre for Crime Reduction. In E. Piza and B. Welsh (eds) *The globalization of evidence-based policing innovations in bridging the research-practice divide*. Routledge.

Tompson, L., Belur, J., Morris, J. and Tuffin, R. (2017) How to make police-researcher partnerships mutually effective. In J. Knutsson and L. Tompson (eds) *Advances in evidence-based policing*. Routledge.

Tompson, L., Belur, J., Thornton, A., Bowers, K., Johnson, S., Sidebottom, A., Tilley, N. and Laycock, G. (2021) How strong is the evidence-base for crime reduction professionals? *Justice Evaluation Journal*, 4(1): 68–97.

West, R. and Michie, S. (2020) A brief introduction to the COM-B Model of behaviour and the PRIME Theory of motivation [v1]. *UCL Discovery*. https://discovery.ucl.ac.uk/id/eprint/10095640/

Wheller, L. and McNeil, A. (2019) *Knife crime evidence briefing*. College of Policing. https://assets.college.police.uk/s3fs-public/2022-03/Knife_Crime_Evidence_Briefing.pdf

Wheller, L. and Morris, J. (2010) *What works in training, behaviour change and implementing guidance?* NPIA Research, Analysis and Information (RAI) Unit. https://library.college.police.uk/docs/npia/What-Works-in-Training-and-Behaviour-Change-REA-2010.pdf

5

The Education Endowment Foundation: building the role of evidence in the education system

Harry Madgwick, Becky Francis and Jonathan Kay

Since its establishment in 2011, the Education Endowment Foundation (EEF) has undertaken an ambitious programme of research with a focus on generating evidence of 'what works' in education. In its first ten years, the EEF commissioned over 160 randomised controlled trials (RCTs), developed an extensive suite of guidance and resources founded upon the best available evidence for teachers and school leaders, and built trusting relationships with stakeholders from across the education sector.

The EEF was set up as an independent charity by the Sutton Trust and Impetus with a £125 million endowment from the Department for Education, which came with a condition to spend £200 million over a 15-year period, and the purpose to improve the educational attainment of socially disadvantaged pupils. In 2013 the EEF was also designated as the What Works Centre for Education, acting as a founding member of the What Works Network. Throughout its lifespan the EEF's mission has been to support high-quality teaching and learning for all, and to challenge the socioeconomic gap for educational attainment. The EEF's story is therefore one of two gaps: closing the evidence gap to help close the disadvantage gap.

The attainment gap between disadvantaged pupils and their peers begins early. On average, reception age children are

4.6 months behind their better-off classmates. Over the next 11 years of full-time schooling, this learning gap widens and by the time children take their GCSEs, the gap has increased to 18.4 months (Hutchinson et al, 2018). More than two-thirds of 16-year-olds who have been eligible for free school meals leave school without attaining the grade 5 or above in English and maths GCSE that can constitute a 'good standard' of attainment (DfE, 2021a). These academic qualifications are prerequisites for progressing into secure, good-quality employment, including apprenticeships, further study and higher education.

As the most impactful within-school influence on pupil attainment (Hattie, 2003), teaching has the potential to reduce attainment gaps and secure improved outcomes for disadvantaged young people. Across England, schools have demonstrated an ability to close learning gaps through high-quality teaching, targeted interventions and wider strategies that remove barriers to learning (Hutchinson et al, 2018). Yet, to do so, schools and teachers require reliable information on the practices that are most likely to have a positive impact on pupils' learning (Gu et al, 2021).

Working with limited budgets and resources, schools also need to know how best to distribute their annual spend to bring about the biggest benefits for pupils. When the Pupil Premium was introduced in 2011 as a supplementary source of funding to help schools overcome barriers to learning experienced by pupils from families of lower socioeconomic backgrounds, little information or evidence was available on what might comprise effective ways of spending this money.

Since then, the EEF has sought to redress these gaps in research evidence. It has populated a previously sparse field of RCT studies in UK education research, involving 16,000 schools and 1.7 million pupil participants. It develops the Teaching and Learning Toolkit with Professor Steve Higgins and Durham University – which is used by over two-thirds of school leaders in England and is translated for 18 countries across five formal partnerships. Alongside this it has built a network of Research Schools to support the system in making best use of available research evidence.

In 2020–2021, £2.44 billion of Pupil Premium funding was allocated to boost the attainment of around two million pupils eligible for free school meals. By assisting the professional judgement of school leaders and teachers with trustworthy information founded upon rigorous research evidence, the EEF promotes effective and efficient use of the Pupil Premium across local and national levels.

By identifying effective approaches and disseminating insights from research activities to schools and policy makers, over the past decade the EEF has established itself as a go-to source for evidence generation, synthesis and mobilisation (Qu, 2021; Sutton Trust, 2021; DfE, 2022). We take a deeper dive into each of these areas in the following sections, reflecting on the EEF's influence on the education system and some of the challenges experienced along the way.

Evidence generation

RCTs remained very rare in UK educational research prior to the EEF's establishment (see, for example, Oakley et al, 2005). However, in the intervening decade the EEF has commissioned 166 high-quality, large-scale experimental trials (Edovald and Nevill, 2021). RCTs offer several key benefits as a robust method for evaluating practice. By allocating participants randomly to treatment and control groups, RCTs can eliminate selection bias. Such trials can offer teachers, school leaders and policy makers causally robust data on the effectiveness of programmes or interventions, which, when aligned with information on cost and implementation successes and challenges, may provide insights into 'best bets' for future practice.

RCTs are not all the same quality, however. Historically RCTs in education were often conducted by delivery organisations – the people who design and deliver the interventions – rather than independent evaluators, and best practice methods such as pre-specification of analysis was uncommon (Slavin et al, 2021). Such processes reduce the likelihood that research is biased by those invested in the outcomes from it. This is why the EEF has always ensured that it sets the highest sector standards for research transparency, pre-specification and reporting, seeking the least-biased methods for estimating the effectiveness of approaches to teaching and learning (Nevill, 2019).

The move towards more experimental evidence generation has not gone without criticism. One argument is that RCT use in education is unethical as pupils in either control or treatment groups may be disadvantaged by their (in)access to a potentially harmful or effective intervention (see discussion reported by Oakley, 2006). However, without robust evidence we cannot know whether an intervention is effective, or whether it is the control or treatment group that is being disadvantaged by their allocation (Hutchison and Styles, 2010). The EEF has also trialled approaches which are not entirely 'novel', such as those already being used in some schools, but not in others. In this sense, the effect of the trial is to generate knowledge by replacing arbitrary assignment with random assignment.

Another criticism of RCTs in education and other domains of social policy has been that the production of quantitative estimates on programme effectiveness can act as a 'black box'; we can learn whether a particular approach works or not but have little to no information why or how it did or did not work (Siddiqui et al, 2018). To address this issue, the EEF regularly refines its guidance to researchers on how best to collect data on the processes underlying pedagogical approaches, and has gradually extended its emphasis on process evaluation, subsequently providing the sector with more nuanced and robust information on the ways in which programmes and interventions are implemented.

By assessing the level of compliance and fidelity with which approaches are put into practice, and the specific mechanisms and theories thought to generate change in practice and learning (Nevill, 2019), the EEF has ensured that trials can not only inform schools about what programmes have or have not worked, but also why these were successful or not, and which specific mechanisms, practices and actions enhance the likelihood of this success.

Conducting research in education is nevertheless highly complex and fraught with practical challenges. School leaders and classroom teachers tend to be time-poor professionals whose primary concern is the needs of their pupils, so to set up school-based RCTs the EEF has been required to proactively encourage teachers to participate in such experiments. For example, agreeing to participation and randomisation may mean that schools are not able to implement a programme that they are keen to make use of, often even after the trial has finished. One way the EEF has remedied this concern is through waiting-list trial designs that enable all schools to access the programme following the trial (Coe et al, 2013). While helpful in addressing schools' reluctance to participate, this approach also eliminates researchers' ability to study the long-term effects of programmes through further long-term post-hoc analysis.

Another common challenge of conducting RCTs in education is attrition. Retaining schools, teachers and pupils throughout the entirety of a trial, and ensuring pre-specified assessments are carried out as planned, is vital to source the necessary statistical power[1] for statistically significant results, and for generating findings that are more generalisable across different types of schools. Yet, schools are busy places with lots going on and many competing priorities. In early trials, average attrition was 24 per cent (Edovald and Nevill, 2021). In order to tackle this obstacle, the EEF has implemented the following measures:

- Financial incentives have been used to encourage participation and cover administration and time costs of trial involvement.
- Schools are recruited to the evaluation (not just the project): schools that have 'bought in' to the idea of building evidence through evaluation are more likely to stay committed to the evaluation regardless of whether they are allocated to receive the project.
- Control schools are shown to be as valuable to the evaluation as treatment schools: it is important that schools understand that schools in the control group are as valuable to the evaluation as schools in the treatment group. The data collected from control schools allows us to understand the effect of the project. Without control schools we are unable to have a robust evaluation.
- The requirements of trial involvement are explained before schools sign up: schools that are aware of the demands of the evaluation and are enthusiastic about the evaluation are less likely to drop out. It is helpful if the project and evaluation teams work closely to ensure that whoever is recruiting is able to explain the evaluation clearly and communicate the requirements of the evaluation.

Average attrition was reduced to 17.8 per cent by 2019 – a 25 per cent drop – and often the result of challenges linking data rather than large numbers of pupils or schools dropping out of trials. The efficacy (Sibieta et al, 2016) and effectiveness (Dimova et al, 2020) trials of the Nuffield Early Language Intervention (NELI) demonstrate how research can engage schools in the processes and outcomes of evidence generation. The NELI programme is designed to improve the language skills of reception-aged (4–5-year-old) pupils using scripted individual and small-group language teaching sessions, delivered by trained teaching assistants. The NELI trials commissioned by the EEF showed that the programme had consistently positive impacts on learning: the efficacy and effectiveness trials involved over 2,000 pupils from over 4,000 schools and found that the intervention had between three and four months of additional progress within an academic year, respectively. This provoked the Department for Education to fund a countrywide scale-up of the programme in 2020, which the EEF assisted with the University of Oxford and educator training provider Elkan. Schools with high proportions of disadvantaged pupils were given priority access to the ring-fenced funding provided to the programme, illustrating how robust research evidence coupled with targeted government spending can work to address educational inequalities (see Figure 5.1).

A key lesson from the first ten years of the EEF is that while RCTs provide rigorous impact estimates, they may not always be appropriate or even possible. One example was an attempt to evaluate later school start times (based on neuroscientific evidence on teenage circadian rhythms). Schools may have been willing to change their start times – but they were not willing to explain to parents and governors that the school time would be dictated by the coin flip of whether they were allocated to treatment or control. The trial aimed to recruit 100 schools – by the time the trial was abandoned, only 12 had signed up. Responding to these challenges, the foundation has also commissioned different types of research and developed more advanced requirements for process evaluations. Both moves have been motivated by a drive to conduct research that is both feasible, and relevant for and supportive of the working practices of teachers and school leaders.

Figure 5.1: Nuffield Early Language Intervention scale-up timeline

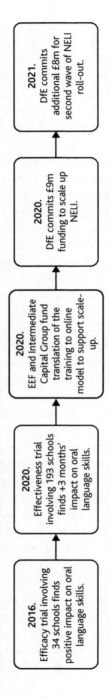

2016.
Efficacy trial involving 34 schools finds positive impact on oral language skills.

2020.
Effectiveness trial involving 193 schools finds +3 months' impact on oral language skills.

2020.
EEF and Intermediate Capital Group fund translation of the training to online model to support scale-up.

2020.
DfE commits £9m funding to scale up NELI.

2021.
DfE commits additional £8m for second wave of NELI roll-out.

For example, quasi-experimental designs have been used to explore variations of practice that already exist within the English education system, such as whether and how schools teach in mixed attainment classes (Roy et al, 2018). In 2019 the EEF embarked upon a new avenue of research named 'Teacher Choices' – a series of projects that sought to test the impact of practices that are already commonplace in classrooms across the country (Coe, 2019); for example, is it better to start a lesson using a retrieval quiz or with a discussion-based activity. By engaging practising teachers in the development of research topics and questions, such trial methodologies can enhance research-informed professionalism in the sector, while also ensuring that evidence generated is highly relevant for everyday classroom practice.

The most effective way of engaging schools in a trial and in valuing the results of evidence generation is to ensure that research answers the questions that schools care about. The first ten years of the EEF has been focused on assessing what aspects of current practice work through evaluating popular education programmes and submissions from schools. In the future, an explicit research agenda will identify what questions practitioners care most about and hence which research can leverage the biggest impact. The most rigorous and appropriate methodology for answering the questions will be selected after this exploratory engagement with practising teachers, ensuring that research methods and trial designs are employed with a specific purpose in mind.

Evidence synthesis

The generation of research evidence on the effectiveness of programmes, approaches and practices has provided schools with much richer information on effective uses of time and money. However, most 'off the shelf' programmes are not available in every area of the country due to market supply, meaning that some schools may not be able to implement those that are found to be successful, even if they wanted to. It is therefore vital that school leaders have access to evidence on the likely effectiveness of more general approaches to support pupil learning that are not wedded to specific programmes or organisations whose capacity is limited.

The EEF's Teaching and Learning Toolkit fulfils this objective, providing high-quality evidence on the prior effectiveness of pedagogical and other within-school approaches that may benefit pupil outcomes. Established and led by Professor Steve Higgins and his team at Durham University, with support from the Sutton Trust, the toolkit synthesises existing research evidence using meta-analyses to assist and inform decision making in schools. The preliminary development of the toolkit built upon a database of educational meta-analyses compiled by Higgins and colleagues and funded through the Economic and Social Research Council's Researcher Development Initiative from 2008 to 2011 (Higgins, 2018).

By aggregating the impact of research trials within 30 overarching approaches that schools may choose to employ, the toolkit has become a go-to source for teachers, with 69 per cent of school senior leaders now using the toolkit to inform their decision making (Sutton Trust, 2021).

Also included within the toolkit's headline impact findings for each approach – which is communicated in a more school-friendly months' progress figure rather than the raw effect size – is a security of evidence rating and cost ranking. By combining these three sources of information on specific teaching practices and engaging with the additional findings from the research that underpins the toolkit, school leaders can make informed professional judgements about how to spend finite time and money in a way that is most likely to improve pupils' learning (Higgins et al, 2012).

The original Teaching and Learning Toolkit derived the average impacts of approaches through the aggregation of effect sizes taken from existing meta-analyses and systematic reviews: synthesising evidence at the 'meta-meta-analytic level'. In 2021, though, the EEF updated the entire resource by 'unzipping' the original meta-analyses and reviews to aggregate effect sizes at the study level. This refined methodology enabled a much more thorough and robust analysis of study quality and risk of biases, as well as allowing for a more nuanced exploration of factors that explain variation in outcomes within approaches, such as age, subject and specific strategy type (for example, the impact of written or oral feedback rather than just feedback overall). Rather than siloing studies into separate reviews across different topic areas, the EEF has built a central living database of over 2,500 studies, which will form the basis of the underlying evidence infrastructure of the organisation and allows for cross-topic research on methodology and transferability.

In practical terms, the toolkit's new update provides school leaders with far greater detail on the evidence of approaches and the applicability of the existing research to each user's context. As critics of meta-analysis have argued, when synthesising evidence in education, it is essential to consider the relevance of context (Wiliam, 2019); this is why the toolkit clearly communicates how and where approaches have been trialled and uses contextual factors to explore the causes of variation by examining the influence of covariates that may moderate impacts. Put together, this enables school leaders to make professional judgements about which findings are most relevant to their schools, teachers and pupils.

While originally developed for the English school system, in part due to its conducive pairing with the Pupil Premium policy and funding to schools, the toolkit has also proven to have great functionality to education systems and schools around the world (Higgins, 2019). Through the establishment of international partnerships with education and research organisations across the globe, the EEF has licensed the toolkit to many different contexts, including sub-Saharan Africa and South America. These translated toolkits include global and local evidence – transparently communicating the source of evidence and potential relevance to context or research question.

Other countries and governments have also made use of the EEF's Teaching and Learning Toolkit. Most recently, the Dutch government and Ministry of Education have drawn upon the toolkit to guide recovery spending following the COVID-19 pandemic: the approaches taken from the EEF's website have been aligned with other sources of evidence to provide a menu of teaching and learning methods that schools can choose to spend additional funding on.

Evidence mobilisation

The EEF's generation and synthesis of evidence has gone a long way in addressing the existing evidence gaps in the sector. This said, the production and collation of evidence is not enough to develop a system-wide adoption of evidence-informed practice. Schools are extremely busy places, staffed by teachers with a finite amount of time and attention. The EEF has developed four approaches to ensure knowledge brokerage and secure impact.

To address the challenge of mobilising the EEF's guidance and resources to teachers and school, in 2015 it established a network of Research Schools who act as a focal-point for evidence-based practice in their region. Building affiliations with large numbers of schools and supporting the use of evidence at scale, the Research Schools play three key functions in the school system:

1. Disseminate evidence-based programmes and practices, and support their effective use through events, school-to-school support, training and professional development.
2. Model and develop evidence-based practice, involving the production of guidance and support for within-school implementation and evaluation.
3. Bridge the gap between research and practice by developing innovative practices and interventions based on the latest research, including the capturing and codification of effective approaches to enable replicability.

To instigate wide-scale and long-lasting change in the school system, the EEF works with the Research Schools to establish localised partnerships that broker knowledge and facilitate more effective evidence through a regional strategy. As such, the Research Schools Network has acted as the EEF's conduit for engaging and communicating with the wider school system (Gu et al, 2021); and provided an invaluable sounding board for the EEF regarding schools' needs, and the usefulness or otherwise of its resources. Research Schools are system leaders in evidence implementation, having developed specialist expertise in monitoring and adjusting the way in which research findings are translated and applied to real-school and classroom contexts.

They provide continuing professional development and partner with other local schools and stakeholders to develop evidence-led initiatives.

In addition to this localised approach to evidence mobilisation, the second method EEF uses to encourage impact is its resources and materials. These include, of course, the Teaching and Learning Toolkit itself; but also a suite of guidance reports, evidence reviews, teaching materials and other resources, which draw from research evidence to support teaching and learning. Recent research for the Department for Education (DfE, 2022) on schools' recovery strategies during the COVID-19 crisis found that the EEF was cited most frequently as the most useful resource used by schools to support their delivery and planning for recovery during the pandemic.

Third, the EEF has more recently sought to support evidence-informed policy making, to achieve its mission by influencing the operationalisation of evidence at a national policy level. Despite being funded initially by the Department for Education, the endowment model means that the EEF is independent of government and the Department for Education cannot make direct decisions on the EEF's research agenda or activities. The EEF instead engages with the Department for Education as an independent partner when policy can be an effective route to achieving the EEF's mission.

As a notable example, given the evidence of impact of teaching quality on pupil progress – and especially for pupils from disadvantaged backgrounds – the EEF has supported the Department for Education by curating the research evidence for a suite of national career development programmes for the teaching profession, including for the Early Career Framework and reformed National Professional Qualifications. As such the EEF has evolved an 'evidence guardian' role, a position it could not play without the sector's respect for the foundation's bipartisan stewardship of robust research evidence that minimises political biases.

Through this emerging role, the EEF has:

1. Quality assured the statements and research evidence underpinning policy frameworks. These frameworks prescribe

the knowledge and skills teachers should learn and master by enrolling upon career development programmes – see the Early Career Framework as an example (DfE, 2019).

2. Advised Department for Education officials on how to critically appraise the operationalisation of evidence to assist the procurement of programme providers.

3. Reviewed the materials developed from the previously approved frameworks, ensuring that all framework statements are covered in full, and that underpinning evidence is presented with appropriate fidelity to the original research papers.

The EEF has extended this policy-support approach to Pupil Premium development, and to educational recovery during the COVID-19 pandemic.

And, fourth, the EEF seeks to support effective practice to scale. Examples include the government funding of 'Magic Breakfast' following the EEF's trial, and more recently the government's provision of the NELI as a national programme to support educational recovery, following two successful EEF trials of the programme. Whereas these examples focused on existing interventions, in the case of the National Tutoring Programme the EEF and its charity partners built a programme based on existing research on effective tuition provision, which was rolled out nationally with government funding during the pandemic. At the time of writing the EEF is leading the establishment of the Department for Education's 'Accelerator Fund' project that seeks to scale up evidence-informed programmes in the North, East Midlands and Humber, and the West Midlands.

These approaches to mobilisation of research evidence for the education sector often inter-relate. For example, the Research Schools Network has been instrumental in supporting the extension of these programmes to 'hard to reach' areas and schools.

The future of evidence in education

Nobody would deny that the English education system has changed significantly over the past decade, and many would say that the use of evidence in schools and policy making has acted as one of the most significant thrusts of this transformation. Yet, while caution should be exercised when making parallels between health and education, it remains true that our system does not embed and sustain evidence use in the same way as medicine. While we are making important strides in the right direction through the empowerment of teachers to engage in, critique and interpret evidence to the benefit of their pupils' learning, there remains much variation in practice across the system – some of it healthy and some less so.

For the EEF to fulfil its mission of closing the gap between evidence and practice – in order to narrow the attainment gap – it will be vital to provide information that is valued by schools and that can directly inform decision making. Building upon the Teaching and Learning Toolkit's success in synthesising high-quality global research evidence that is communicated with brevity and clarity, the EEF is working internationally to build a global evidence ecosystem in which multiple partner organisations curate an accessible evidence base as a global good for education. By expanding its reach throughout and beyond the country, aided by the Research Schools Network and its ever-expanding suite of evidence-informed guidance reports, research summaries, and practical teaching or leadership tools, the EEF can also cement itself as a 'go-to' source for reliable information for all teachers and school leaders. And finally, by refining its processes for commissioning research, adopting a more proactive approach that focuses on addressing topics most likely to challenge the attainment gap, the EEF can hope to target its resources and expertise towards areas that will have the highest leverage for improving the learning and outcomes of socioeconomically disadvantaged pupils.

Note

[1] The 'power' of a given trial is how likely it is to be able to identify an effect of a given size, if one exists. Sufficient power is needed to guard against the possibility of a type 2 error, or 'false negative'. As such, 'underpowered' studies are more likely to incorrectly conclude that an effective intervention *doesn't* work.

References

Coe, R. (2019) Teacher choices: can we make complex findings actionable? *Education Endowment Foundation* [blog], 14 October. https://educationendowmentfoundation.org.uk/news/eef-blog-teacher-choices-can-we-make-complex-findings-actionable

Coe, R., Kime, S., Nevill, C. and Coleman, R. (2013) *The DIY evaluation guide*. The Education Endowment Foundation. educationendowmentfoundation.org. uk/uploads/pdf/EEF_DIY_Evaluation_Guide_2013.pdf

DfE (Department for Education) (2019) *Early career framework*. Department for Education. https://assets.publishing.service.gov. uk/government/uploads/system/uploads/attachment_data/file/978358/Early-Career_Framework_April_2021.pdf

DfE (Department for Education) (2021a) *GCSE English and maths results, in 2019 to 2020 academic year*. www.ethnicity-facts-figures. service.gov.uk/education-skills-and-training/11-to-16-years-old/a-to-c-in-english-and-maths-gcse-attainment-for-child ren-aged-14-to-16-key-stage-4/latest

DfE (Department for Education) (2021b) *Understanding progress in the 2020/21 academic year: Complete findings from the autumn term*. https://assets.publishing.service.gov.uk/government/uploads/system/uploads/attachment_data/file/991576/Understanding_Progress_in_the_2020_21_Academic_Year_Report_2.pdf

DfE (Department for Education) (2022) *School recovery strategies: Year 1 findings*. www.gov.uk/government/publicati ons/school-recovery-strategies-year-1-findings

Dimova, S., Ilie, S., Brown, E.R., Broeks, M., Culora, A. and Sutherland, A. (2020) *The Nuffield early language intervention*. https://educationendowmentfoundation.org.uk/public/files/Nuffield_Early_Language_Intervention.pdf

Edovald, T. and Nevill, C. (2021) Working out what works: The case of the Education Endowment Foundation in England. *ECNU Review of Education*, 4(1): 46–64.

Gu, Q., Seymour, K., Rea, S., Knight, R., Ahn, M., Sammons, P. et al (2021) *The research schools programme in opportunity areas: Investigating the impact of research schools in promoting better outcomes in schools*. University College London.

Hattie, J. (2003) *Teachers make a difference, What is the research evidence?* University of Auckland.

Higgins, S. (2018) *Improving learning: Meta-analysis of intervention research in education*. Cambridge University Press.

Higgins, S. (2019) The Teaching and Learning Toolkit Q&A with lead author Prof Steve Higgins. *Evidence for Learning*. www.yout ube.com/watch?v=mHm7SiR_Xv0

Higgins, S., Kokotsaki, D. and Coe, R. (2012) *The teaching and learning toolkit*. Education Endowment Foundation and Sutton Trust.

Hutchinson, J., Robinson, D., Carr, D., Crenna-Jennings, W., Hunt, E. and Akhal, A. (2018) *Education in England: Annual report 2018*. Education Policy Institute.

Hutchison, D. and Styles, B. (2010) *A guide to running randomised controlled trials for educational researchers*. NFER.

Nevill, C. (2019) Randomised controlled trials: 3 good things, 3 bad things, and 5 top tips. *Education Endowment Foundation* [blog], 31 October. https://educationendowmentfoundation.org.uk/news/eef-blog-randomised-controlled-trials-or-how-to-train-your-dragon

Oakley, A. (2006) Resistances to 'new' technologies of evaluation: Education research in the UK as a case study. *Evidence & Policy*, 2(1): 63–87.

Oakley, A., Gough, D., Oliver, S. and Thomas, J. (2005) The politics of evidence and methodology: Lessons from the EPPI-Centre. *Evidence & Policy*, 1(1): 5–32.

Qu, H. (2021) Endowment for a rainy day? An empirical analysis of endowment spending by operating public charities. *Nonprofit Management and Leadership*, 31(3): 571–594.

Sibieta, L., Kotecha, M. and Skipp, A. (2016) *Nuffield early language intervention: Evaluation report and executive summary*. Education Endowment Foundation.

Siddiqui, N., Gorard, S. and See, B.H. (2018) The importance of process evaluation for randomised control trials in education. *Educational Research*, 60(3): 357–370.

Slavin, R.E., Cheung, A.C. and Zhuang, T. (2021) How could evidence-based reform advance education? *ECNU Review of Education*, 4(1): 7–24.

Sutton Trust (2021) *School funding and pupil premium*. National Foundation for Educational Research.

Wiliam, D. (2019) Some reflections on the role of evidence in improving education. *Educational Research and Evaluation*, 25(1–2): 127–139.

6

Audiences first, evidence second: lessons from the Early Intervention Foundation

Jo Casebourne

Introduction

When we talk about early intervention we mean identifying and providing effective early support to children and young people who are at risk of poor outcomes. We are not just focused on early years, although they are especially critical – we believe early intervention can improve the lives of children and young people at any age, so we are focused on children from pregnancy to age 18.

Early intervention is about providing support before problems become entrenched and costly. The kind of support that is more targeted and intensive than universal services, but is less intensive than the support that is needed when problems are already acute. Early intervention covers a broad range of activities, such as home visiting programmes in the early years, schools-based programmes to improve children's social and emotional skills, and mentoring schemes for young people at risk of crime. It is important to note that not all early intervention is effective or has yet developed evidence of effectiveness and at the Early Intervention Foundation (EIF) we focus on *effective* early intervention, which leads to positive impacts on children and families.

We've learned a lot of lessons since the EIF was set up, but looking back, five of these really stand out.

Start with what your audiences' need

What Works Centres exist to bridge the gap between evidence, policy and practice. To do this well, it's crucial to start by defining who your audiences are and to then work to understand what they need.

Early intervention is a cross-sectoral (and cross-governmental) issue, and can help improve outcomes in early years services, schools, policing, the National Health Service, local authority early help services and children's social care (EIF, 2018). This means that EIF has a wide range of audiences and a line of sight that extends from politicians and Whitehall policy makers across a number of different government departments, right through to many different types of local service managers and frontline practitioners.

To influence the frontline practice of social workers, midwives, health visitors, teachers, family support workers, mental health workers and the police, our audiences at the national level include those who 'set the rules of the game' and can prioritise and invest in evidence-based services. These are the national politicians, policy makers, sector and workforce bodies, research funders and charities. Audiences at the local level include those who can set a vision and strategy which mobilises services and resources and can commission and evaluate services. These are the local politicians, system leaders, commissioners and service managers. We also work closely with others in the evidence community and with opinion leaders to influence our audiences. Our audiences are set out in Figure 6.1.

Once you've identified your audiences it is vitally important to understand the context that they are working in. The better you understand their context, the better you will be able to support their evidence use. Otherwise, you can fall into the trap of misdiagnosing the problem or making assumptions about what is getting in the way of evidence use. For example, you might design a project to persuade a group of teachers of the value of using evidence-based approaches to supporting their pupils' mental health, when in fact the teachers are already persuaded but are struggling with the practicalities of implementing these approaches – what they actually need is a short, practical guidance

71

Figure 6.1: Map of the Early Intervention Foundation's stakeholders and audiences

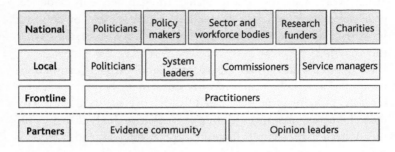

document that sets out a range of evidence-based strategies that they can use without needing any specialist training.

It is therefore important to always start with a good understanding of the real-world context facing policy makers and practitioners – what they are trying to do to improve outcomes for children, how the wider system is impacting on their ability to do this, how evidence features in what they are trying to do, what questions they have that evidence could answer, what kinds of evidence they need, and how the system is incentivising (or not) evidence use. This enables you to assess what is needed to drive the use of evidence. Having decided who your audience are for a particular piece of work, you can stand in their shoes and ask: 'What are they trying to do, and how is the wider system impacting on their ability to do it?' You can (and should) also ask: 'How does evidence feature in what they are trying to do and how is the system encouraging (or discouraging) evidence use?' (Waddell, 2021). Primary qualitative research, primary quantitative research and secondary data analysis can all help to understand that context. Our work on school-based approaches to supporting pupil mental health and wellbeing, to continue with this example, has been shaped by direct engagement with teachers and other school staff through surveys, qualitative research and co-production approaches, supplemented by rapid literature reviews, to pick up insights from implementation science and more widely about the delivery of approaches to supporting mental health in schools.

However, starting with what your audiences need doesn't mean you should not also work to build demand for evidence in these audiences, especially in areas of practice where there is not a strong culture of evidence. That can mean working with national policy makers and funders to use their levers to bake-in evaluation into national funding and programmes and it can also mean working directly with local audiences, as we have done with local councillors who have lead responsibility for children's services, to make the case for why evidence can help them in a time of increasingly constrained resources and increasing demand for services.

Be clear what you mean by evidence

Different kinds of evidence can help you answer different kinds of questions. For example, quantitative data can help answer questions about how prevalent a problem is, or what its root causes are, and qualitative research can shine in-depth light both on issues about access to services and the experiences of children and families. Many different methods have a value and a place in helping practitioners to make informed decisions. It is important to look beyond 'traditional' research evidence to broader forms of knowledge, such as practice experience and expert opinion, and consider how you can help your audiences to integrate these different perspectives into their decision-making processes. But to understand impact, or 'what works', quasi-experimental and experimental methods such as randomised controlled trials are needed. In our view, experimental methods are the only routes to proving that an intervention is effective, through rigorously establishing causality (Waddell, 2021).

One of the key things that EIF did early on was establish evidence standards (EIF, 2017a) to underpin our work – standards which still live on today. These needed to be recognised as high-quality and rigorous, to ensure that the organisation and our recommendations were viewed by policy makers as objective, robust and independent. This was an important foundation to lay down. These evidence standards were operationalised to create the EIF *Guidebook* (EIF, 2022). The *Guidebook* provides information about over a hundred early intervention programmes that have been evaluated and shown to improve outcomes for children and young people. Developing the *Guidebook* was a really complex exercise and there is still a lot of work today involved in maintaining the *Guidebook* and adding to it. Applying our evidence standards to real programmes and working with the organisations that developed and deliver those programmes takes a lot of time, diplomacy and back-and-forth. To help with this, we now have a well codified and open programme assessment process to make sure people know that their programme is being treated rigorously and fairly. This process rigorously assesses the strength of the evidence and the *Guidebook* then shares information about the programme and the quality of evidence underpinning it. This provides independent information (from an intermediary who is not selling a product) to commissioners, policy makers and practitioners on the quality of evidence underpinning programmes designed to support children and young people.

This activity was a key focus in the first few years of the EIF. When we came to refresh our strategy four years after we were founded, we widened our view of evidence, to make sure we were providing what our audiences needed. This meant taking a broader view of evidence and going beyond primarily focusing on evidence-based programmes to also consider evidence-based practice. We had realised that, increasingly, people were asking us different kinds of questions: not just 'Which evidence-based programme should I commission?'. Commissioners wanted to know how to transform entire systems to put early intervention at the centre, or how to use evidence to develop their workforce.

As a result, we now have a number of different ways of generating evidence. Alongside our work assessing evidence-based programmes we are putting more of an emphasis on helping others to generate evidence themselves (Asmussen et al, 2019) – building the evidence base by providing support and guidance for the evaluation activity that will be essential if we're going to increase the supply of high-quality evidence. Where there are gaps in knowledge about how best to intervene to support children and families and very few well specified or evaluated approaches, evaluation support can help to improve the evidence 'pipeline', by helping services define their theory of change and improve their evaluation. EIF's Evaluation Hub brings resources to do this into one place and we have produced subject-specific evaluation guides and have worked intensively with local places to support this work.

Evidence generation also means conducting new trials or evaluations. Where there is limited data on impact or efficacy, randomised controlled trials or quasi-experimental research are needed to generate what works evidence.

Synthesising existing evidence is also a core part of our work in subject areas where high-quality evidence exists, but has not yet been brought together or made accessible. For example, our recent review on adolescent mental health (Clarke et al, 2021) drew on evidence from 34 systematic reviews published since 2010 and 97 primary studies published over the previous three years, to produce the most comprehensive review of the evidence on adolescent mental health support approaches and interventions in the UK for at least a decade, and the first to focus squarely on the secondary school age group and setting. Systematic and rapid reviews can collate what we know about what programmes and approaches with families work to improve outcomes for children and can highlight where evidence gaps exist.

Finally, we are beginning to experiment with distilling the common elements (Ghiara and Clarke, 2020) of programmes – where there are a set of well-evidenced programmes which have been found to be effective, we are starting to identify if there are common elements across these effective programmes that could be used to influence practice and services more widely. For example, we are currently conducting a project that aims to support the development of children's skills and capabilities through strengthening the quality of early childhood education in the UK, by systematically identifying and coding the common skills and practices used in the most effective programmes that enhance children's cognitive and social-emotional development. Common elements approaches may be able to help where evidence-based programmes are not perceived as feasible and may be a way of bringing practitioners closer to evidence-based practices.

Focus on getting evidence used

After building and collating the evidence, it's important to invest sufficient resources in getting evidence used, so you can actively engage your audiences and align your efforts with others in the evidence ecosystem to turn evidence into the tools and resources that your audiences will find practical and useful. It is then possible to test different ways of getting the evidence out there, into the hands of those people who make important decisions about commissioning and funding. We have done this with our work on early years – evaluating the effectiveness of our Early Years' Transformation Academy on supporting evidence use in systems planning and development (Lewis and LaValle, 2021) and learning lessons from the evaluation on how best to mobilise evidence.

We all know it isn't enough just to put evidence on a website and expect people to come and find it and we know that too many research reports end up sitting on shelves and not making a difference to policy and practice. To avoid this, it's important to develop 'knowledge mobilisation' plans (Waddell, 2021). To get evidence used nationally and locally to narrow the gap between what is currently being delivered and what has the best evidence requires you to engage your audiences and select and sequence knowledge mobilisation activities in response to an understanding of the context they are working in. These activities may include:

• Producing accessible evidence-based resources such as guidance, planning tools, maturity-matrices,[1] commissioner-guides, policy briefings, events and webinars.
• Facilitating networks: bringing together people involved in similar roles to discuss applying evidence to their work.
• Workforce development: partnering with sector and workforce bodies to build evidence into their professional learning and development programmes, and partnering to deliver training to change the practice of those commissioning and delivering early intervention.
• Implementation support: supporting local areas intensively to use evidence to change commissioning and frontline practice.

We've done a lot of work to bring evidence to life and make it accessible over the years. We've produced planning tools, for example, to support local authorities and their partners to deliver a system-wide approach to reducing the negative impact of conflict between parents on their children. We've developed maturity matrices to support local areas to take a system-wide approach to improving outcomes for children and families. We've produced commissioner guides to directly address the questions that commissioners want an answer to, whether that is to develop their understanding of the evidence or to find ways to measure the impact of what they are doing. Each question also has links to further detail, and tools and resources that can help commissioners. Alongside this, we've produced more 'traditional' evidence outputs, such as briefings and webinars.

We've taken evidence out to our audiences through roadshows, and we've partnered with the organisations our audiences are already listening to. For example, in our efforts to reach councillors who are lead members for children, we have worked with the Local Government Association to build our evidence into their professional learning and development programme. We've worked intensively with groups of local places, like our Early Years Transformation Academy (Lewis and LaValle, 2021), which seeks to get the evidence used to transform local services, and we have run networks, like the Police Leaders academy.

Build strong partnerships and relationships

It is also really important to build strong relationships with your audiences. We have a close relationship with national government, which is crucial, given that we are trying to influence national policy as well as local practice. A strength, and challenge, of early intervention is its cross-cutting nature. We have relationships with a number of different government departments (including the Department for Education, Department for Work and Pensions, the Department for Levelling Up, Housing and Communities, the Home Office, and Department for Health and Social Care), as no single department is responsible for vulnerable children. This means we are able to support government to think about vulnerable children in a cross-cutting way and to help to make links between different policy areas, which is particularly important, given that government does not always effectively communicate across departments. The EIF's close involvement with each of the main government programmes that provide support to vulnerable children and families enables us to play a unique role in helping government to join them up.

These relationships mean that we are able to push for evaluation of government programmes that we are involved with and can support Whitehall departments by becoming a strategic partner in government programmes: providing flexible and responsive policy advice based on the evidence, as a 'critical friend' to government policy teams. We have worked hard to build strong relationships with local places to understand how we can support their work.

As well as building strong relationships with your audiences, it is also important to think about who you can partner with. We are never going to achieve our mission alone, so we are always looking for partnerships where each partner brings clear strengths and expertise. It is really helpful to think about who else you can partner with within the evidence ecosystem, who can help you to influence your audiences. This is also valued by funders, who welcome organisations with different experience coming together. This means we work closely with a range of different academics, research centres and other What Works Centres. Being able to pick the brains of other What Works Centres has been invaluable in being able to shortcut how to solve common challenges.

We also have some formal mechanisms to bring partners into our work. We have an Evidence Panel which advises us on our work, while individual academics are also involved with our programme assessment process where programmes are assessed for our *Guidebook*. Most of our evidence projects also have academic advisory groups and we have a number of academics on our board of trustees.

Measure your impact

Last but not least, it is important to be clear in your organisation's mission about the change you are trying to achieve, to consider ways to measure your own impact, and to invest in evaluation of your own work wherever possible. This is not easy, given the complexity of the landscape we are often operating in, and the practical challenge of finding funding for evaluation of our own work, but it is clearly important for What Works Centres, given the time they spend telling others about the importance of measuring the impact of their services. We must practice what we preach. Evaluation of your own work can help you understand what is working to drive change, so you can reflect and refine your approach.

We therefore set about designing an impact strategy for EIF that, while being realistic about what we could and should measure, set a framework against which we could develop stronger, more consistent project-level theories of change and design evaluation approaches. This is the first step in a journey for us. In common with other centres and most other organisations in the business of supporting evidence use in policy and practice, we remain a way away from being able to determine the causal impact of our work. But the clarity in our impact strategy does gives us a firm foundation on which to build.

Having agreed a new mission in our refreshed strategy, we decided to think about our impact in terms of influencing behaviour change among our key audiences, which felt more measurable and attributable than trying to measure our impact directly on child outcomes in the UK. We then delved into the behavioural science literature to help us consider the aspects of behaviour change that we could measure. We found that it – and the Capability Opportunity Motivation – Behaviour (COM-B) framework, developed by Professor Susan Michie and colleagues (2011), in particular – offered us a structure against which we could usefully think about and clearly and confidently describe our organisational aims at a level below our mission statement. The COM-B framework sets out three factors which interact to generate behaviour:

- Capability – the individual's psychological and physical ability to engage in the desired behaviour, including having the right knowledge and skills.
- Opportunity – all the factors that lie outside the individual – that is, features of their external context – which facilitate or acts as a barrier to engaging in the desired behaviour.
- Motivation – the individual's intention to perform the behaviour, often driven by desires and impulses, as well as beliefs about what is good or desirable, or bad or undesirable.

The COM-B framework helps us structure how to think about short-term impact measures that enabled the overall behaviour change we were seeking. So, for example, our longer-term behaviour change impact goal may be that local commissioners commission more evidence-based programmes to support families with complex needs. Our short-term impact goals may be about capability – that commissioners understand more about what these programmes are and what they can achieve, for example, about opportunity – that national levers have been used to enable local areas to commission more of these programmes (perhaps national government has brokered arrangements with providers, for example, or made a grant stream available to part-fund these programmes), or motivation – that commissioners are more persuaded by the benefits of commissioning evidence-based programmes in this space (perhaps we have successfully tackled misconceptions about how difficult they are to implement, or how costly they are). These short-term goals can become part of a sound theory of change for a given project, and of course are relatively easy to measure through pre–post evaluation approaches.

These factors are then underpinned by a set of hygiene factors on which the rest of the impact framework rests – to influence behaviour change, the EIF needed to be financially sustainable, to produce high-quality work, to be a place that people wanted to work, and so on. Measures of our organisational reach and influence, such as downloads of reports, press mentions and so on, also sit at this level (it is worth noting that this is *all* that many organisations measure).

We have published our impact strategy (EIF, 2017b) and publish an impact report annually, which sets out each year how we are doing against our own impact goals – including reflections on the progress we are making and where we still have further to go.

What we haven't done enough of yet is to use impact evaluations of our activities to increase evidence use, to see which approaches are the most effective. It's important to invest in evaluation of this kind of activity and share the results with others. We have taken recent steps towards this, for example, through a formative evaluation of our Early Years Transformation Academy (Lewis and LaValle, 2021), and user testing of the EIF *Guidebook* (EIF, 2022), but we plan to do more.

Conclusion

We have evolved a lot since our founding in 2013 and we plan to keep doing so. We want to stay focused on our audiences and make sure that we are meeting their ever-changing needs and to do that we are constantly examining our methods and approaches and asking whether they are fit for purpose. Learning whatever we can from others in the What Works Network and beyond is a critical and ongoing part of this process.

Note

[1] A maturity matrix is a way of categorising how developed an intervention is, starting from an idea through to a fully realised and manualised, evidence-based programme.

References

Asmussen, K., Brims, L. and McBride, T. (2019) *10 steps for evaluation success*. Early Intervention Foundation. www.eif.org.uk/resource/10-steps-for-evaluation-success

Clarke, A., Sorgenfrei, M., Mulcahy, J., Davie, P., Friedrich, C. and McBride, T. (2021) *Adolescent mental health: A systematic review on the effectiveness of school-based interventions*. Early Intervention Foundation. www.eif.org.uk/blog/picking-out-the-golden-threads-a-common-elements-approach-to-supporting-childrens-development

EIF (Early Intervention Foundation) (2017a) *Evidence standards*. Early Intervention Foundation. https://guidebook.eif.org.uk/eif-evidence-standard

EIF (Early Intervention Foundation) (2017b) *Our strategy 2018–2023*. Early Intervention Foundation. www.eif.org.uk/about/our-strategy#measuring-our-impact

EIF (Early Intervention Foundation) (2018) *Realising the potential of early intervention*. Early Intervention Foundation. www.eif.org.uk/report/realising-the-potential-of-early-intervention

EIF (Early Intervention Foundation) (2022) *Guidebook*. Early Intervention Foundation. https://guidebook.eif.org.uk/

Ghiara, V. and Clarke, A. (2020) *Picking out the golden threads: Supporting a common elements approach to supporting children's development.* Early Intervention Foundation. www.eif.org.uk/blog/picking-out-the-golden-threads-a-common-elements-approach-to-supporting-childrens-development

Lewis, J. and LaValle, I. (2021) *Evaluation of the early years transformation academy.* Early Intervention Foundation. www.eif.org.uk/report/evaluation-of-the-early-years-transformation-academy

Michie, S., Van Stralen, M.M. and West, R. (2011) The behaviour change wheel: A new method for characterising and designing behaviour change interventions. *Implementation Science*, 6(1): 1–12.

Waddell, S. (2021) *Supporting evidence-use in policy and practice: Reflections for the What Works Network.* Early Intervention Foundation. www.eif.org.uk/report/supporting-evidence-use-in-policy-and-practice-reflections-for-the-what-works-network

7

Overcoming the youth employment evidence challenge

*Jane Colechin, Catherine Fitzgerald, Chris Goulden,
Ryan Howsham and Anna Round*

Introduction

The Youth Futures Foundation was set up in 2019 to narrow
employment gaps for young people by identifying what works
and why, investing in evidence generation and innovation, and
igniting a movement for change, so that young people[1] have
fair access to good quality jobs. We want to improve the whole
youth employment and training system by working in partnership
with policy makers, employers, practitioners and young people
themselves, to remove barriers, expand opportunities and support
more young people from marginalised backgrounds to be ready
for work.

This is a complex mission and vision for a What Works Centre.
There are three specific challenges that we face:

1. Needing to generate evidence within a fragmented policy and
   practice space and a fluctuating labour market – something
   that has become particularly acute because of the COVID-
   19 pandemic.
2. Aiming to get more employers doing things backed by
   evidence to effectively recruit and retain young people from
   marginalised backgrounds.

3. Getting young people with direct experience of disadvantages relating to employment and skills to participate meaningfully in our work.

This chapter sets out how we are approaching these challenges, balancing the need to always take a rigorous, evidence-led approach within a volatile context and with some stakeholders that may (understandably) not always have evidence and the scientific method first and foremost in their minds. The next sections explore these three challenges in more detail and our responses to them, before concluding with a summary of how we plan to develop further and take them on as a What Works Centre.

Generating evidence in a fragmented policy and practice context and a fluctuating labour market

There is no single government department with overall responsibility for youth employment, with policy spanning the Department for Education, Department for Work and Pensions (DWP), HM Treasury, Department for Digital, Culture, Media and Sport – via whom we are funded, through dormant assets – Department for Business, Energy and Industrial Strategy and Department for Levelling Up, Housing and Communities. Other departments are responsible for some young people who may face difficulties in accessing the job market – for example, the Ministry of Justice and people leaving young offending institutes. Additionally, there are policy and delivery differences regionally, according to a patchwork of mayoralties, local governments, and pots of money from national and European funders distributed according to the boundaries of different agencies. Policy silos, fragmentation and low strategic coherence can mean that some parts of the policy system pull in different directions or displace activities and interventions in another part of the system or area.

Young people navigate a complex landscape of support. Interventions that seek to improve young people's job and career prospects span a wide age range, from secondary school careers guidance through to further and higher education, and into adult learning and employment services. There is a mixed economy of support and different levels of consistency in services across target age and places. Services range from nationally directed employment support offered in the network of Jobcentre Plus offices (for example, CV and job search support from Youth Employability Coaches and programmes such as the 13-week Youth Employment Programme), centrally commissioned large employment support contracts delivered by private and third sector providers like the Work and Health Programme[2] to patchworks of small-scale Voluntary, Community and Social Enterprise and local authority support services funded through European Social Funding or DWP Flexible Support Funds. Young people moving between different departmental responsibilities (particularly education and adult employment services) can fall through the cracks of different services and opportunities for contact.

There are several implications of this complex patchwork of policy and support for our work as a What Works Centre.

First, our lens for intervention and evidence generation is necessarily wide, but also deep. We fund and evidence the effectiveness of support interventions for young people aged 14–24, which includes those both in and outside of statutory education or training. It is important for us to work with younger groups, as well as those in the labour market, as the evidence shows that young people aged 14–18 from disadvantaged backgrounds are more likely to be not in education, employment or training (NEET). Analysis of large national and representative datasets shows few marginalised young people escape the long-term scarring effects of early disadvantage (Gregg and Tominey, 2005; Tumino, 2015; Impetus, 2019; Anders and Macmillan, 2020). There is a weight of evidence about the importance of the role of early intervention and follow up with these young people who are most vulnerable at the early stages of their unemployment or inactivity (Maguire, 2021).

Second, there are many kinds of early intervention (before a young person becomes NEET) and traditional employability interventions to test but the current evidence base is low. In the UK, there are many kinds of generic and specialist support interventions for young people that have been delivered over decades but given a focus on delivery over measuring impact within the sector, we do not have a clear idea of which are good quality factors of good practice, nor a clear idea of the underlying theories of how they achieve outcomes.

Our initial evidence scoping, and recently published Evidence and Gap Map (Youth Futures Foundation, 2022a), shows that there is good (international) evidence of the effectiveness of active labour market policies (Kluve et al, 2019) (which include job-search assistance; training programmes; subsidised employment; direct job creation and public employment programmes; and start-up subsidies, self-employment assistance and support). However, a major problem with these policies is that they tend to focus on those who are able to take up a job immediately, putting harder to help and harder to reach groups at a disadvantage (Maguire, 2021). Moreover, the map shows that there are few robust studies of youth employment initiatives successfully conducted in the UK in the last two decades. Partly this can be explained by the data complexity of working across different government departments responsible for education and employment – and dataset changes associated with major policy changes such as the introduction of Universal Credit (which moved benefit records from referring to an individual to referring to their household). Some departments such as the DWP prefer to conduct impact assessments in-house given the sensitivity of the data (DWP, 2016). However, recent initiatives such as the Longitudinal Educational Outcomes dataset, DWP data lab and work being undertaken by Administrative Data Research UK (ADR UK) are promising initiatives that will allow independent or academic evaluators the ability to robustly assess the impact of youth employment interventions. It is more common in the UK for government-commissioned trials of employment services to be large-scale (thousands of participants receiving treatment), and while these typically have sufficient observations of participants to 'power' a study to show a clear result, these can suffer from problems of low compliance, intervention fidelity or compliance with randomisation protocols, as delivery is at several removes from policy makers. In the example of the recently published evaluation of the Youth Employment Initiative, an overall impact assessment showed a positive effect, due to the range of different types of intervention, support and delivery, the report highlighted that is difficult to show which kinds of delivery models were most effective (DWP, 2022).

In contrast, in the US there is a much larger evidence base in employability, built from multiple high fidelity, smaller scale trials (with hundreds, rather than thousands, treated). For instance the current UK interest in Individual Placement and Support, which is the subject of two large-scale trials,[3] was developed from the US evidence base. It may therefore be prudent to start smaller, focus and build up to scale, hopefully in concert with government departments as we develop.

From development to impact

Given these challenges, our first round of grant and evaluation investment, initiated in 2020 (Development and Impact Grants in our What Works Programme[4]) was designed to focus on small-scale specialist interventions, supporting young people who were more likely to be NEET, and young people with additional or complex needs or marginalised from mainstream employment, education and training opportunities (Youth Futures Foundation, 2020). We are mindful of the different policy and statutory support services for different cohorts of young people (particularly for care leavers, young people with experience of the criminal justice system and those with education and health-care plans), and we have funded at least two studies for each of these cohorts of young people.

Given the low base of evidence and theoretical understanding of which delivery models achieve employment, education and training outcomes, we have sought to build theory from the ground-up through our development stream, moving onto pilots and efficacy studies when we have a good understanding of intervention effectiveness and plausibility.

Understanding the youth employment system

Given policy fragmentation and the persistence of high NEET levels, particularly along the lines of demographic characteristics and geography, it is likely that there are systematic or place-based factors that affect marginalised young people's ability to have good education and employment outcomes in addition to specific types of intervention or programmes. In 2022, we launched our system change fund, Connected Futures,[5] to begin to unpick some of the known issues of policy and support fragmentation and to understand some systematic biases for marginalised young people. We recognise that it will take us a long time to build up a picture of the effects of different interactions and interventions and we must be mindful of the dependencies and potential displacement effects.

Fluctuating labour markets

A further complication to our work is that national youth employment policy is intimately connected to fluctuating labour market conditions. Depending on the economic cycle, policy makers' needs for different types of robust evidence of what works can rapidly change in response. As Youth Futures commenced its work in 2019, employment across all age groups was at a decade-high of over 75 per cent with overall low unemployment (3.8 per cent). This is a rate that most economic and policy commentators would consider close to 'full employment' (that is, realistically, employment is not going to get much higher than that in a market economy). While the unemployment rate for young people was still two and half times higher (10 per cent), investment in new employment initiatives was not a priority for the government.

A stable economic context and generally 'quiet' national policy environment is advantageous to embarking on a focused programme of evidence generation. The last major national youth employment policy – the Youth Obligation – had fully rolled out in 2018 (Work and Pensions Committee, 2019), making it (relatively) easy to identify and measure the impact of interventions supporting young people further from the labour market into good work.

Just as we launched the What Works Programme in March 2020, however, that labour market stability radically shifted due to the impact of COVID-19. Our evidence strategy necessarily had to pivot to include typically less disadvantaged young people. Economists predicted large rises in unemployment and that the young would be hit by a perfect storm of weak demand in the economy and high competition for available jobs – particularly in entry level jobs in shut down sectors (Joyce and Xu, 2020). Longitudinal evidence from previous recessions highlighted the likely fiscal and scarring impact of long-term/repeated spells of unemployment on young people (Youth Employment Group, 2020).

With four other organisations,[6] we rapidly convened the Youth Employment Group (Youth Futures Foundation, 2022b) and collated evidence of what worked to prevent that scarring in previous recessions. To offset the risk of long-term unemployment we advised the government to invest in building on the existing Youth Obligation policy to include a job guarantee through a wage subsidy programme, a programme that became the national Kickstart programme, and we were also supportive of the development of Youth Hubs to connect young people to support and opportunities.

While the right thing to do for young people, there have been impacts on the interventions funded through the first What Works Programme. In addition to the impacts of COVID-19 lockdowns, many of our projects have suffered from recruitment issues as young people are directed towards Kickstart or Youth Hubs instead. This highlights the interaction of policy and labour market context that is the complex backdrop to our evaluation ambitions.

Next steps

We have laid the groundwork to begin to understand both the youth employment landscape and establish an evidence base of what works within it. We are now seeking to accelerate our evidence generation through a second What Works Programme. This will take a more evidence-led approach (employing our curated evidence base) and be co-designed with a stronger intent alongside our delivery and evaluation partners. We anticipate this will also include the crucial role of employers.

Engaging employers in evidence

Employers have a vital part to play in realising systemic change in youth employment. For Youth Futures, employers must be both a core partner in our aim to understand and spread good practice, and a key audience, whose practice is improved by evidence on what works. This differentiates us from most of the rest of the What Works Network where, for other centres, the ultimate implementing partner of recommendations is public sector – local authorities, national government, schools, hospitals or police forces. Whereas for Youth Futures, we need to in the end influence thousands of firms in the private sector (and other sectors).

User research conducted on behalf of Youth Futures by FutureGov identifies the crux of the challenge that we face with regards to engaging employers with our evidence base. The research found:

- Traditional What Works Centre toolkits will be unlikely to meet the needs of employers, who require more practical, immediately applicable guidance.
- Employer engagement with research is driven by whether they have the capacity, capability and motivation to spend time doing so; there are also other necessary conditions for change, including a 'non-traditional' organisational culture, leaders who drive change and financial incentives.
- However, even where the conditions are in place for an employer to engage in research, they may still choose to trust and seek out support from other sources (for example, buy in bespoke support).

The research directed us to consider how we can convene best practice (via robust primary and secondary research sources and methods) from across industry sectors, producing and disseminating an evidence base that can be easily applied to the employer context, in addition to the other important users of our evidence on what works.

The coming years will be a crucial time for us to accelerate our engagement with employers and those supporting them to improve practice, to effectively share what we know and begin to realise behavioural change across the system. This will include activities focused on tailoring parts of our evidence base to specific industry users, disseminating our evidence base in ways accessible to key employer audiences, and building deeper partnerships with employer intermediary organisations (that is, those organisations that employers look to for support, advice and guidance on recruitment and retention practice).

To date, we have laid the foundations in two main ways: we have established an 'Employer Advisory Board' (EAB) and undertaken two 'Rapid Evidence Assessments' (REAs) exploring the scientific literature on employer practice.

Employer Advisory Board

Our EAB is made up of 12 employers and employer intermediaries (Youth Futures Foundation, 2022c). Its membership includes representatives from private, public and third sector organisations, located across England and operating in a diverse range of industries. Set up during 2021, the function and remit of the EAB continues to be refined. However, at its heart, the Board is an opportunity for collaboration and mutual learning, which exists as a testbed for Youth Futures' ideas around our work with employers and a channel through which we can gain insights into how organisations recruit and work with or learn from young people.

Already, the EAB have contributed real-world insight to Youth Futures' evidence, sharing their experience of what works in light of research findings. The EAB has also functioned as an important sounding board, helping us to refine our theory for how best to communicate our evidence base with a wider pool of employers, based on their understanding of other employers in their industries and beyond. For example, the EAB gave a clear steer that they engage primarily with employer intermediaries that are either place-focused (for example, local Chambers of Commerce, Local Enterprise Partnerships) or industry-focused, rather than major national intermediaries, when seeking support for recruitment and retention practices. Youth Futures has subsequently focused on developing our emerging relationships with intermediaries on this basis, exploring opportunities for partnership and joint working to better support employers such as those on our EAB. The trusted relationships formed with employers via the Employer Advisory Board serve to enhance Youth Futures' credibility in future interactions with employers.

Rapid Evidence Assessments

In addition to generating real-world insights from our EAB, recognising the need to identify and leverage existing academic evidence about employer best practice, Youth Futures commissioned two REAs of employer practice. The insights and recommendations from these REAs reflect the findings from over 1,000 empirical studies. Over 100 single studies and meta-analyses were assessed by independent reviewers from the Center for Evidence-Based Management based on predetermined quality criteria.

These REAs are intended to provide both immediate insights for Youth Futures to disseminate to employers and employer intermediary organisations, as well as a longer-term 'bedrock' on which we can develop the evidence base, filling gaps and refining what is already established in the literature for our context and audiences. The REAs cover 'recruitment and selection' and 'retention and inclusion' of marginalised young people respectively, producing detailed findings on evidenced best practice across the whole journey of the young person into good work.

The REAs are a perfect example of Youth Futures taking on a convener role, drawing together a disparate evidence base for the benefit of all our stakeholders. We have already begun disseminating our findings: we have worked with the Chartered Institute for Personnel and Development on its 'One Million Chances' campaign for young people. The evidence was sent out to 250,000 contacts through their online newsletter. Through this, the Chartered Institute for Personnel and Development has highlighted the evidence and practical guidance that employers and recruiters can use to give marginalised young people the fair chance they need to land good jobs (Youth Futures Foundation, 2022d). But it's not just important to involve employers in our work, we have also found ways for young people themselves to participate in the generation of evidence.

Involving young people in what works

Alongside policy makers, practitioners and employers, the involvement of young people across all our activities is important both ethically and practically. Ethically it makes sense to listen to those whose lives we are trying to improve, modelling their empowerment and the removal of barriers. In practical terms, their engagement gives us access to current, nuanced and relevant information about their situation. Many organisations that seek to generate robust evidence for policy and practice follow this principle of 'doing with, not doing to'. Such a commitment brings many advantages, but doing it well also raises questions and tensions, some of which are particularly marked in the field of youth employment.

The young people we aim to support are a highly diverse group, who face different kinds of marginalisation (and intersections between these), as well as diverse challenges around job-seeking and skill-building. The issues they face are similarly varied, and subject to change over time due to wider social trends as well as the fluctuating nature of the labour market (discussed earlier in this chapter). And their involvement with public services, civil society and employers places them in multiple complex relationships of power, agency and citizenship. They connect us as independent workers and learners, service users and clients, students and employees, assets to their employers and – in some discourses at least – 'problems' to be solved. In addition, the years between 14 and 24 span multiple aspects of personal and social development (see Kirschner and O'Donaghue, 2001; McLaughlin, 2009). Our engagement with young people needs to reflect this range, and to be agile enough to capture emerging issues and ongoing developments.

These considerations amplify some of the factors that are common across situations where researchers and policy makers work with the people affected by policy. We also need to make sure that we reach a balance between the kind of evidence gathered through young people's involvement with the methodologically rigorous findings generated through formal evaluations, trials, reviews and other research activities. Our challenge is to create a space where the immediate, experiential and authentic voice of young people sits alongside findings from research and evaluation.

Key questions include:

- How do we work with young people in ways that are ethical and fair, and that build trust in us and our work?
- How can we position youth voices strategically within our work, engaging them in ways that are proportionate and maximise the learning?
- How can knowledge that is generated through methodologically rigorous research and evaluation be brought together with the

personal and experiential knowledge that young people can bring to our work?

• How do we learn from and amplify individual voices and experiences in ways that offer reliable insights into the broad landscape of youth employment?

The nature of the relationship between Youth Futures and young people is crucial, as we aim to put young people with direct experience of the issues we address at the heart of our work. We seek the kind of meaningful involvement where they are not just present, but have a genuine influence across our range of activities and decisions (Halsey et al, 2006; Blakesee and Walker, 2018). For example, we have established a Future Voices Group, whose members collaborate with Youth Futures staff and board members across a range of issues. Among other activities, they offer input into advisory, policy and influencing activities, and act as champions and ambassadors for our work. The Future Voices Group is supported by Youth Futures in partnership with the British Youth Council, who bring expertise in working with young people. We have also set up similar groups in relation to specific projects, including a Youth Reference Group who are working alongside evaluators on a large-scale grant programme to make sure that the evaluation reflects their perspectives and insights.

The positioning of young people's involvement in our projects is also planned to make sure that their experiential knowledge complements findings from our research and evaluations. Essentially this involves balancing two different kinds of evidence; findings from methodologically rigorous research in which data relating to large numbers of people are mediated using well-established and tested approaches, and learning from individual lives that is mediated initially through individual reflection. Each offers insights that are both valuable, and *not* available from the other. Inevitably tensions between the two remain; however, these can to some extent be resolved by adding a layer of mediation to the 'experiential' learning by working alongside young people, building their skills and reflecting on how we use the evidence that they bring.

Participation in practice

In one project, the lead researcher describes the young people who took part as 'coming on a journey' with us through the lifecycle of a project, following a 'route map' tailored to the specific opportunities and nature of the research. In this case, a group of young people initially helped to choose research directions and design research instruments, using *both* reflection on their direct experience *and* guided engagement with relevant literature. Once a project plan was in place, they received training in commissioning and worked alongside the research team as co-commissioners, building their understanding of how to select a research partner. They also joined reviewers with other (often more conventional) kinds of expertise in preparing the research report. Following publication, they were supported to use their communication skills so that they could take part in dissemination activities in a literal amplification of 'youth voice'. This combination of skills building and participation in the project lifecycle is both practical and empowering (see de Graaf et al, 2018).

Establishing relatively long-term relationships with young people in our work helps to build trust through 'deep' engagement and the development of their expertise and understanding, to maximise the visible impact of their involvement (Kirschner and O'Donoghue, 2001; Burke et al, 2017). It allows us to involve them in ways that are foundational rather than tokenistic. Young people have the time and space to develop skills that enhance their contribution to our work, while improving their employability and their empowerment to articulate aspects of their experience and their views on the policies and practices that affect them (Serido et al, 2009). This includes an understanding of how robust evidence is generated and used. At the same time, we plan on building our knowledge of how best to work with young people by commissioning research into the impact of 'user voice' and participant engagement in research.

Overall, the way we listen to 'youth voice' is important. *Individual* narratives and experiences need to contribute to an understanding of *general* societal trends and policy impacts, translating research into policy and practice through the medium of expertise (Brody, 2021). We aim to place the contributions of the young people we work with in their wider context, considering both the experience and the social and policy circumstances that shape it, in an approach that reflects the 'embeddedness' of youth voice (McIntosh and Wright, 2019; Frechette et al, 2020). The stories of these young people are also part of a larger story about the way those aged 14 to 24 learn, earn, find and sustain work. As we gather and interpret evidence directly from young people, we seek to make the connections between their voices and the findings that emerge from data, analysis and secondary sources, amplifying and exemplifying key issues. We also try to empower young people to use their agency and critical reflection to make these connections themselves (Jennings et al, 2006).

Conclusion

We have decided to first and foremost take a *pragmatic* approach to being a What Works Centre. Given the uncertainty of the external backdrop of the labour market and the fragmentation of policy for young people, we need to be flexible in setting up evaluations and bring a wide range of methodologies to bear to make sure that we are extracting as much learning as we can from our investments. That includes codifying the components of employment and training interventions through a realist approach to evaluation that takes account of context as well why different mechanisms do or don't work.

Another underlying principle to our approach with employers is to find a group of interested partners who want to come with us on the journey to building evidence-based practice for recruitment and retention of marginalised young people. Through them and by building wider employer networks, we aim to scale up effective practice. Finally, we take the same practical approach with the young people who are helping to frame and steer what topics matter and where their direct involvement can help us understand problems better and avoid pitfalls in delivery and implementation. We hope they learn from us as much as we learn from them.

By cementing the views of our stakeholders at the heart of our approach – with policy makers, employers, young people and those who deliver services to them, we hope to make the evidence on what works usable at scale to make serious inroads into reducing the numbers of young people who are in neither a good job nor helpful education and training.

Notes

1   Aged 14–24.
2   www.gov.uk/work-health-programme
3   www.isrctn.com/ISRCTN68347173
4   https://youthfuturesfoundation.org/our-work/invest/development-impact/
5   https://youthfuturesfoundation.org/our-work/invest/connected-futures/
6   Impetus, Institute of Employment Studies, Youth Employment UK and The Prince's Trust.

References

Anders, J. and Macmillan, L. (2020) The unequal scarring effects of a recession on young people's life chances (CEPEO Briefing Note Series 6). London: UCL Centre for Education Policy and Equalising Opportunities.

Blakeslee, J. and Walker, J. (2018) 'Assessing the meaningful inclusion of youth voice in policy and practice: State of the science'. Research and Training Centre for Pathways to Positive Futures, Portland State University.

Brody, A. (2021) *Youth, Voice and Development, A Research Report by the British Council and Changing the Story*. University of Leeds.

Burke, J., Greene, S. and McKenna, M. (2017) 'Youth voice, civic engagement and failure in participatory action research', *Urban Review*, 49: 10.

de Graaf, M., Stoopendaal, A. and Leistikow, I. (2018) 'Transforming clients into experts-by-experience: A pilot in client participation in Dutch long-term elderly care homes inspectorate supervision', *Health Policy*, 123(3): 275–280.

Department for Work and Pensions (2016) 'Sector-based work academies: A quantitative impact assessment'. https://assets. publishing.service.gov.uk/government/uploads/system/uplo ads/attachment_data/file/508175/rr918-sector-based-work-academies.pdf

Department for Work and Pensions (2021) 'Over 110 new Youth Hubs offer job help'. www.gov.uk/government/news/ over-110-new-youth-hubs-offer-job-help

Department for Work and Pensions (2022) 'Youth Employment Initiative: Impact evaluation'. www.gov.uk/government/publi cations/youth-employment-initiative-impact-evaluation/youth-employment-initiative-impact-evaluation

Frechette, J., Bitzas, V., Aubry, M., Kilpatrick, K. and Lavoie-Tremblay, M. (2020) 'Capturing lived experience: Methodological considerations for interpretive phenomenological inquiry', *International Journal of Qualitative Methods*, 19: 1–12.

Gregg, P. and Tominey, E. (2005) 'The wage scar from male youth unemployment', *Labour Economics*, 12(4): 487–509.

Halsey, K., Murfield, J., Harland, J. and Lord, P. (2006) 'The voice of young people: an engine for improvement? Scoping the evidence'. National Foundation for Educational Research Northern Office.

Impetus (2019) 'Research Briefing 1: Establishing the employment gap'. www.impetus.org.uk/assets/publications/Report/Youth-Jobs-Gap-Establising-the-Employment-Gap-report.pdf

Jennings, L., Parra-Medina, D., Messias, D. and McLoughlin, K. (2006) 'Towards a critical social theory of youth empowerment', *Journal of Community Practice*, 14(1/2): 31–55.

Joyce, R. and Xu, X. (2020) 'Sector shutdowns during the coronavirus crisis: which workers are most exposed?' https://ifs.org.uk/publications/14791

Kirshner, B. and O'Donoghue, J. (2001) 'Youth-adult research collaborations: Bringing youth voice and development to the research process'. Paper presented at the Annual Meeting of the American Educational Research Association, Seattle, 10–14 April. https://files.eric.ed.gov/fulltext/ED457181.pdf

Kluve, J., Puerto, S., Robliano, D., Romero, J.M., Rother, F., Stoterau, J., Weidenkaff, F. and Witte, M. (2019) 'Do youth employment programs improve labor market outcomes? A quantitative review', *World Development*, 114: 237–253.

Maguire, S. (2021) 'Early leaving and the NEET agenda across the UK', *Journal of Education and Work*, 34(7–8): 862–838.

McIntosh, I. and Wright, S. (2019) 'Exploring what the notion of lived experience offers for social policy analysis', *Journal of Social Policy*, 48(3): 449–467.

McLaughlin, H. (2009) 'What's in a name: "client", "patient", "customer", "consumer", "expert by experience", "service user" – what's next?', *British Journal of Social Work*, 39: 1101–1117.

Serido J., Borden, L. and Perkins, D. (2009) 'Moving beyond youth voice', *Youth and Society*, 20(10): 1–20.

Tumino, A. (2015) 'The scarring effect of unemployment from the early '90s to the Great Recession', No 2015-05, ISER Working Paper Series, Institute for Social and Economic Research. https://EconPapers.repec.org/RePEc:ese:iserwp:2015-05

Work and Pensions Committee (2019) 'Universal Credit and the youth obligation: A welfare reform update'. https://committees. parliament.uk/committee/164/work-and-pensions-committee/ news/98089/universal-credit-and-the-youth-obligation-a-welf are-reform-update/

Youth Employment Group (2020) 'Securing a place for young people in the nation's economic recovery: A rapid response to COVID-19'. https://youthfuturesfoundation.org/wp-cont ent/uploads/2020/05/Youth-Employment-Covid19-Respo nse-FINAL-.pdf

Youth Futures Foundation (2020) 'Young, vulnerable, and increasing – why we need to start worrying more about youth unemployment'. https://youthfuturesfoundation.org/wp-cont ent/uploads/2020/04/YFF_NEET_Report51.pdf

Youth Futures Foundation (2022a) 'Evidence and gap map'. https://youthfuturesfoundation.org/our-work/identify/evide nce-and-gap-map/

Youth Futures Foundation (2022b) Youth Employment Group. https://youthfuturesfoundation.org/our-work/ignite/youth-employment-group/

Youth Futures Foundation (2022c) Employer Advisory Board. https://youthfuturesfoundation.org/our-work/ignite/emplo yer-advisory-board/

Youth Futures Foundation (2022d) 'Recruiting young people facing disadvantage: an evidence review: Scientific summary'. https://youthfuturesfoundation.org/wp-content/uploads/2022/ 03/Recruiting-young-people-facing-disadvantage.pdf

8

'Pulling rather than pushing': a demand-led approach to evidence mobilisation

Steve Martin

Introduction

The Wales Centre for Public Policy (WCPP) generates evidence that is designed to help improve both national policy and local practice. Based in Cardiff University and with core funding from the Economic and Social Research Council and Welsh Government, the WCPP was established in 2017 to build on the success of the Public Policy Institute for Wales, which was created four years earlier to provide Welsh Government ministers with authoritative independent evidence (Bristow et al, 2015). The WCPP continues to work with ministers but also provides evidence for local government, the health service and other public bodies. And rather than producing evidence and then 'pushing' it out to policy makers, it starts by working closely with them to identify their priorities and then generates, synthesises and mobilises evidence that addresses these issues.

The WCPP's demand-led approach is designed to increase the chances that policy makers get evidence that is relevant and timely and therefore act on it. This way of mobilising evidence is informed by the 'two communities' concept which makes the oversimplified, but nevertheless useful, observation that 'social scientists and policy makers live in separate worlds with different and often conflicting values, different reward systems, and different languages' (Caplin, 1979, p 459). There are heroic individuals who manage to straddle both worlds, but they are exceptions. Most policy makers work to much shorter timescales than researchers and they prize practical, politically expedient answers to 'real world' problems. By contrast, academics are rewarded for publishing theory-driven research, which can take years to produce and rarely offers straightforward answers (Oliver et al, 2014). As a result, even if policy makers are aware of evidence that is being generated in universities, they struggle to penetrate the journal paywalls it is published behind and the academic jargon it is couched in, and are unlikely to find that it offers clear-cut 'actionable recommendations'.

In recent years, researchers in the UK have been encouraged to pay more attention to the practical implications and potential applications of their research. The UK's Research Excellence Framework, which rates each universities' research output and allocates funding accordingly, now gives credit for impact beyond academia, and research councils ask grant recipients to specify the commercial and/or public policy benefits of their work. However, because policy making is not a linear, rational or uncontested process, and evidence is just one of many competing influences on policy decisions (Cairney, 2016; Ingold and Monaghan, 2016), it remains rare to have a clear line of sight between research and policy.

The WCPP addresses this challenge by focusing on five main activities (see Table 8.1):

- *Identifying* policy makers' evidence needs and mobilising evidence to meet them.
- *Convening* activities that bring policy makers and experts together to analyse and apply evidence.
- *Communicating* evidence in user-friendly formats.
- *Advancing* understanding of what works in evidence mobilisation.
- *Advocating* for evidence use.

This chapter describes the way in which the WCPP goes about these activities, explores the factors that have contributed to its success, and discusses the challenges it has encountered.

Table 8.1: Wales Centre for Public Policy activities

Identify	Convene	Communicate	Advance	Advocate
We work with ministers, officials and public service leaders to identify their evidence needs	We act as a bridge between evidence producers and policy makers/ practitioners	We communicate evidence that supports better policy making and public services	We conduct research on how evidence can inform policy and practice	We promote evidence use by showing how it can support policy makers and practitioners
We identify leading policy experts who can meet evidence needs	We work with policy experts to synthesise the best available evidence	We publish evidence reviews, reports and policy briefings	We evaluate how our work makes a difference so we can keep improving what we do	We enable researchers to engage with policy makers and practitioners
We identify and work with policy makers, practitioners and academic networks to mobilise evidence	We support policy makers and practitioners to access and apply the evidence	We disseminate evidence through events, blogs and social media	We study how other evidence centres work	We encourage policy makers and practitioners to use evidence
We monitor policy developments so we can anticipate future evidence needs	We bring experts and policy makers together to discuss how to apply the evidence in Wales	We share evidence in user-friendly formats that can speak to a broad audience	We disseminate what we learn through academic networks and journals	We sponsor research apprenticeships and PhD placements to build capacity

Source: WCPP (2020)

Identifying evidence needs

The WCPP identifies evidence needs through analysis of policy documents, monitoring policy developments and debates, horizon scanning and dialogue with government ministers, civil servants and public service leaders. Some of our work is undertaken in response to requests from policy makers, while some we initiate ourselves in light of our reading of policy priorities. In both cases, one of the keys to success is understanding the policy imperatives that lie behind policy makers' evidence needs. Although they may not express it in quite this way, we have found that policy makers are typically interested in one of four key questions:

1. 'Is there a problem?' Policy makers often need evidence to enable them to understand the nature of a problem and assess whether it demands action from them. They are interested in what the issues are, the scale or prevalence of the problem, whether it is getting worse, and who is affected by it.
2. 'What can I do about it?' Where policy makers are already committed to addressing an issue, they often want to know what has worked elsewhere and whether it could be effective in their own locality/region/country.
3. 'What will happen if …?' A third type of question seeks evidence about the likely impact of an intervention that policy makers are already actively considering. In this case they want to know will it work, who will benefit, will anyone lose out, and what the risks are.
4. 'How do I …?' Where policy makers have already decided on a course of action, they may ask for evidence to inform policy implementation. Questions include who needs to be involved, what resources are required, and what obstacles will have to be addressed.

Open and direct dialogue with policy makers is key to differentiating between these different types of evidence needs. Letting us in on their thinking requires trust on the part of policy makers, but it helps to ensure that our work addresses the issues they are most concerned about. As an example, we were asked by a minister for evidence on how to increase the number of credit unions in Wales. Discussion with him revealed that he saw this as a way to reduce low-income households' reliance on 'pay-day loans' (a form of high interest, short-term, unsecured credit designed to be repaid within a month). A rapid review of the evidence and a series of discussions with experts suggested to us that expanding credit unions would not achieve the desired result. So, with the minister's agreement, we commissioned research to understand why households use pay-day loans and identify interventions that could provide better alternatives. Realising that the policy question was 'What can I do about X?', rather than 'How do I do Y?', enabled us to avoid conducting research that would have amounted to 'digging in the wrong place' and probably resulted in a policy that wouldn't have tackled the underlying problem.

In addition to ensuring that we understand policy makers' evidence needs, we also test whether we are best placed to address it. Occasionally we have found that a question posed by policy makers can be answered by referring them to existing reports. As already noted, it is difficult for ministers and officials to keep abreast of research undertaken in universities. They may also be unaware of work undertaken in another part of government or by their predecessors. For example, when a minister asked us for evidence to help develop a food strategy we found that an earlier expert report commissioned by one of her predecessors provided all the answers she needed. In such cases, evidence intermediaries provide a kind of 'external hard drive' that retains information lost from the organisational memory as politicians and officials rotate to new roles.

Sometimes we conclude that there are others (including other What Works Centres) who are better placed than us to meet an evidence need and rather than take on the work ourselves, we broker links between them and the policy makers. For example, in the case of pay-day loans described earlier, we worked with a research council to initiate research that was undertaken by a team of researchers from an independent research organisation who interviewed low-income households to discover why they preferred this form of lending over borrowing from credit unions and what other alternative forms of credit they would find more attractive.

Our demand-led approach helps to secure ownership of our work but raises important issues about how to maintain our independence. The topics that we work on are dictated, directly or indirectly, by policy makers' needs. However, our findings and recommendations are always based firmly on the best available evidence. Reports are peer-reviewed by academics. A publications protocol, agreed with the Welsh Government, ensures that ministers cannot amend, delay or veto reports that they find inconvenient or uncomfortable. And all outputs are published on our website so that the evidence is freely available for all political parties, scrutiny committees and other policy actors, and can be scrutinised by researchers to ensure its reliability and robustness.

These arrangements require bravery on the part of policy makers, but they know that safeguarding and demonstrating our independence is important to our ability to work with world-leading experts, many of whom would not be prepared to collaborate with us if they believed that they might be subject to political pressure. Funding provided by the Economic and Social Research Council has been important to signal our commitment to providing authoritative independent evidence, as is the fact that we are based in a university. However, the politics of evidence use are never easy to navigate, and evidence centres like ours need to be politically aware while remaining scrupulously non-partisan. Our work produces evidence which can be unpalatable for policy makers, and some of our reports have been used by opposition parties to attack government policies, particularly in the run up to elections. When this happens, it is important that policy makers stand by their commitment to our independence. And for our part we need to be prepared to accept that while the evidence we produce will be heard it won't always be heeded because policy decisions are influenced by a host of other factors. Researchers with strongly held views backed by robust evidence sometimes find this difficult to accept. We are careful to avoid conflating communicating evidence with campaigning for policies because we understand that blurring the line between these activities would erode the trust that policy makers have in our impartiality which is in turn key to our effectiveness as evidence intermediaries.

Convening evidence

The WCPP is currently the only member of the UK's What Works Network with a specific geographical focus – our work can cover any policy area that is devolved to the Welsh Parliament (including health, social care, education, housing, local government, agriculture, and some key aspects of environmental policy, the economy and skills). It is unrealistic to expect to develop in-house expertise across such a broad range of topics, so much of our work is undertaken in collaboration with experts, including other What Works Centres, universities and independent researchers from across the UK and internationally. Drawing on data and insights which these experts have already generated enables us to respond much more rapidly to policy makers' needs than studies which involve gathering new primary data (see WCPP, 2019b). But our reliance on existing evidence makes it important that we identify and work with the best available experts in a field, and it also has implications for our approach to evidence standards.

The question of what counts as evidence is an important one and different evidence intermediaries have different answers to it. We have adopted a pragmatic approach which accepts that the type of evidence we need to provide varies depending on the type of question that we are addressing. The answer to 'Is there a problem?' requires data about Wales. The answer to 'What can I do about it?' is likely to call on evidence about interventions in other countries. 'How do I …?' questions probably require input from practitioners. Our reliance on existing evidence means that there are some questions we can't answer, and others where we can only provide partial answers. However, our view is that some evidence is better than no evidence, so long as we give clear advice about its limitations. Policy makers are, of course, accustomed to dealing with uncertainty and we have found that they don't necessarily expect or need clear-cut answers, and in cases where the evidence is incomplete, contested or of variable quality, roundtables have proved a valuable way to enable policy makers and experts to work through the issues about which there is disagreement or uncertainty.

Once we are confident that we understand the evidence gap and have the skills needed to address it, we usually conduct a rapid review. We use a range of conventional search engines complemented by one-to-one discussions with academic experts in the field. We focus on social science research and include both academic and 'grey' literature (for example, evaluations conducted on behalf of governments). Sometimes we commission experts to produce reviews, sometimes we produce them in-house. All reviews are then peer-reviewed to ensure that the evidence is reliable and is being interpreted correctly. In addition we may bring together experts and policy makers to assess whether the evidence is applicable to Wales. This is important because policy makers need to understand the extent to which interventions will work in their own context. Roundtables provide a 'safe space' for open discussion about this and we adopt the 'Chatham House rule' which stipulates that while participants may use information from one of these discussions, they will not reveal the identity or affiliation of the source.

Bringing together a range of experts and policy makers in this way means that we can draw on insights from a variety of disciplines and on experience from a range of countries. It also enables us to address different dimensions of complex policy challenges where no individual expert has all of the evidence that is needed. Some experts are surprisingly reticent about engaging directly with policy makers in this way, and we work closely with them in advance to ensure that they understand the evidence need, the Welsh policy context and why their expertise is relevant.

We have found that Welsh policy makers have a real appetite for learning from elsewhere. Context matters, and there are some important differences in the political culture, values and priorities between different parts of the UK. However, they face similar societal and economic challenges and have shared legal frameworks and administrative traditions. Evidence centres funded by Whitehall departments are inevitably focused primarily on the needs of policy makers and practitioners in England so we act as a 'bridge' helping other What Works Centres and evidence producers to spot when their work is relevant to Wales and introducing them to policy makers who we know will benefit from it.

Communicating evidence

Presenting evidence in a concise and accessible way is key to gaining policy makers' attention and interest and therefore influencing their behaviours and decisions. Even experienced academics with a track record of policy engagement sometimes want to include descriptions of their research methods and long list of caveats to their conclusions, and some find it difficult to shed academic 'jargon'. Because of this, we provide detailed guidance about length, language, style and format. We also invest a lot of time in editing draft reports to ensure that what we present to policy makers is as accessible, clear and concise as possible. We use graphic designers to produce attractive formats and communicate evidence through a range of media including reports, policy briefings, social media, commentaries and podcasts, our own online and in-person events, and contributions to conferences organised by others. We run 'lunch and learn' sessions in the Welsh Government's offices, which are advertised on its staff intranet and open to all civil servants. And we have found that one of the best ways to reach practitioners is to offer presentations, panel discussions and workshops at events convened by their own professional bodies or representative organisations. 'Piggy-backing' on events that feature ministers or other 'big name' speakers has also proved to be an effective mode of dissemination.

We know that communicating evidence through reports and presentations is rarely sufficient to influence national policy decisions or local practice and we have experimented with a variety of forms of engagement. Roundtables are one means of achieving this. In addition some ministers value in-person briefings which give them the chance to ask questions that go beyond and behind what is presented in a written report/briefing. We have also cultivated strong links with professional networks (such as the All Wales Heads of Children's Services Group) and representative organisations (including the Welsh National Health Service Confederation, Welsh Local Government Association and Wales Council for Voluntary Action). They have both shaped our understanding of their evidence needs and been key users of our work on topics such as how to improve outcomes for children and young people in local authority care and ways to reduce loneliness and social isolation.

Advancing understanding of evidence use

The WCPP is unusual in having a small team of researchers whose primary role is to evaluate our ways of working and our impact.

They do this combing the academic literature for lessons which can inform our practice, conducting structured reflection sessions on each project that we complete, and interviewing a sample of the intended evidence users. Their findings inform our day-to-day practice and longer-term strategy and are shared through academic papers and conference presentations in the hope that they provide useful insights for other evidence intermediaries. The team has, for example, analysed the benefits of integrated data for local policy making (Durrant et al, 2018) and conducted an assessment of how knowledge brokering can support evidence-based policy (MacKillop and Downe, 2022). It is currently working on papers on local knowledge mobilisation, the practices employed by evidence intermediaries, and activities of university-based policy engagement teams.

Because we know that the ways in which we communicate evidence must be attuned to the capacity and capability in the civil service, local government and other public services, we also conduct research on policy making and implementation in Wales (Connell et al, 2019; Connell et al, 2021; Nesom and MacKillop, 2021). This work recognises that an intervention which has worked well elsewhere may be a non-starter if Wales lacks the organisational culture, finances, collaborative capacity and accountability mechanisms that led to its success elsewhere. But conversely, the small, relatively tight-knit policy community in Wales may be able to make a success of initiatives that have languished in other settings because of what List et al (2019) call the 'scale-up problem'.

Advocating for evidence use

The WCPP seeks to demonstrate through its own work that evidence can and does make a useful contribution to policy decisions. Policy makers often have mixed experiences of working with researchers and may initially be sceptical about our ability to deliver timely, balanced evidence which addresses real-world challenges.

Some of our work has failed to meet their expectations. For example, a former minister started a briefing session that we arranged with a leading expert on enterprise zones by dropping his report on the table and declaring 'Well, there's nothing in here that we can use' (although we and our expert succeeded in changing their mind by the end of our half-hour meeting). In another case, an evidence review that we conducted on the physical punishment of children did not provide the unequivocal empirical evidence to support outlawing smacking which ministers had anticipated and was quietly shelved by the government (though not by a lobby group that was campaigning vociferously against the proposed ban).

However, there are numerous other examples where ministers and/or public service leaders have reported that our work has had a significant impact on policy decisions. The First Minister has stated that 'The work of the Wales Centre for Public Policy greatly strengthens our policy-making in Wales. It gives us high-quality independent evidence to challenge current assumptions and improve our decisions' (WCPP, 2019a), and we frequently receive unsolicited letters from ministers thanking us for reports and explaining how they have informed policy decisions. Some examples of work that has had tangible impacts on policy include:

- Our modelling of the impact of free child care (Paull and Xu, 2016), which led the Welsh Government to rethink a commitment to provide a universal offer and to target support on working parents instead.
- Work on preventing youth homelessness (Schwan et al, 2018), which the Minister for Housing and Regeneration told the Welsh Parliament informed her decision to introduce a £4.8 million innovation fund to develop housing and support options.
- Analysis of the economic impact of Brexit (Johnson and Tilley, 2021), which the Director responsible for European Transition reported showed the 'huge impact which the WCPP has made on the creation of what has been an almost entirely new – and strategically vital – policy agenda'.
- Work we conducted on using behavioural science to increase waste recycling (Webb, 2018), which the First Minister said 'made a valuable contribution to helping the Welsh Government and its partners understand how to increase recycling rates among residents'.

Conclusion

The examples we have given in this chapter – and numerous others – have raised awareness among politicians, civil servants and public service leaders of the potential value to them of research evidence, which in turn helps to fuel future demand for it.

As we have said, our mission is often a bridging one – between academics and policy makers; between What Works Centres disproportionately focused on Wales, and between the wider world of evidence and the needs of the people of Wales. In this way, we ensure that Welsh policy making is both effectively and efficiently evidence based wherever possible.

References

Bristow, D., Carter, C. and Martin, S.J. (2015) Using evidence to improve policy and practice: The UK What Works Centres. *Contemporary Social Science*, 10(2): 126–137.

Cairney, P. (2016) *The politics of evidence-based policymaking*. Palgrave.

Caplin, N. (1979) The two communities theory and knowledge utilization. *American Behavioral Scientist*, 22(3): 459–470.

Connell, A., Martin, S.J. and St. Denny, E. (2019) Can meso-governments use metagovernance tools to tackle complex policy problems? *Policy and Politics*, 47(3): 437–454.

Connell, A., St Denny, E. and Martin, S.J. (2021) How can subnational governments develop and deliver distinctive policy agendas? *International Review of Administrative Sciences*. https://doi.org/10.1177/0020852321996429

Durrant, H., Barnett, J. and Rempel, E.S. (2018) Realising the benefits of integrated data for local policymaking: Rhetoric versus reality. *Politics and Governance*, 6: 18–28.

Ingold, J. and Monaghan, M. (2016) Evidence translation: An exploration of policy makers' use of evidence. *Policy & Politics*, 44(2): 171–190.

Johnson, C. and Tilley, H. (2021) *Brexit and Wales*. Wales Centre for Public Policy.

List, J., Suskind, D. and Al-Ubaydli, O. (2019) The science of using science: Towards an understanding of the threats to scaling experiments. *Research/BFI Working Paper*, Becker Friedman Institute for Economics, University of Chicago.

MacKillop, E. and Downe, J. (2022) Knowledge brokering organisations: A new way of governing evidence. *Evidence & Policy*. https://orca.cardiff.ac.uk/147103/

Nesom, S. and MacKillop, E. (2021) What matters in the implementation of sustainable development policies? Findings from the Well-Being of Future Generations (Wales) Act, 2015. *Journal of Environmental Policy and Planning*, 23(4): 432–445.

Oliver, K., Lorenc, T. and Innvær, S. (2014) New directions in evidence-based policy research: A critical analysis of the literature. *Health Research Policy and Systems*, 12(1): 12–34.

Paull, G. and Xu, X. (2016) *Childcare policy options for Wales*. Wales Centre for Public Policy.

Schwan, K., French, D., Gaetz, S., Ward, A., Akerman, J., Redman, M. and Stirling, T. (2019) *Preventing youth homelessness*. Wales Centre for Public Policy.

WCPP (Wales Centre for Public Policy) (2019a) About us. Cardiff: Wales Centre for Public Policy.

WCPP (Wales Centre for Public Policy) (2019b) Wales Centre for Public Policy acclaimed for outstanding impact on policy in Wales. Cardiff: Wales Centre for Public Policy. www.wcpp.org.uk/news-and-media/news-article/wales-centre-for-public-policy-acclaimed-for-outstanding-impact-on-policy-in-wales/

WCPP (Wales Centre for Public Policy) (2020) Using evidence to improve public services and government policies. Wales Centre for Public Policy

Webb, J. (2018) *Increasing household waste recycling using behavioural science*. Wales Centre for Public Policy.

9

The What Works Centre for Local Economic Growth: some lessons from the first ten years

Danielle Mason, Max Nathan and Henry G. Overman

Introduction

What can policy do to increase local economic growth? This is a question that has challenged decision makers and academics for decades. It's also a fundamental question today, when the UK government has made economic growth one of its priorities – in the face of a decade of slower growth and tight budgets.

Research and evaluation have a crucial role to play in providing answers and increasing the effectiveness of policy making. Unfortunately, making sense and making use of the evidence is not easy, especially for those tasked with delivering better economic outcomes for their communities.

The What Works Centre for Local Economic Growth (known as What Works Growth) was founded in 2013 to work with policy makers and help address these challenges. This chapter summarises what we have learnt from our first three phases of activity.

Phase 1: Evidence reviews – what works?

An evidence centre needs evidence. So our first task was to review what is known about the impact of local economic policies. After developing, testing and iterating our review methodology, we published 14 reviews in two years covering areas including employment training, business advice, estate renewal, broadband and area-based policies. We would argue that was good progress for a small team (roughly five full-time staff) covering a vast policy literature. We made several key decisions early on that helped us do this, but which also had implications for our work that resonated well beyond this first phase.

Systematic evidence reviews

The first decision concerned the kind of reviews we would produce. For people to have some confidence in our objectivity we felt that the reviews had to be systematic – by which we meant rules-based and summarising all available literature that met those rules. But there are different ways to do systematic reviews. For example, the Alliance for Useful Evidence distinguishes between 'exploratory' approaches – describing who's doing what in different places – and 'structured' approaches, which draw on studies which use more formal methods to test policy effectiveness.

We decided to take a structured approach for several reasons. Most importantly, in 2013 exploratory work on local economic policy was common, with far fewer structured reviews – something which remains true today. Structured approaches also played to the comparative advantage of our core academic team, and structured approaches provided the best fit with the What Works Network requirements.

A focus on impact evaluations

Our second big decision was to focus on a specific type of evidence – impact evaluation evidence. Impact evaluations seek to identify and understand the causal effect of policy interventions and to establish their cost-effectiveness. To put it another way, they ask: 'Did the policy work?', 'How did it work?' and 'Did it represent good value for money'?

While all the What Works Centres recognise the central importance of impact evaluation, some also draw heavily on other types of evidence. These include correlational evidence – which identifies factors which are *related* to the outcomes of interest,

114

but does not demonstrate a causal effect – and process evaluation evidence, which is designed to investigate *how* interventions are delivered and explain *why* they are effective or not. Both of these provide valuable complements to impact evaluation, but we felt that within local economic policy, the evidence gap was most pronounced for impact evaluation. We also felt it was important to have a clear focus on evidence which demonstrates whether a policy has been effective, which neither of these other evidence sources can do.

Traditionally, local economic policy making has *not* drawn much on evidence which uses causal methods. Governments around the world increasingly have strong systems to monitor policy inputs (such as programme spend) and outputs (such as the number of programme participants). However, they are weaker on identifying policy outcomes (programme effects) and, in particular, many government-sponsored evaluations that look at outcomes do not use credible strategies to assess the causal impact of policy interventions. By highlighting the importance of impact evaluations and demonstrating their uses, we hoped to achieve a change in culture, as well as shifting specific practices.

Pinning down causality is a crucially important part of impact evaluation. To assess causal impact requires an estimate of the difference that can be expected between the average outcome for individuals 'treated' in a programme, and the average outcome they would have experienced without it. Establishing causality requires the construction of a valid counterfactual – that is, what would have happened to programme participants had they not been treated under the programme. So, we organised our reviews around the credibility with which evaluations establish causality: our reviews include any evaluation that compares outcomes for people, firms or places receiving treatment (the treated group) after an intervention with outcomes in the treated group before the intervention, relative to a comparison group used to provide a counterfactual of what would have happened to these outcomes in the absence of treatment.

It has been argued that our evidence standards are set too high. For evaluations of some area-based initiatives – such as infrastructure and sports and culture programmes – finding suitable comparison groups is challenging. However, internal exercises we ran on evaluations for sporting and cultural events and facilities strongly suggest our evidence standards are not the problem. Instead, a clear pattern emerged that most of the studies we found, particularly for events, modelled the possible impacts before they were in place ('ex-ante' appraisal). But precious few evaluations look at the actual impacts after the event ('ex-post' evaluation). A small but growing body of impact evaluations for transport – as covered by our transport evidence review – shows that there *are* impact evaluation methodologies which can be applied to interventions like these.

Arguably, the barrier is not that impact evaluation is not possible, but that it is seen as less necessary, or less appealing, in a policy area where there is particularly intense focus on up-front economic *appraisal* – the quantitative modelling of *potential* impacts. The focus on appraisal is not surprising: policy makers are, perhaps understandably, more interested in figuring out ways to assess new projects, rather than discovering whether their estimates were right after the money was spent. But for future policy to be credible, rather than just plausible, it needs to be built on an understanding of what has worked in the past.

A focus on key economic outcomes

A third key decision was to emphasise outcomes that most directly capture change in a local economy: wages, employment and productivity. There are, of course, many other important ways in which places differ. But ultimately, if policy isn't increasing wages, employment or productivity, it's hard to claim that it's improving local economic growth.

That said, we were still interested in other outcomes. Sometimes, because they act as proxies for the effect on local economic performance: for example, if business advice increases firm sales, then this may translate to improved local economic performance. But we always need to be careful with such proxies. For example, if business advice boosts domestic sales at supported firms, these sales may simply be at the expense of other firms nearby. Good for the supported firm, not so good for the unsupported. There are also policy areas – such as estate renewal and sports and culture – where our evidence reviews suggest that spending tends to have a limited impact on the local economy but which might have plenty of other potential benefits, including environmental, health, crime and wellbeing. And there may be indirect links from these benefits to our core outcomes (for example, economic benefits from improved health).

Piloting, scoring, iterating, updating

Having made these big calls, and refined a list of topics with practitioners, we carried out two pilot reviews – one on employment training and the other on business advice – issuing calls for evidence and searching the academic literature, think tank reports and policy evaluations.

Even with our high evidence standards, the initial literature searches were vast: we covered evidence from all Organisation for Economic Co-operation and Development[1] countries, with no pre-set time limit (although we focus on more recent evidence when summarising findings). The first review, for example, generated a longlist of over a thousand studies. We narrowed this down to a shortlist by sifting on titles and abstracts, then conducted a full appraisal of each shortlisted study (a few hundred), collecting key results and giving robustness scores – based on an adjusted Maryland Scientific Methods Scale – that reflected both the quality of methods chosen and quality of implementation. We also developed detailed scoring guidance, in consultation with our academic panel, and tested it using double-blind trialling of scoring by team members. It's important to note that the ranking of individual studies is not an exact science and often involves a degree of judgement. Indeed, anyone who has attended an academic seminar will know the extent to which such issues can be hotly disputed. Nevertheless, on average our scoring tended to produce rankings on which many evaluation experts would broadly agree.

Crucially, we allowed the way we classified and presented findings to evolve, as we looked for the most helpful approach to present evidence and lessons across different subject areas. When we published what turned out to be our final evidence review, we revisited the early reviews and brought our findings into line with our latest methodology. Fortunately, in practice, this mostly resulted in minor changes to our findings. In several cases these changes strengthened our initial findings, although they also weakened others due to a change which meant we classified more studies as having mixed findings rather than positive or negative.

Phase 2: Toolkits – what works best?

In 2016 we entered a second phase. Our evidence reviews provided a solid base for understanding the impact of a variety of individual local economic policies including employment training, business advice, estate renewal, broadband and area-based policies. Overall, they suggested that deep scepticism about policy effectiveness is not justified: in just about every evidence review, around half of the high-quality evaluations that we reviewed find positive effects on local economic outcomes, the remainder mostly find zero effects with a few finding negative effects.

At this point we made our first major pivot, away from systematic reviews towards more specific 'toolkits'. That is, we moved from answering the high-level question – 'Does this policy work?' – to more detailed questions of policy design – 'In this policy area, what works best?'

There were two reasons for this shift. First, the fact that the evidence base was mixed for many of our topics – with some of the studies showing positive results and others not – meant that the answer to the first question could be uninformative, while there was much that could be usefully said in response to the second.

Second, at a practical level, many of our users were responsible for spending programme budgets. Rather than deciding whether to spend money on a given policy area (as users in central government sometimes do), they wanted to know *how best* to spend the resources they *did* have for a particular policy area that had already been chosen.

In many cases, the reviews found enough evidence to give additional guidance of this type. For example, our employment training review suggests that in-firm, on-the-job programmes outperformed classroom-based ones, and short training courses may be more cost-effective than longer ones; our access to finance review found some evidence that loan finance programmes were more likely to be successful than equity finance programmes; and our review of Enterprise Zones suggested that local employment conditions can influence the extent to which employment effects are felt locally. Our toolkits – which constituted the bulk of our work in this phase – are designed to summarise this type of evidence where it is available and make it accessible to users with no background in evidence.

But the toolkits are far from comprehensive. Anyone looking to develop an effective employment training programme will want to know about the costs and benefits of short- and long-term approaches, but they may also want to know, for example, about the selection of participants, about how they are assigned to a specific training programme, and about how they are supported during their training. We do not have high-quality evidence to address all of these topics.

Of course, appetite remains for simpler answers to the big questions: Does transport investment work? Do regeneration schemes work? Do cultural interventions work? Questions this broad are hard for all What Works Centres to answer, but the limited availability of high-quality impact evaluation for some types of local economic policy makes it a particular challenge for What Works Growth. For example, the question of whether education interventions 'work' may seem as difficult to answer as the question of whether transport investment 'works'. However, for education, it is possible to fund many smaller trials, to dig down into the evidence, to examine what might explain the variation in results across studies and to focus on particular outcomes. You can't say whether education interventions 'work' in general, but you can say that education interventions which teach 'phonics' *do* work to improve literacy, based on data from hundreds of studies. Unfortunately, for many policies, the local growth evidence base is not developed enough for us to delve down and provide these more nuanced answers. But we think the toolkits undermine any suggestion that the mixed nature of the evidence base means that 'nothing works' when it comes to local growth.

Phase 3: Demonstrators and evaluation support – helping to fill the evidence gaps

Our work in Phases 1 and 2 delivered 14 reviews and over 30 toolkits. But many gaps remain. There are several challenges in *generating* impact evaluation evidence, both structural and practical, and many of these are particularly pronounced for local economic policy. We flag a number of these, then discuss What Works Growth's evolving response.

The 'gold standard' of impact evaluation is the randomised controlled trial. Fundamentally, randomisation is challenging for capital investments (like transport infrastructure) and for area-based economic initiatives (such as Enterprise Zones). For these, the size, 'lumpiness' and longevity of interventions makes experimentation tricky (to say the least). However, this does not necessarily rule out high-quality evaluation. Quasi-experimental methods currently available (and more being developed) exploit pre-existing features of the policy, such as an eligibility cut-off, or staged roll-out to construct counterfactuals. More traditional approaches, such as propensity score matching, use data on non-participants to the same end. Such approaches are often applied even when randomisation would be feasible but has not been implemented.

All these approaches to impact evaluation are technically complex, and not usually straightforward for local governments to implement. Even *commissioning* high-quality evaluation requires some evaluation expertise – that's why central government employs many analysts and researchers to do just that. It's very hard to buy in this type of expertise on a temporary basis, and many local partners find it impossible to justify permanent staff given financial constraints. Those larger places which do have this type of capacity are better placed to deliver impact evaluations that can help to fill the evidence gaps.

Another practical issue is that impact evaluation almost always has resource implications. These include not just the financial cost of commissioning or delivering an evaluation, but also the additional resource required when delivery needs to change to accommodate evaluation design or data collection. Relatedly, local delivery partners can also be resistant to impact evaluation if they feel that the resources required for evaluation come at the cost of delivery. Both these issues affect the local economic policy especially hard, particularly given the impact of significant funding cuts to councils since 2010.

Central government has a role to play in solving these issues, for example by coordinating impact evaluations across local areas or by providing sufficient resources as part of central government funding schemes, earmarked for evaluation at the outset. Coordination between different places doing similar interventions may also help solve a frequent methodological constraint faced by local evaluations when the size of local schemes mean the sample will be too small.

There are also political and presentational challenges. The downside risk of being found to spend public money on something that 'didn't work' is substantial, while an upside to positive findings is often missing or limited. While this applies to many other policy areas, the balance of costs and benefits may make local evaluations particularly tricky. For example, centrally funded interventions which are shown to have been effective come with no guarantee of continued central support – what's the point of knowing something works if you can't afford to carry on doing it?

Randomisation presents a particular challenge as it is often viewed as unfair or politically unfeasible to give some eligible individuals, businesses or communities an intervention and not others, even when the intervention is not known to be effective. There *are* cases where central government has built in random allocation to the policy, but we know of no examples for local growth programmes led by local governments.

A simple illustration of the fact that there are significant barriers and disincentives to doing high-quality impact evaluation of local growth interventions at the local level comes from a recent mapping exercise. Between December 2019 and March 2020, we contacted local authorities, combined authorities, local enterprise partnerships and central government departments, as well as other organisations all over the country to see what evaluations they had undertaken. In total, we sent emails to 1,329 people from 416 different organisations, and also conducted in-depth interviews with some of the respondents. A call for evidence, including to all local and combined authorities and local enterprise partnerships, resulted in 46 evaluations from 31 different organisations. None of these met the minimum standards we use for robust evaluation.

What Works Growth has gradually evolved its 'offer' to users in the face of these challenges, complementing training and capacity-building with dedicated support on demonstrator projects, and in

Phase 3, a dedicated fund for delivering evaluations. There were two main reasons for this pivot. First, in many policy areas we had gotten about as far as we could with the existing evidence base (although we have still added new areas). Second, because we discovered – through hard experience – that training and materials for evidence generation were not enough to get new evaluations off the ground in serious numbers without direct support and funding.

All What Works Centres face evidence gaps, but only a few are resourced to carry out the new evaluations needed to fill those gaps. The Education Endowment Foundation, for example, is spending down a £125 million endowment on hundreds of evaluations of specific education interventions designed to improve pupil attainment. The Education Endowment Foundation identifies evidence gaps (for example, what works to ensure pupils don't fall behind during the transition to secondary school) and issues public calls for relevant interventions which they can evaluate. They then fund schools to deliver a range of promising interventions as randomised controlled trials, so that high-quality evidence of their effectiveness can be collected and added to the evidence base.

Unfortunately, such an extensive exercise is beyond the budget of most of the What Works Centres. For these other centres, their primary option for filling evidence gaps is to identify promising interventions at the design stage – or, failing that, interventions already being delivered – and encourage the funders or deliverers to commission a high-quality evaluation. We support this approach by providing pro-bono support via our evaluation panel, composed of experts covering a range of policy areas. Supported by our funders, we have also created a 'stimulus fund', which allows us, for the first time, to cover the financial costs of a small number of evaluations undertaken with local partners, rather than simply providing support and advice.

In parallel with enhancing our offer to local partners, we have increasingly moved to working directly with central government programme funders. This second, more gradual pivot has also been essential in evidence generation because it has allowed us to influence the monitoring and evaluation frameworks around economic development programmes such as the Levelling Up Fund.

We think there is still more that could be done to leverage this existing spending on local growth interventions to get more good evaluation. For example, the current batch of central funds aiming to deliver levelling-up could be designed to support impact evaluation of the vast array of local growth interventions that they will fund. This can be done partly by building better incentives (and requirements) for evaluation into the design of the funds. In some circumstances it also requires central government to play a coordination role that no individual local partner can play.

Conclusions

A lot has changed in the last ten years. When we started, the evidence base was much thinner than most people would assume in some areas. For example, when we published our transport evidence review, in 2015, we found just 11 studies that looked at the economic impact of rail investments and met our evidence standards. As we write in 2022, our recent rapid evidence review on rail investment found an additional 18 studies. Our original business advice evidence review found no UK-based randomised controlled trials of business support. By 2019 the first two rounds of the Department for Business, Energy and Industrial Strategy's Business Basics Programme had funded 11 trials and 26 proofs of concept. In short, more impact evaluations are happening.

But the barriers to local evaluation remain substantial. Our offer of technical advice through the evaluation panel and even financial support for demonstrators has not yet delivered a step change in the number of local growth evaluations of the type that we have seen for education evaluations over the last ten years. We need to undertake far more high-quality evaluations of the large amounts that we spend on local growth. We also need to place far more emphasis on experimentation, piloting and evaluation at the early stages of policy development and on ensuring that lessons learned feed back into decisions about scaling up (or down) and into improving policy design. We suspect that additional resources and coordination and improved incentives will all be needed to achieve such a shift.

While there's still a long way to go in shifting people's understanding of the role that evaluation can play in helping improve local economic policies, a small but growing group of practitioners in both central and local government are trying to improve evaluation and embed it in the policy design process. Pre-pandemic, we put in place our evaluation panel and stimulus fund to respond to this growing demand. Hopefully, our attention can soon turn back to supporting efforts to better evaluate and improve our understanding of what works for local economic growth.

Disclaimer

The What Works Centre for Local Economic Growth is funded by a grant from the Economic and Social Research Council, the Department for Business, Energy and Industrial Strategy, the Department for Levelling Up, Housing and Communities and the Department for Transport. The support of the Funders is acknowledged. The views expressed are those of the authors and do not represent the views of the Funders.

Note

[1] The Organisation for Economic Co-operation and Development is often described as a 'group or club of rich countries'.

PART II

10

Criticisms and challenges of the What Works Centres

Michael Sanders and Jonathan Breckon

In the first part of this book we have looked at the history of the What Works Centres, and heard from some of the chief executives, and other senior members, from a large number of the extant centres in the UK.

By far the most investment and activity around producing and synthesising evidence has been in the health sector (see Chapter 3), with the National Institute for Clinical Excellence (NICE) sitting at the centre of this activity. NICE inspired the creation of the other centres, but each centre has developed its own way of working. It has not been a 'case of cut and paste' from health to other areas of social policy (Chapter 3, this volume). There has been a wide diversity of different models inspired and informed by, but not following, the NICE model (Chapter 2, this volume). All centres are dedicated to evidence synthesis, generation, transmission and adoption, but there is no rigid blueprint for the way in which they work, and they each employ somewhat different standards of evidence systems.

The centres are primarily focused on supporting the evidence needs of practitioners and service delivery organisations, but some of their outputs are useful for and aimed at policy makers too. More specifically, the What Works Centre in Wales (Chapter 8, this volume) has provided Welsh ministers with an on-demand evidence service. All of the centres can be understood as evidence intermediaries. Many see their role as not only as supplying relevant evidence to policy makers and practitioners but also as encouraging and enabling evidence use, by interpreting research findings to provide actionable evidence and sometimes offering implementation advice and support. They are complemented in their endeavours by a wide range of other initiatives aimed at encouraging evidence use.

Reflecting on the current state of the network, we can see reasons for hope for the future. Every study completed is another piece of the jigsaw in trying to improve the way that public service functions. The number of centres trying to enter the network is impressive and gives ground for hope.

So too does the chatter about new centres, which seems constant. Whether that's University College London and Nesta attempting to start a What Works Centre for 'net zero' carbon emissions, the Neighbourly lab and others attempting to establish a centre for social cohesion, and the Social Mobility Commission's recommendation for a further education focused What Works Centre, evidence in general, and What Works Centres in particular, are being proposed as partial solutions to some of the biggest challenges faced by our societies.

Against this backdrop, it might be hard to think about the failures, and criticisms, of the network. However, these cannot be ignored, and focusing on how to respond to them is the focus of the remainder of the book.

There are many criticisms levelled at the 'what works' methodology, from various disciplines and practice areas (for example, Cartwright and Munro, 2010; Cartwright and Hardie, 2012; Pampaka et al, 2016; Knutsson and Tompson, 2017) and a weighty literature on the barriers, misunderstandings and fundamental challenges of the whole project of evidence-based policy (for example, Oliver et al, 2014; Cairney, 2016; Parkhurst, 2016). For some, evidence-based policy is ultimately impossible and naive. A school of thought has arisen that rejects the very idea of evidence-based policy (French, 2018). This chapter could not concern itself with all of these criticisms, and nor do we want to indulge in some of their inaccuracies. Instead, what we will do here is to set up ten common challenges that have been alluded to in Part I, combined with our own experiences of leading What

Works for Children's Social Care (WWCSC; Michael as founding chief executive, Jonathan as founding board member), and also highlight some key findings from independent evaluations and reviews of the UK What Works Centres, before leading into the next section which sets out some ways forward.

Ten challenges and criticisms

1. Audiences and coverage: the challenge of focus

One area of confusion arises from the wide array of thematic and geographical coverage of the What Works Centres. Who exactly they are trying to influence – and at what level? Are the centres trying to change the behaviour of national policy makers at the top of government, or the frontline such as teachers, police officers, nurses and other 'street level bureaucrats' (Lipsky, 1980).

Most of the What Works Centres are thematic, that is, they focus on a subject area, such as early intervention, wellbeing or crime reduction. But some themes are much broader than others. Improving educational outcomes in English schools (the Education Endowment Foundation [EEF] – see Chapter 5, this volume) is, for example, more tightly defined than boosting the entire nation's wellbeing (Chapter 14, this volume). The list of potential audiences for some centres can be multitudinous. The Early Intervention Foundation has a commendable cross-sectoral theme (Chapter 6, this volume) that bridges multiple government departments, at both national and local level, and seeks to influence a whole area of audiences, in early years services, schools, policing, the National Health Service, local authority early help services and children's social care (Chapter 6, this volume). Whatever the scale of your resources, that is a challenging number of audiences for one body.

Such broad cross-cutting themes make prioritising audiences hard. With limited time and budgets, you cannot reach everybody. And some What Works Centres have taken an even more ambitious perspective by covering whole countries – such as all of Wales (Chapter 8, this volume) or Scotland (Chapter 2, this volume). The potential list of topics tackled by the Wales Centre for Public Policy (WCPP), for instance, are enormous, covering any policy area that is devolved to the Welsh Parliament, including health, social care, education, housing, local government, agriculture, and some key aspects of environmental policy, the economy and skills. It is unrealistic to expect to develop in-house expertise across such a broad range of topics.

However, such breadth does not have to be a barrier to success. A 2022 evaluation of some of the What Works Centres for the Economic and Social Research Council suggested that geographic centres – like the WCPP – have been very effective at developing a strong local presence and relationships with local partners. This has facilitated coordinated, whole-systems thinking on cross-cutting policy matters (Frontier Economics, 2022). What Works Centres have not followed a narrowly defined audience and 'preach to the converted' but cast the net widely. The College of Policing bravely made a choice to be relevant to the entire rank and file of police officers, not just their superiors. The College moved from just focusing on the smaller groups of easier-to-reach early adopters and evidence champions, seeking wider buy-in from across the police forces of England and Wales (Chapter 4, this volume).

While in hindsight we could have done more to make 'audiences first, evidence second' (Chapter 6, this volume), the centres have learnt to adapt their products and processes to the frontline. Rather than summarising purely academic themes, the EEF's toolkit has 30 overarching approaches that schools may choose to employ – in language relevant to any teacher. The EEF claims the toolkit has become a 'go to' source for teachers, with 69 per cent of school senior leaders now using the toolkit to inform their decision making (Chapter 5, this volume).

Unlike others, such as the US What Works Clearing Houses, the UK What Works Centres have placed more onus on evidence-informed *practices* – such as classroom teaching techniques, or neighbourhood crime-reduction measures – rather than packages of manualised 'off the shelf' evidence-based programmes, like the Nurse Family Partnership or Multidimensional Family Therapy, that often come at a cost and with copyright protection. The Early Intervention Foundation pivoted away from its early focus on programmes, towards practices. Their audience of commissioners were not asking 'Which evidence-based programme should I commission?'. But different questions, such as how to transform entire systems to put early intervention at the centre, or how to use evidence to develop their workforce, and they are starting to experiment with distilling the common elements, skills and building blocks that make for successful ways of working (Chapter 6, this volume).

2. The marmite factor: criticism of randomised controlled trials

One common concern is around the implementation and public perception of randomised controlled trails (RCTs). Even NICE itself can no longer rely as heavily as it once did on what was once seen as the 'gold standard' of double-blind trials (Chapter 3, this volume). Some claim that randomisation is often harder outside medicine. We have certainly found first-hand that people tend to love or hate them. Like the much loved (or loathed) yeast-based black sticky Marmite that some spread on toast, people can have strong views on RCTs, particularly around randomisation. A lot of the anti-RCT critique is visceral, gut-based and rooted in deep-seated epistemological differences. We are unlikely to change their minds. And so do not attempt to do so here.

But what we will do here is cover some common practical and perceptual challenges with RCTs flagged up in the chapters so far. Although the EEF has helped set up nearly 200 large-scale trials in the UK, they do recognise that experimental evidence generation has not gone without criticism. One argument is that RCT use in education is unethical as pupils in either control or treatment groups may be disadvantaged by their (in)access to a potentially harmful or effective intervention (Chapter 5, this volume). However, as the EEF points out, without robust evidence we cannot know whether an intervention is effective, or whether it is the control or treatment group that is being disadvantaged by their allocation (Hutchison and Styles, 2010). And uncontrolled experimentation and randomisation are happening already. The EEF has also trialled approaches that are already being used in some schools, but not in others. In this sense, the EEF says the 'effect of the trial is to generate knowledge by replacing arbitrary assignment with random assignment' (Chapter 5, this volume).

While the EEF has been world-leading in running trials for schools, it has found in its decade-long experience that RCTs can be fraught with practical challenges. They can be time-consuming to set up and classroom teachers are time poor. In early trials, the drop-out rate from trials – or attrition – was 24 per cent (Edovald and Nevill, 2021). A school may be keen to run an exciting innovation that they have heard about in other parts of the UK or overseas – but don't want to be part of a trial.

One way the EEF has remedied this concern is through waiting-list trial designs that enable all schools to access the programme following the trial (Chapter 5, this volume). The EEF has also learnt as it evolved – an important feature in our view of all What Works Centres – adapting to experience and feedback. The EEF sets out some of the measures it has now deployed to manage attrition, including paying participants and promoting buy-in in schools into the whole ethos of the trial. Where randomisation is hard to implement or sell, the EEF has also started to use quasi-experimental designs (Chapter 5, this volume).

3. The evidence won't travel: the contextual challenge

A common theme for some centres is how to make the research relevant to the needs of practitioners. There is the challenge of so-called black box of trials, when there is no information on why or how something did or did not work. There has been more emphasis in some centres on getting inside the black box of RCTs and meta-analysis. The What Works Centre for Crime Reduction has, for instance, taken a more 'realist' approach (Pawson, 2006), setting out some of the mechanisms and contextual factors in its commissioned systematic reviews (for example, Sidebottom et al, 2018) and crime reduction 'toolkit' (Chapter 4, this volume). The assessment from the College of Policing is that taking a few extra days or weeks to pay careful attention to mechanism and implementation creates both a stronger evaluation, but also a better chance of delivering impact (Chapter 4, this volume). The EEF has updated its toolkit to provide school leaders with far greater detail on the context and relevance of the evidence of approaches. It is then left to school leaders to make professional judgements about which findings are most relevant to their schools, teachers and pupils (Chapter 5, this volume).

Much of the available existing evidence comes from certain countries, such as the US, and so may not travel to other countries.

And much of the What Works Centres have focused on England. The WCPP has thus taken on a translation role as a 'bridge' between English evidence and the difference in political culture, values and priorities in Wales and the rest of the UK. The WCPP has helped other What Works Centres and evidence producers spot when their work is relevant to Wales and introduced them to policy makers (Chapter 8, this volume).

4. Confusing methodological pluralism: what counts as evidence?

One response to the criticism outlined in the previous section of the 'black box' of trials and meta-analysis has been in diversifying the types of research undertaken. The EEF has begun to commission more different types of research and put more emphasis on process evaluation, 'providing the sector with more nuanced and robust information on the ways in which programmes and interventions are implemented' (Chapter 5, this volume). The Early Intervention Foundation has moved towards doing more primary qualitative research, primary quantitative research and secondary data analysis, which can all help to understand that context (Chapter 6, this volume). The What Works Centre for Crime Reduction is merging trials, and systematic reviews – on topics like knife crime or crime during the COVID-19 pandemic – with promising emerging practice from the frontline police that has not yet been formally evaluated (Chapter 4, this volume). But this spreading methodological pluralism does raise the issue of what counts as high-quality and trustworthy evidence of 'what works'. How inclusive of different types of research should we be?

To navigate through the varieties of evidence, some centres have produced formal frameworks and hierarchies of evidence (see, for example, Chapter 6, this volume). But they can be confusing and contradictory, making differing judgements about the quality of evidence across centres. There are at least 18 different evidence frameworks in UK social policy, and growing roughly at two a year (Gough and White, 2018; Puttick, 2018), with a growing library of different manuals and guidelines describing how research should be undertaken (Gough et al, 2018, chapter 4).

Some have used pre-existing frameworks, like the NICE adoption of the Grading of Recommendations Assessment, Development and Evaluation (GRADE) framework (Breckon and Ruiz, 2014), or the use of the Maryland Scale by the What Works Centre for Local Economic Growth. Others have invented their own. The Early Intervention Foundation says that one of its most valuable early foundations was to establish evidence standards to underpin all of its work (Chapter 6, this volume). Others have avoided creating evidence standards altogether. The WCPP took a pragmatic approach which accepts that the type of evidence we need to provide varies depending on the type of question it is addressing. Its view is that some evidence is better than no evidence, so long as it gives clear advice about its limitations (Chapter 8, this volume).

Considering the diversity of What Works Centres' aims and functions, it is not surprising that there is no unifying framework. It would be hard to have consistency of standards when their functions, forms and policy areas with the evidence 'ecosystem' are so diverse (Gough et al, 2018). However, some greater coordination – particularly when doing joint trials, research or reviews across centres – would be valuable, and we return to this in Chapter 18.

5. Empty reviews and evidence gaps

A core part of the What Works membership model is to generate high-quality, accessible evidence syntheses, drawing on systematic reviews and meta-analyses (Cabinet Office, nd). Yet many centres have struggled to synthesise when the evidence is not there in the first place. Unlike health, where there was a large body of research for NICE to summarise and communicate (Chapter 3, this volume), other sectors have had a gap in the evidence 'pipeline' of trials and high-quality impact studies. There is a particular deficit in economic research on the costs and value for money of different interventions – and most What Works Centres have not been able to include research on cost-effectiveness.

An evaluation of the Economic and Social Research Council-funded What Works Centres concluded that it is not useful for a centre to spend substantial time synthesising an evidence base only to end up with a key finding that 'there is no evidence of sufficient quality' to answer the decision maker's question (Frontier Economics, 2022, p 3). This was the experience of the What Works Centre for Local Economic Growth, which wisely changed direction; it started by commissioning a range of expensive and timely systematic reviews but struggled to find other high-quality impact evaluations to populate them. After an initial five years, it pivoted towards helping to grow the skills and capacity to do more primary research (Chapter 9, this volume).

Other centres have also run training and helped build the confidence, skills and funding for frontline practitioners to help to build the evidence themselves, such as the Research Schools Network of the EEF, and the Early Intervention Foundation's Evaluation Hub of resources on methods and advice. Such bottom-up practitioner-led evidence generation may help with implementation, and the wider scaling and take-up of evidence, as professionals are brought into the research culture and objectives (Chapter 4, this volume).

There could, however, be much more funding in some sectors to help people conduct this research. The What Works Centre for Crime Reduction has been savvy about leveraging other external funding sources to help with this evaluation pipeline, such as founding the £10 million 'knowledge fund' in 2010, supported by the Home Office and Higher Education Funding Council for England (Chapter 4, this volume).

This support for building evidence from the ground up – rather than leaping to empty reviews – has been the experience of others, including ourselves when leading What Works for Children's Social Care. Although we did find summaries of existing evidence useful, we changed towards filling the large evidence hole of RCTs and other research in our sector. Running a full-blown systematic review can be a time-consuming one – they can take at least six months, and often more. So more rapid reviews are useful, even if they cut some methodological quality. The Wales Centre for Public Policy (WCPP) believes that rapid reviews can provide a helpful snapshot of what we know and don't know, and cover both academic and 'grey' literature (Chapter 9, this volume), and faster scoping reviews of the evidence landscapes, or evidence-gap maps, that we discuss in the next section of this book (see Chapters 11 and 17).

Meta-analysis and reviews can also omit crucial details to help decision makers, a challenge touched on in the previous section on the 'black box' challenge. The original Teaching and Learning Toolkit worked at a very high 'meta-meta-analytic level' level, bundling up average impacts of approaches through the aggregation of effect sizes taken from existing meta-analyses. In 2021 they went into 'nuanced exploration' of factors by 'unzipping' the original meta-analyses that explain variation in outcomes, such as age, subject and specific strategy type (Chapter 5, this volume).

6. Failing on scaling

Perhaps the most damning failure of the network is our failure to scale evidence-based interventions, with a few notable exceptions. These include NICE, whose different status to the other centres gives it more authority, and which was discussed in Chapter 3. They also include the What Works Centre for Crime Reduction, whose role in shaping the training for new police officers gives them substantial sway, albeit concentrated among more junior police officers (Chapter 4, this volume). Beyond this, successful examples of scaling are few and far between – but some are covered in previous chapters. The National Tutoring Programme, begun during the 2020 pandemic, is a triumph for the Education Endowment Foundation's toolkit, as is the expansion of the Nuffield Early Language Intervention (Chapter 5, this volume). The 2010–2015 coalition government's funding of parenting support programmes is arguably a success of the Early Intervention Foundation and its evidence base, but take-up of the intervention itself was remarkably low.

As well as shortcomings in the number of interventions that are taken to scale, the manner of this scaling also leaves something to be desired. The EEF's Octopus trial that aimed to increase take-up of evidence-based interventions by schools did not show substantial improvements in this area (Lord et al, 2017), and rigorous evaluation of the EEF's research school model, or the WWCSC's Evidence Ambassador programme, has yet to be produced. Anecdotally, the experience of scaling the 'Magic

Breakfast' programme following a successful trial result was beset by growing pains as a small organisation sought to grow rapidly, creating technical and logistical barriers to success. There is also a more general phenomenon, noted by Chicago economist John List, of interventions' effectiveness declining as time goes on, and as interventions scale. One potential route to improve the quality and reliability of scaling is in implementation science, which is the topic of Chapter 13.

7. Policy influence: the difficulty of biting the hand that feeds you

Most What Works Centres were not designed to focus purely on influencing the central government alone. The goal was to influence leaders of public services, commissioners and frontline professionals; to put these 'users' at the 'heart of everything' the centres do (Cabinet Office, nd). Yet changing national and local policy is unavoidable. You need to be engaging with policy makers if you want to influence the minds of those who 'set the rules of the game' and invest in evidence-based services (Chapter 6, this volume).

For those that do go after policy, the track record on impact has been decidedly mixed. There are some notable success stories. For example, the What Works Centre for Wellbeing successfully promoted the use of wellbeing as an aim of public resources as defined in HM Treasury's Green Book (Chapter 14, this volume). But an evaluation of the Economic and Social Research Council-funded centres was unable to identify clear examples of policy impact for all centres (Frontier Economics, 2022, p 5). The Institute for Government think tank (Haddon and Sasse, 2018) has highlighted the need for the centres to be better at developing stronger routes into policy making (Haddon and Sasse, 2018).

Part of the problem is the fundamental different cultures and mutual suspicions of policy makers and researchers (Chapter 8, this volume) and it can feel like 'shouting from different hilltops' (Chapter 4, this volume). But perhaps a more profound difficulty is the challenge of 'biting the hand that feeds you'. Many centres have been directly funded by Whitehall government departments, arm's-length bodies, or the devolved governments of Scotland and

Wales. Even if governance and funding mechanisms are in place to buffer government meddling in to the work of What Works Centres – such as creating independent funding sources via an endowment – it is hard in practice to be openly critical of elected officials and the government of the day. Most of the influence goes on quietly and diplomatically behind closed doors, rather than open criticism. NICE has been a rare example of countering the wishes of the government, such as in the cancer drug fund controversy (Chapter 3, this volume) but there were never any open political or media battles with ministers.

That said, the centres have defended their independence. Even when the topics are dictated by policy-makers' needs, as with the WCPP, measures are in place to safeguard neutrality: reports are peer-reviewed by academics and made public, and the Welsh Government has agreed a protocol that ensures that 'ministers cannot amend, delay or veto reports that they find inconvenient or uncomfortable' (Chapter 8, this volume).

But politics is still hard to avoid. The WCPP work has been used by opposition parties to attack government policies, including in the run up to elections. Scrupulous transparency in the research methods is also required – not just to maintain independence from government, but also from others with vested interests such as businesses and consultancies that offer paid-for services for the public sector. Historically, trials in education were prone to bias as they were often conducted by delivery organisations – the people who design and deliver the interventions (Chapter 5, this volume). The EEF has demanded that all of its research has high levels of transparency, pre-specification and reporting.

8. A failure to measure outcomes

If we are interested in the causal impact of interventions, we need to know what we're hoping to have an impact on. As with public services in general, the broad goal is to increase quality of life and net happiness. If everyone can agree on this, there is much less consensus on what exactly this means, and importantly, how it can be measured.

At some level, there is clear failure in the network's attempts to measure outcomes and impact. Although happiness and wellbeing are central to the mission, these are very rarely measured by trials – in part because wellbeing is not routinely measured, and there is substantial inconsistency in the way that it is measured in those studies that do so. Methodological questions still remain about our ability to measure wellbeing, and the extent to which it should be measured contemporaneously, or retrospectively. Later in the book, Nancy Hey, director of What Works Wellbeing, discusses this particular measurement challenge and what is being done to address it (see Chapter 14, this volume).

The complexity of measuring the higher order end of happiness and wellbeing naturally leads us to focus on more concrete, intermediary measures – things like educational attainment, participation in crime, or income. These measures are more commonly routinely collected, and so are easier to use in large trials where attrition could be a problem. They are also likely to be 'important' in some sense. Administrative datasets are costly and burdensome to produce – and so they tend to exist for a reason. The UK's National Pupil Database contains information on students' grades, attendance and exclusions, because these things are viewed as important by the government. With half of all social mobility being driven by differences in education (Blanden et al, 2007), and with school absences being a strong predictor of involvement in youth violence, these things matter. These things might only be proxies for the thing we care about really – as exam grades are only a proxy for learning – but they are widely used proxies, which have an impact on later outcomes – because they are the main source of information that people in, for example, the labour market, have to go on. Nonetheless, our reliance on many and varied proxies for true outcomes of interest should be acknowledged.

9. Short-termism

Another failing of the network, at least as it stands at the moment, is in its short-termism. Some centres can be distracted by chasing short-term funding or keeping multiple funders contented. The centres can be constrained by the timescales of the funding cycles they work to, as well as the degree of freedom they have on budget allocation. The Early Intervention Foundation was required to negotiate funding with increased frequency with government departments (Gough et al, 2018, p 109). This can limit its capacity to be strategic and longer-term, while the negotiations themselves require a substantial share of resources. A review by the Economic and Social Research Council found that longer-term financial commitment was necessary to enable proper establishment of the centres. Improving evidence production and use was seen as a 'long-term project that required long-term support' (Economic and Social Research Council, 2017, p 2).

Funding cycles, even for the endowed centres, mean that outcomes are often collected a small number of months after an intervention. Given the difficulty in changing people's lives for the better, and the potential compounding of effects over time, this may mean that we miss out on interventions that are effective, spuriously concluding that because they do not produce effects rapidly, they do not produce them at all. Even where interventions are found to be effective in the short term, we might seriously underplay the cost-effectiveness of interventions, if they have compounding effects, or effects that spill over into different domains. For example, if an intervention increases engagement with school, it might achieve a short-term increase in attainment, but longer-term impacts on university attendance, employment and even criminality. Downstream centres, like the Centre for Transforming Access and Student Outcomes, might take up the baton of trials conducted previously, to improve our understanding of longer-term effects – this is discussed in Chapter 11.

10. Erasure

The final failure of the network is one of erasure. The role of statistics is to shine a light into the world and reveal patterns that might otherwise be hidden. For example, the beauty of a randomised trial is that we can, with relatively few assumptions, cleanly identify the impact of interventions on outcomes, by moving beyond the experience of individuals. The process of conducting this research – and especially of conducting it well – is to keep it simple. We minimise the number of statistical tests that we conduct, the number of outcomes we look at, and the number of different groups that fall under our gaze. Doing so is the source of our rigour and the cleanliness of our tests – by reducing dimensionality, we improve clarity.

It is easy to lose track in all of this of the reason why we do the work that we do. Most of us are motivated by improving the lives of individuals, not achieving statistical significance in a regression analysis. Taking a step back, we can recognise the importance of individuals' experiences, and of the tapestry of human experience. We can also recognise that effects can differ widely between individuals and groups. Gender, class, sexual identity of orientation, race and ethnicity change the way that the world interacts with us, and the way that we interact with the world. It is important that we do not erase these differences, and the narrative of everyday life, in our search for statistical parsimony. More researchers and centres are thinking about how to retain the network's rigour, while also incorporating inequalities into our framework. Chapter 16 considers the present and future of this work.

References

Blanden, J., Gregg, P. and Macmillan, L. (2007) Accounting for intergenerational income persistence: Noncognitive skills, ability and education. *The Economic Journal*, 117(519): C43–C60.

Breckon, J. and Ruiz, F. (2014) *The NICE way: Lessons for social policy and practices from the National Institute for Health and Care Excellence*. The Alliance for Useful Evidence. www.alliance 4usefulevidence.org/publication/the-nice-way-lessons-for-soc ial-policy-and-practices-from-the-national-institute-for-hea lth-and-care-excellence/

Cabinet Office (nd) *What Works Network membership requirements*. GOV.UK. www.gov.uk/government/publications/what-works-network-membership-requirements/what-works-network

Cairney, P. (2016) *The politics of evidence-based policy making*. Palgrave Pivot.

Cartwright, N. and Munro, E. (2010) The limitations of randomized controlled trials in predicting effectiveness. *Journal of Evaluation in Clinical Practice*, 16(2): 260–266.

Cartwright, N. and Hardie, J. (2012) *Evidence-based policy: A practical guide to doing it better*. Oxford University Press.

Economic and Social Research Council (2017) *What Works strategic review and investment framework.* Economic and Social Research Council. www.ukri.org/what-we-offer/supporting-collaboration-in-the-uk/supporting-collaboration-esrc/what-works/investment-framework/

Edovald, T. and Nevill, C. (2021) Working out what works: The case of the Education Endowment Foundation in England. *ECNU Review of Education*, 4(1): 46–64.

French, R. (2018) Lessons from the evidence on evidence-based policy. *Canadian Public Administration*, 61(3): 425–442.

Frontier Economics (2022) *ESRC investment in What Works Centres: Evaluation report for the ESRC: Executive summary.* Frontier Economics.

Gough, D. and White, H. (2018) *Evidence standards and evidence claims in web based research portals.* Centre for Homelessness Impact. www.homelessnessimpact.org/post/evidence-standards-in-web-based-research-portals

Gough, D., Maidment, C. and Sharples, J. (2018) *UK What Works Centres: Aims, methods and contexts.* https://eppi.ioe.ac.uk/cms/Portals/0/PDF%20reviews%20and%20summaries/UK%20what%20works%20centres%20study%20final%20report%20july%202018.pdf?ver=2018-07-03-155057-243

Haddon, C. and Sasse, T. (2018) *How government can work with academia.* Institute for Government. www.instituteforgovernment.org.uk/publications/how-government-can-work-academia

Hutchison, D. and Styles, B. (2010) *A guide to running randomised controlled trials for educational researchers.* NFER.

Knutsson, J. and Tompson, L. (eds) (2017) *Advances in evidence-based policing.* Routledge.

Lipsky, M. (1980) *Street-level bureaucracy: Dilemmas of the individual in public service.* Russell Sage Foundation.

Lord, P., Rabiasz, A. and Styles, B. (2017) *'Literacy octopus' dissemination trial: Evaluation report and executive summary.* Education Endowment Foundation. https://eric.ed.gov/?id=ED581230

Oliver, K., Innvar, S., Lorenc, T., Woodman, J. and Thomas, J. (2014) A systematic review of barriers to and facilitators of the use of evidence by policymakers. *BMC Health Services Research*, 14(1): 2.

Pampaka, M., Williams, J. and Homer, M. (2016) Is the educational 'what works' agenda working? Critical methodological developments. *International Journal of Research & Method in Education*, 39(3): 231–236.

Parkhurst, J. (2016) *The politics of evidence: From evidence-based policy to the good governance of evidence*. Routledge.

Pawson, R. (2006) *Evidence-based policy: A realist perspective*. SAGE.

Puttick, R. (2018) *Mapping the standards of evidence used in UK social policy*. Nesta: Alliance for Useful Evidence. www.nesta.org.uk/report/mapping-standards-evidence-used-uk-social-policy/

Sidebottom, A., Tompson, L., Thornton, A., Bullock, K., Tilley, N., Bowers, K. and Johnson, S.D. (2018) Gating alleys to reduce crime: A meta-analysis and realist synthesis. *Justice Quarterly*, 35(1): 55–86.

11

Higher aspirations: growing from a university home to an independent body

Eliza Kozman and Omar Khan

Education and social mobility are so closely linked, that many conversations about the latter focus consistently on the former. This makes sense. Jo Blanden and colleagues (2007) find that half of all social *immobility* flows through differential access to, and success in, education. Although there is much to be done, progress has already been made in this area in Britain. Making education universal to 18, and mostly doing away with grammar schools, has served to create a more level playing field in primary and secondary education, albeit one in which competition for the best school places in the state sector remains fierce, and plays out through the housing market.

The last, or perhaps merely the next, frontier in educational expansion is therefore into higher education. This area too has seen a large-scale increase in participation, from 3.4 per cent in 1950 to more than 50 per cent in 2019. However, despite some calls for a comprehensive higher education system, higher education in general, and universities in particular, remain highly selective, and tuition fees, even structured as they are, mean that such education is not freely available to all.

The growth of the proportion of young people taking part in higher education has two major drivers. Expansion of providers, both at the intensive and extensive margin (there are now more higher education institutions, and universities are on average larger) is one cause, and so too is the change in a large number of professional qualifications to reclassify them as 'degree level' subjects, including nursing, midwifery and social work.

The increase in student numbers is, almost mechanically, a tool for widening participation to groups who otherwise would not have been able to participate previously. Despite claims of meritocracy, university education in previous decades was predominantly the domain of a privileged few. Yes, students had achieved good grades, but they were also overwhelmingly White, male and middle class. To take an extreme example, the vast majority of students studying at Eton, an elite private school, attend university, both in the 1950s and in the 2020s. Almost any expansion of higher education participation *must* reach people who are less privileged than students from this kind of rarefied environment. Recent years have indeed seen record numbers of disadvantaged young people enter higher education. However, 2020 marked the final dip in a decline in the 18-year-old population and, as the pool of young applicants grows, we must remain vigilant to ensure that disadvantaged students are not squeezed out when capacity constraints bite.

The conversion of formerly vocational qualifications – like nursing – to degree level status has attracted less support, with some arguing that it amounts to 'watering down' the quality of degrees. This viewpoint misses, first, that this was not merely a rebadging but a substantial change in the nature of the course; and, second, that the beneficiaries of these changes are disproportionately female, people from lower-income families, and members of ethnic minorities – all of which are overrepresented in the caring professions. Law, medicine, accounting and other courses are similarly 'professional' in nature and among the most valued by students, parents and employers. To the extent that education conveys an individual's status, this was a straightforward way to make a substantive change.

The concentrated effort by government, universities, schools and the third sector to widen participation is nothing new, but it has taken on a different energy since approximately 2012. With the introduction of £9,000 tuition fees for undergraduates by the coalition government in 2010, institutions wishing to charge the higher rate of fees needed to invest a proportion of this funding in widening participation, and to describe their activities through their access and participation plans to be approved by the government regulator for higher education, the Office for Students (OfS). Subsequent regulatory changes have softened the requirement for investment, moving away from set expectations about the level of spending, and towards more of a focus on outcomes. Policy in this area continues to evolve, but providers are still expected to articulate and deliver on clear targets to diversify their intake and support their students.

These changes have seen a great deal of both energy and money driven towards increasing the representativeness of student cohorts. Much of this work has been developed with the best of intentions at its heart, with increases in the kinds of activity that were already being undertaken – like summer schools – and substantial innovations – like ambitious programmes of curriculum reform.

While this activity is to be applauded, there is no guarantee of its effectiveness at achieving its goals. In earlier stages of education (pre-school through to secondary school), only about one in five robustly evaluated interventions has been shown to have a positive effect. Without rigorous evidence, we should be sceptical about the difference being made by all of this new money, attention and programmes to boost access and success. Even where things are, and have been found to be, effective, this is not enough. The higher education sector is fragmented, with responsibility for widening participation divided between hundreds of different organisations. We therefore need to ensure that good, impactful practice is widely adopted, adapted appropriately for different contexts and subject to ongoing evaluation, so we can be sure we are doing the best by students across the sector.

It was to achieve these goals – of building evidence and ensuring that it spread across the higher education sector – that the OfS commissioned an 'Evidence and Impact Exchange (EIX)', to fill the existing gap in the market and become a What Works Centre for higher education. At the end of 2018, a consortium led by King's College London and Nottingham Trent University won the right to lead the establishment phase of this new centre, and in January 2019, the Centre for Transforming Access and Student Outcomes in Higher Education (TASO) was born.

The team was led during its establishment phase by Susannah Hume, the director of evaluation at King's College London, and before long, a permanent director (Omar) joined from the Runnymede Trust, and a deputy director for research (Eliza) joined from the Behavioural Insights Team. The team was set up with three main goals – to collate everything that we currently know about the efficacy of interventions to widen access and promote student success; to create new evidence to fill gaps that currently exist; and to engage and enthuse the sector about what works type evidence and build grassroots demand and, ultimately, supply.

In the intervening three years, a few things have not gone according to plan – not least the COVID-19 pandemic sweeping the world and transferring most lectures – and most open days – from campuses and lecture theatres to bedrooms and laptop monitors. Not only was the higher education sector unprepared for the effects of a global pandemic – how could it have been? – the evidence base that we had amassed was ill-suited to offering concrete advice on how they should adapt to this 'new normal'.

Nonetheless, we have achieved some notable successes. We've published evidence summaries collating what we know about a range of topics, including interventions focused on young people with care experience, summer schools, financial support – and even online teaching and learning. Our toolkit captures this evidence base in clear format, following the practice of other What Works Centres, and is updated regularly to cover new topics and as we learn more about what works. At the same time, we've launched a series of new evaluations, looking at the efficacy of summer schools, of financial capability training for students, and targeted outreach for potential medical school applicants, among others. Our conferences and workshops have had attendees from across the sector, with over 1,000 attending in total from over 100 higher education institutions, and all of our evaluations and projects are conducted in partnership with higher education institutions.

Alongside our successes, three years in we have a clearer sense of our priorities and the challenges we face – some of which we have tried to articulate here.

The importance of empiricism

It might go without saying that as a What Works Centre, we believe that empiricism, and particularly causal impact evaluation, is an important part of our work, but it bears repeating. Outreach activities are developed by intelligent and passionate people and organisations determined to make a difference in the world. Unfortunately, as we've learned from other fields, and increasingly in our own, passion, intelligence and drive do not always translate into success. Dispassionate empirical analysis is the only reliable way we have of teasing out effective practice from well-intentioned yet ultimately fruitless uses of time and resources. Every field develops its own sacred cows and whether these survive and spread needs to be determined by more than just the charisma of their advocates.

This unwavering commitment to empiricism isn't just about cutting things that don't work, but about having a more honest debate about what does. It is an accepted truism that bursaries and other financial inducements – which are costly, but potentially appealing and easy to administer – are ineffective. However, if we review the evidence for and against bursaries in a clear-eyed way, the findings are much less conclusive, with much of the case against bursaries based on simply comparison of means without a good counterfactual group. A prominent paper compares university attendance rates for people who are eligible for bursaries, with that of those who are not eligible, and finds no differences, concluding that the bursaries are ineffective. However, because bursaries are targeted at lower-income students – as well as often at members of other underrepresented groups in higher education – we might reasonably expect *lower* attendance by people eligible for bursaries in the absence of bursaries – so, having the same level of attendance might reasonably be considered to be a success. This is not conclusive evidence that bursaries *are* effective, but it does mean that we should not consider this conversation over.

A similar argument plays out when we consider tuition fees, which have been raised from £0 in 1996 to £9,250 per year (in England) at the time of writing, via increases to £1,000 and £3,000 along the way. Many passionate advocates for widening participation, not least student bodies, argue that tuition fees stand in the way of a more equal higher education participation based purely on merit, and that they discourage attendance by poorer young people. The decision by the Conservative-Liberal Democrat coalition to raise tuition fees to £9,000, in spite of a manifesto pledge by the Liberal Democrats not to, contributed to the disillusionment of younger voters with the Liberal Democrats. The gradual, and fairly consistent, widening of participation over this time period does not appear to support the fear of mass discouragement, but more rigorous empirical research is once again needed if either side is to be convinced.

Longer-term thinking

Alongside rising interest in widening participation, and greater investment in these kinds of activities, there has been an increasing focus in widening participation activities starting earlier in a child's life. There are good reasons to think that this makes sense. Only about 60 per cent of 19-year-olds had qualifications at level 3 (equivalent to A levels) in 2019. As some level 3 qualification is almost always a requirement for entering higher education, this provides an effective ceiling on potential attendance. While higher education attendance at 19 in 2019 was around 40 per cent, progression to higher education conditional on studying for A levels was 77.9 per cent in that same year. Even allowing for differences in attendance within this cohort by different groups of students, there is more ground to be made up earlier in the school journey to give a greater number of students the chance of attending higher education, than there is at the point where, aged 18, students are taking their A levels and other level 3 qualifications.

We can see evidence for this looking further back. The Longitudinal Study of Young People in England finds big differences in students' aspirations and expectations of attending higher education even at the beginning of secondary school aged 11, and these gaps widen substantially over time, so that, for example, care experienced and lower-income students think themselves much less likely to attend university than their peers at age 16 and 18. As student and family expectations of attendance are important early predictors of progression, addressing these expectations early might yield greater rewards, while a summer schools activity aged 17 might be too late for the vast majority of young people. Raising these expectations is not simply a case of encouraging young people to 'dream big', but rather ensuring that we are providing them with the tools, knowledge and support that they need to hold expectations that are both high and realistic.

This situation has seen widening participation departments reaching further back into the lives of young people to increase participation in the somewhat longer term. This approach brings a number of challenges for a What Works Centre. First, when intervening in a child's life when they are 11 years old (for most, the first year of secondary school), there will be at least seven years until attending higher education can be measured as an outcome. This means either we need to design very long-term trials (more than twice the length of TASO's original funding period), or rely on intermediate outcome measures, like expectations and grades. In practice, we will need to do both if we are to have any actionable findings in a timely way, while being confident in the long term that we are having meaningful effects on the outcomes we really care about. We also need to strengthen our understanding of how intermediate outcome measures, which sometimes use self-report instruments, map onto our more concrete long-term behaviours and outcomes – and we intend to publish our work to build and validate scales for exactly this purpose in the first half of 2022. Ultimately, our projects also need not just to be longer than we might typically see in education, but larger – a long-term study is more susceptible to attrition, measurement error and attenuation of effects over time. All else being equal, this means larger investments in fewer projects than we might otherwise conduct, or that our sister centre at the Education Endowment Foundation will typically fund.

Widening participation teams reaching back further and further also brings up important questions of comparative advantage. Institutions might excel at academic education and research, but teaching at degree level is a very different task to teaching 11-year-olds. The level of specialisation that a degree or other higher education qualification brings is neither plausible nor desirable in younger pupils. The focus on independent learning that is sensibly a focus in higher education, due to the age of the students and very often the size of a lecture, is clearly not appropriate for young pupils. It is therefore sensible that the teaching of younger students is left to their teachers and, concurrently, that universities try to add value in those areas where they can – perhaps through interventions which nurture expectations, or aspects of learning that require the resources and equipment to which most schools do not have access. There are as many ideas on how to do this as there are institutions attempting to do it. TASO is developing a typology of the range of such interventions, outlining the existing evidence base and working with partners in higher education and outside to further improve this evidence in order to differentiate between wheat and chaff.

Student success

It's not enough just to get students into higher education – they have to succeed once they arrive. If we are able to help a student get a place at university, but they subsequently attend and drop out, then they will have debt from their student loans and living expenses but no degree to show for it. By choosing a route into university, they will also have forgone other potentially successful pathways, at least temporarily, incurring less tangible opportunity costs. When a student does not flourish in higher education, efforts to promote their entry may have ultimately made their life worse. This is a common finding from the US efforts to increase university attendance – although we should note that drop-out rates are much higher there in general.

Testing interventions to keep students enrolled is important for these reasons, but is made more complicated by the fact that (thankfully) drop-out rates are in general low in most UK higher education institutions, making improvement difficult to detect statistically; and (less thankfully), by the fact that many institutions, and particularly higher-tariff ones, have fairly few students from widening participation backgrounds enrolled – meaning that research will need participants from a large number of institutions to provide robust evidence. This need for many partners also produces challenges in research governance.

Two projects show how we are approaching the question of student success. First is our project on curriculum reform, an area that our evidence review suggested had some promise of addressing the long-standing and persistent degree-awarding gaps between Black, Asian and minority ethnic students and White students. Second, our work on online teaching and learning, an issue that has perhaps always deserved greater focus, but that has become particularly relevant and urgent given the switch to wholly online teaching and learning during the first COVID-19 lockdown in 2020. While we can expect in-person teaching to remain a preferred default in many circumstances, online teaching and learning is here to stay, even if we are not yet certain about how it can best be delivered to tackle, rather than worsen, existing inequalities.

Research ethics

After a year of independent operations, we have learned a lot about the various challenges of delivering on effective evaluation, and how we can respond to these to support partners and produce the best evidence we can.

The first challenge is around research ethics, an issue that we have confronted in our own work, and that has arisen among potential partners. We therefore prioritised producing ethics guidance for the sector, which will be published in spring 2022.

It is vital that research is carried out in an ethical way, and that the ethics of an intervention and a research design are considered properly prior to any study beginning. This is especially the case when we are conducting randomised controlled trials, in which participants have some chance of an intervention they could potentially benefit from, and may have actively tried to access, being denied to them in order to ensure the robustness of the evaluation. University ethics committees are well placed to assess the ethics of this kind of research.

However, conducting research in widening participation and student success raises ethical challenges that are not so common in the other areas covered by the What Works Network. First, those carrying out the research have a duty of care to the young people, particularly when we consider research on student success interventions which can involve institutions experimenting on their own students, and/or otherwise using students' data for research purposes – something which many institutions heavily restrict. Unlike carrying out a multi-site project in schools, each institution involved in delivering the work will have its own ethics committee and processes, and will very likely require separate ethical approval to be sought. Given that ethical clearance can take months, this can dramatically slow down the process, presenting particular problems for a What Works Centre like ours with fairly limited time horizons in terms of funding. Having multiple independent committees means that they may each need different changes to be made to the research process before they are willing to grant approval – meaning that each site may conduct the research or the intervention in different ways, reducing the extent to which broad conclusions can be drawn.

Data collection/harmonisation

Another area that has consistently raised challenges is data collection and harmonisation. Those conducting impact evaluation in primary or secondary education benefit from the National Pupil Database, while most of the outcomes being measured in interventions are related to attainment or attitudes within schooling. There is no similar 'national student database' for higher education, and more need to measure longer-term outcomes, including in the labour market. Even where data exists, for example on graduate labour market outcomes and, for example, a particular providers' access and participation activities, it can be difficult to access in a way that allows apples-to-apples comparisons. This is a challenge across the What Works Network, to consider how we might make better use of longitudinal datasets.

Regulation

One final challenge we have experienced is the role of regulation – or at least the perception of regulation. The government established the OfS as a regulator to focus on addressing inequalities in student outcomes, while all providers must produce access and participation plans to outline their targets as well as how they might achieve those aims. Some in the sector feel that there is a tension between demonstrating how they are reducing inequality and developing innovative impact evaluations that might instead show that their interventions may not be working. We, and OfS, are working to communicate that effective evaluation *is* a priority, but this cannot wholly ease this tension.

Partnerships

The flip side of the ethical and logistical complexity of working in higher education is that many of our projects benefit from an embarrassment of riches, with institutions – both on the academic and professional services sides – being packed with professionals with a good understanding of research, and an enthusiasm for producing evidence, as well as a good grasp of the theoretical underpinnings of the work they are doing. Where other centres might struggle to work with stakeholders to formalise an intervention via a theory of change, this has proven more straightforward with partner universities, and ideas are able to be both theorised and refined to give them the best shot at succeeding.

These partnerships, with around 20 universities working directly with us on our summer schools, curriculum reform, multi-intervention outreach and mentoring, and financial capability student success projects, have led us to conduct more interesting and more ambitious projects than we might otherwise have been able to. The challenges that we have described in this chapter are more than compensated for by the energy and intellect that our partners bring to the table.

Conclusion

As we write this chapter, TASO is three years old, and nearing the end of its initial funding period. Although we could not have predicted or prepared for a global pandemic that has radically transformed every aspect of our society, including higher education, our track record gives us substantial cause for hope for the future. The original King's College London/ Nottingham Trent University bid to the OfS reflected the fact that high-quality causal evidence was sorely lacking in the field of widening participation and student success. At that time, and since, we have argued that the idea of an 'Evidence and Impact Exchange' (as TASO was initially to be called), would be reduced to the role of a 'what *doesn't* work' centre, bemoaning the absence of high-quality evidence, and finding little to share with the sector. Instead, we have attempted to start on the front foot – to collaborate widely, to review the evidence where appropriate, but most importantly to actively build new evidence, and empower others to build their own, reflecting on and responding to the challenges of doing so in the field. A passion for partnership, combined with a ruthlessness about rigour, are what we believe will see TASO, and the wider What Works Network, flourish in years to come. Ultimately, this will also result in tackling some of the most persistent and long-standing inequalities in our society, including those in higher education.

Reference

Blanden, J., Gregg, P. and Macmillan, L. (2007) Accounting for intergenerational income persistence: Noncognitive skills, ability and education. *The Economic Journal*, 117(519): C43–C60.

12

Using evidence to end homelessness

Lígia Teixeira

The Centre for Homelessness Impact (CHI) was founded in 2018, establishing itself as an independent entity having been incubated within Crisis (one of the UK's largest homelessness charities), and joining the What Works Council (the grouping of What Works Centres recognised by the UK Cabinet Office) in 2019.

The centre's objective is simple – to create a society in which any experience of homelessness is rare, brief and non-recurring. Despite substantial reductions in homelessness, and in particular rough sleeping in the first part of the 21st century, rates have increased in the UK in recent years.

Homelessness is a complex phenomenon with infrastructural, economic and social causes and outcomes. Although many people's mental image of homelessness is the rough sleeper or the *Big Issue* seller (a magazine sold on the street by the homeless or others marginalised in some way), many people who are homeless live in temporary, unstable or unsuitable accommodation, and are less at the forefront of the minds of both policy makers and the public.

To ensure that our work is aligned with our mission, we work within the SHARE Framework that identifies five focus areas that offer the best chance of driving significant change in ending homelessness. This stands for:

Smart policy
Housing system

All in it together
Relational
Ecosystem of services

Each element of the framework has an important part to play in ending homelessness, and each needs its own evidence base. Naturally, some of these elements already have better evidence than others – for example housing system, for which we have identified 17 indicators – contrasting with smart policy with only two. Given this disparity, our role is to collate the evidence that is available, and to do all we can to generate new evidence in partnership with delivery organisations and evaluators.

For the remainder of this challenge, we will consider our journey as an organisation – what we have learned, where we have succeeded and where we are going. First, it is helpful to consider how CHI differs from many of our sister What Works Centres.

How is the Centre for Homelessness Impact different?

All What Works Centres are distinctive in their own ways – as the introductory chapter of this book suggests, the variety of shapes, sizes and behaviour of What Works Centres is so vast that it could be said that there is 'no such thing' as a What Works Centre.

Even with differences between all the centres, there are a few that stand out for us about our organisation and the way we respond to the world around us. The most obvious point of difference is in the origins of our centre. CHI emerged from the findings of a feasibility report conducted by Crisis and the GHN, which was published in 2017 (Teixeira, 2017). This report, which drew on expertise from across the housing and homelessness sector, as well as existing What Works Centres, drew some clear conclusions. First, that a new approach was needed, drawing more on the scientific method, if homelessness was to be ended. Second, that a What Works Centre for homelessness was needed to achieve this goal, and finally, that the new organisation should be 'sector led and owned'. This is a departure from the vast majority of other centres, which were created following a need identified either in government, or close to it.

The feasibility study also went further in prescribing what it should do compared many of our sister centres – with the initial size and makeup of the team specified, and Scotland being identified as an ideal place to start.

This decision reflects the reality that no nation is free from homelessness, and that even if there are substantial differences between the four nations, they each need and deserve high-quality evidence for tackling homelessness. As well as *making* this choice, we were, crucially, *able* to make the decision.

This is a result of our funding model, in which our core funding comes from philanthropic sources, rather than grants from government departments or research councils. For most centres, the funding is subject to the same conditions as those that apply to the government department sponsoring them. Education and children's social care are devolved in Scotland, Wales and Northern Ireland, and hence funding received by the relevant What Works Centres (What Works for Children's Social Care and the Education Endowment Foundation) from the England-based Whitehall Department for Education cannot be spent outside of England.

As well as allowing us to work with partners across the UK, the nature of our funding – which gives us long-term core funding, but not at the level of the endowed centres like Education Endowment Foundation, Youth Endowment Fund and Youth Futures Foundation – allows us to make long-term plans and invest in thinking about infrastructure and partnership building, in a way that is not possible for organisations with one to three years of funding (as experienced by the smaller centres). The difference this brings is clear from one of our current trials – on cash transfers. This project, which is funded by philanthropic donors and foundations, is a randomised controlled trial of giving substantial cash transfers to people at risk of homelessness in three cities: Glasgow, Manchester and Cardiff. Cash transfers have been shown to be effective, with much the same implementation, in Canada (Kerman, 2021). However, these kinds of transfers are controversial in some quarters, and there is certainly a lot that *could* go wrong when giving vulnerable people, who may not have a fixed abode, a substantial amount of money. Accordingly, it was important that we take the time to get the trial right – ensure that all ethical procedures had been complied with, that all participants were adequately safeguarded, and that processes were in place to identify any adverse events that occur and to respond accordingly. In all, the process of developing the trial took over a year – longer than the funding window of many centres.

More than just the duration of our funding, its nature is also important. One of the values of the What Works Network is independence[1] – something that all centres take seriously, but which is easy for sceptics to question in light of government funding. Our philanthropic funding base means that we can be truly independent, and we can make bolder moves – like funding a cash transfers trial – than we would be able to do if we received more government funding.

The final focus that we think sets us apart from other centres is that we have built in, from the very beginning, an approach that involves working closely with people working on homelessness. This has manifested in a few ways – from ensuring that all of our work observes best practice design principles from the off, to the importance of having staff with lived experience of homelessness, to our work and culture.

While we may be different from our sisters in some ways, we are similar in others, including our commitment to causal methodologies and many of the challenges that we face. It is to these that we turn now.

Challenges

Staffing

Being a small charity always brings with it some challenges – recruiting a team that is small enough to be nimble, but large enough to be effective is a powerful one. This is particularly acute in the What Works Network, where practitioners, who know about the situation on the ground, and feel real empathy for the people we are trying to help, but who may lack a background in rigorous research, meet academics or other researchers, who may lack experience in the substantive area but bring an absolutely essential sense of impact evaluations and statistical rigour. As with many other centres, perfect individuals – who stand astride both of these camps – do not exist, and searching for them is likely to be fruitless. Instead, we have built a team which values its diversity and the varying strengths of its team.

Funding

We are fortunate, as described, to have long-term funding from a philanthropic source. As well as allowing us the ability to make long-term decisions in a way not open to What Works Centres who work on the short budget cycles of research funders or central government (or, rarely in recent years, on the three-year cycle of spending reviews), an individual philanthropist can be more decisive than government. Instead of interacting with junior officials, who must convince senior officials of a course of action, and who in turn need to convince ministers, we have a direct route to a single individual with the will to make decisions – and whose incentives are closely aligned with our own.

However, this source of funding is smaller than other centres. Even non-endowed centres funded by central government receive income several times the size of ours.[2] That means that in order to fund trials – which we believe are urgently needed to understand how to reduce homelessness – we are constrained in what we can do – our core budget only allows us to fund two trials a year if we're funding the intervention as well as the evaluation. This has led us down a similar route that some other centres (including richer ones) are increasingly adopting: funding the evaluation only, and partnering with other funders or agencies themselves to fund the intervention.

This approach is cheaper, but it's also fraught with risk. People delivering interventions – whether in local government or the voluntary sector – often have concerns about the process of randomisation. As people who are passionate about their intervention, they might be reluctant to leave the decision as to who gets it to chance. In some cases, we'll be asking them to not work with the people they believe they can help the most, or even to work with fewer people than they plausibly could. Outcome measures that work for a trial – those that are easy to collect reliably for both treatment and control group – might be appealing to researchers, or even to national policy makers, but seem reductive to people working with the complexities and nuance of frontline practice. If a trial is funded by a What Works Centre, including both evaluation and intervention costs, the centre has quite a bit of power to set the terms. It can be a condition of a grant or contract that (only) a certain number of people need to be treated, and that they must be selected at random. Effectively, all delivery within the scope of the trial becomes a research project.

Lacking this power changes the dynamic between us as a centre, the evaluators and those being evaluated. It forces us to compromise more – not on the rigour of the test, but perhaps on some of the outcomes, on the timing of delivery, the way in which people assigned to the control group are treated, and very often on the questions asked by the qualitative component of the evaluation. This need to be flexible also has human consequences. The people we're working with become genuine partners, brought together by a common cause. Being more flexible means we have to listen more, and be more convincing when we're talking about the benefits of randomisation and rigour. We also need to prioritise working with evaluators who exhibit these same behaviours.

This in turn makes it more likely that our results will be acceptable and accepted by both the partners and the wider sector. When a trial concludes, sometimes inevitably, that an intervention is ineffective, prominent supporters of the intervention will sometimes disown the findings of the study and this can severely dampen the impact that the research has in practice. By building partnerships, rather than mere financial relationships, this is less likely to happen, and partners themselves can become credible and passionate advocates for the value of research evidence.

Data collection

Data collection is difficult in almost all research projects, and is the reason that many researchers and What Works Centres choose to work primarily with administrative data. Data collection is costly – sometimes requiring research assistants to travel to participants' locations and administer a test, which may itself cost money.[3] It is also risky – if a participant is not available when you go to do your data collection, you might spend more money trying to visit them again and again, only to never manage to get their outcome data. Participants may also not understand what they are being asked – especially if they are vulnerable, or have English as a second or additional language – meaning that even if the data are collected, they are of little value. In both of these cases, additional money is spent, and still participants either fall away or provide data which are little more than noise. If this happens, the research becomes less rigorous by virtue of a loss of statistical power. Perhaps more importantly, it may mean that our evidence doesn't speak to the outcomes of particularly vulnerable groups, and so we are failing those who most need the help of evidence-based policy and practice.

These problems are particularly acute in homelessness. Almost by definition, homeless people, and particularly those who are rough sleeping, do not have a fixed location at which they can be found to be counted. Sporadic attempts to move rough sleepers on, the provision of temporary accommodation, and periodically bad behaviour by local areas looking to move the homeless into a neighbouring jurisdiction further confound this challenge. The Combined Homelessness and Information Network[4] multi-agency database of rough sleepers and the wider street population in London is the only example of good quality administrative data in an urban centre in England. Scotland has higher quality data available than is generally possible in England, but across the UK as a whole, the homeless population is underserved by good quality data and, as Sanders and Reid (2019) argue, those who get counted get helped by new policies.

Attempting to improve the quality of data collection, and within this the infrastructure that supports data collection, is therefore a key part of our role as a What Works Centre – and it cannot be separated from the other aspects of our mission to build an evidence base. This data collection has a public good element to it, and we hope that our work in this area will not just improve and lower the cost of our research, but also that conducted by other researchers and agencies.

Ethics

The ethics of conducting randomised controlled trials on people experiencing homelessness also warrant a mention here. Randomisation – and the possibility of informed consent among a very vulnerable population who will often be recruited by comparatively powerful gatekeepers – is difficult to ensure, as is verifying that participants at follow-up have consented in the past.

For people sleeping rough, who may be at their lowest ebb, the assumption of ethical equipoise (a state of genuine uncertainty between different options by the evaluator) might be difficult to justify, as many interventions that simply provide food, shelter or resources may be effective at improving their living conditions, reducing the strength of the argument for testing.

While this issue of ethical equipoise is real and must be considered, the ethics of randomised controlled trials in this area can be flipped on their head. Though we might argue that any help is likely to be beneficial, the reality is that funding for interventions to prevent or reduce homelessness is limited, and prone to squeezes during straitened fiscal times. Living in that reality, it is essential that every pound is spent not just on things that are effective, but on things that are the *most* effective – necessitating an understanding not just of whether an intervention is better than nothing, but also whether it is better and cheaper than the alternatives.

Stronger together

The What Works movement is strongest when it is more than a loose collection of individual centres, and instead works as a network. Although the network to a certain extent replicates the structure of the government departments that fund them, the lives of the people that the network aims to help do not. Nowhere is this clearer than in homelessness. Disadvantage and discrimination in other domains make homelessness more likely – care leavers (Sanders et al, 2022), lesbian, gay, bisexual, transgender, queer and other people (Sanders et al, 2022), and members of ethnic minorities are more likely to become homeless (Heaslip et al, 2022). Poor grades, involvement in criminal activity (and particularly illicit substance use) and unemployment make homelessness more likely, and, in turn, homelessness makes it more difficult to study, find work, and live a healthy and prosperous life. This vicious circle cannot be broken simply by looking at one part of it. This is why we at CHI are among the strongest advocates not just for what works methodologies, but for the What Works Network, and for collaborating with other centres.

Conclusion

CHI is one of the smaller and younger What Works Centres, but we hope that we punch above our weight, and are wise beyond our years. Having spent most of my adult life working on this issue, I know that the causes of homelessness are multifarious and difficult to fight. I also know that producing the evidence we need to win that fight will be hard, and require time, commitment and intellect to be thrown at it in vast quantities.

Nonetheless, I think it is both useful and important to be optimistic. The reason our campaign is called 'end it with evidence' is to be clear and positive about what our objective is. Evidence may lead to incremental change, but in the end, we should hope that evidence can do for homelessness what it did for polio, smallpox and malaria – either eradicate it, or dramatically reduce its toll on human life.

Notes

[1]   www.gov.uk/government/publications/what-works-network-membership-requirements/what-works-network
[2]   The Early Intervention Foundation receives approximately four times our funding per year, while What Works for Children's Social Care receives closer to 30 times our funding. What Works Wellbeing, which is funded by a mixture of funders, is the exception to this rule.
[3]   Many standardised metrics, as well as education and other outcomes, attract a fee *per respondent* from the developer of these tests.
[4]   https://data.london.gov.uk/dataset/chain-reports

References

Heaslip, V., Thompson, R., Tauringana, M., Holland, S. and Glendening, N. (2022) Addressing health inequity in the UK: People who are homeless, from ethnic minority groups or LGBTQ+ communities. *Practice Nursing*, 33(3): 112–116.

Kerman, N. (2021) The role of universal basic income in preventing and ending homelessness. *International Journal on Homelessness*, 1(1): 3–13.

Sanders, M. and Reid, L. (2019) *How data and machine learning can help strengthen communities*. King's Policy Review.

Sanders, M., Whelan, E., and Jones, L. (2022) *Sexuality, gender identity, and homelessness*. Centre for Homelessness Impact. https://uploads-ssl.webflow.com/59f07e67422cdf0001904c14/63317fdfd1d200585b60b1a3_CHI.Sexuality-gender%20ident ity%20and%20homelessness%20policy%20paper.pdf

Teixeira, L. (2017) *Ending homelessness faster by focusing on 'what works': Towards a world-leading centre for homelessness impact.* Crisis.

13

Scaling up: taking 'what works' to the next level

Jane Lewis, Eleanor Ott and Robyn Mildon

Introduction

This chapter sets out a call for What Works Centres to devote more attention and resources to supporting the scaling up of effective approaches – policies, services, practices, programmes and so on – to extend their reach and impact. We pick up the story of interventions at the point where an approach has been shown to have enough evidence behind it to justify its wider use – it has been shown to be effective, usable and implementable. Scaling up is then about expanding the reach and impact of an innovation to foster the greatest possible positive change for diverse groups, including the most marginalised and those with the greatest support needs. (We use the term 'innovation' throughout this chapter, recognising that what is being scaled up might be a policy, programme, service or practice but that it is by definition new to the scale-up setting.)

Of course, not everything *should* be scaled, even if it has been shown to be effective. McLean and Gargani introduce the concept of 'judicious scaling' and make the point that 'scaling is a choice that must be justified' (2019, p 34) and that involves trade-offs. Scaling up an innovation involves opportunity costs and compromises (List, 2022), for example between overall reach, focus on more marginalised groups, quality and cost. It would be very ambitious to scale up very widely, without losing touch with the needs of more marginalised groups, *and* to sustain quality of delivery, *and* to keep costs sufficiently low that demand is not reduced – and in practice choices and compromise are needed. But scaling up is clearly central to the ambitions of What Works Centres: there seems little point in identifying 'what works' without paying at least as much attention to how to achieve levels of reach and impact that are socially significant.

It is, however, a particularly challenging area of work, and in practice few effective innovations reach populations at scale (Fagan et al, 2019; Milat et al, 2020). It is easy to assume that a programme proven to be effective will be taken up by organisations and embraced by the wider system. But this very rarely happens spontaneously, and it cannot be achieved by 'push' alone – disseminating information, resources, making the case for take-up (Proctor et al, 2021). It is simply not the case that 'if we build it, they will come'.

The evidence surrounding scale-up is evolving, and the study of scale-up is approached from varied theoretical perspectives (Green et al, 2009). Greenhalgh and Papoutsi (2019) contrast how scale-up is conceived in different fields. Implementation science (the field of science concerned with how to get effective approaches systematically taken up into routine practice; Eccles and Mittman, 2006) views scale-up as a structured and phased approach based on replicating an innovation in multiple sites. Complexity science views scale-up as an adaptive process of change, requiring attention to the ecology of dynamic systems. Social science views scale-up through the lens of organisational and individual change, attending to the wider forces that shape and constrain it.

The terminology used is also varied. Scale-up has been defined as 'deliberate efforts to increase the impact of successfully tested [health] innovations so as to benefit more people and to foster policy and programme development on a lasting basis' (ExpandNet/World Health Organization, 2010: 2) and as 'efforts to provide access to high-quality, sustained delivery of EBIs [evidence-based interventions] *at the level necessary to produce population-wide improvements in public health and wellbeing*' (Fagan et al, 2019: 1149, emphasis in original). Other terms used include 'diffusion', 'translation', 'transfer', 'spread' and 'replication'.

A distinction is drawn between 'horizontal scaling', meaning replication of a programme in multiple sites, and 'vertical scaling' or 'institutionalisation', meaning integration into the wider policy, legal, regulatory and financial system (ExpandNet/World Health Organization, 2010; Nores and Fernandez, 2018). The replication of the Incredible Years parenting programme is an example of horizontal scaling, and the way in which phonics has been embedded in teaching in the UK is an example of institutionalisation. A rather different distinction is made in terminology between 'spread', which is defined as replication (for example, Incredible Years) and 'scale-up' as building the infrastructure needed to support full-scale implementation (Greenhalgh and Papoutsi, 2019). As we set out in this chapter, in practice attention is needed to all these dimensions: it is very difficult to replicate a programme without also addressing its fit within the wider policy and regulatory system.

In this chapter we use 'scale-up' as an umbrella term for increasing reach and impact, recognising that this might be achieved through replication or institutionalisation, and requires attention to the whole system. We also use the terms 'developer' and 'originating organisation' to refer to those (an individual, team, organisation or partnership) that develop the innovation.

Scaling up requires a whole system approach

In practice, supporting scale-up involves a further set of challenges, and requires different work and skills from what is involved in supporting implementation even for large real-world trials. One of the key challenges is that scaling up requires a whole system approach. Understanding how an intervention fits within the wider system or systems, how these are aligned with and support or inhibit its use, *should* be attended to from the earliest design, development and testing of innovations. But when it comes to scale-up, they must be centre stage.

This is very helpfully conceptualised in the Interactive Systems Framework for Dissemination and Implementation (the ISF; Wandersman et al, 2008), which highlights the need for engagement of and interaction between different systems. The ISF was developed with a focus on prevention approaches but is highly applicable to wider fields, and although it focuses on implementation we use it here to highlight the systems involved in scaling up.

The ISF describes three areas of activity, each primarily the work of a different system:

1. *Distilling evidence about effective practices – the Synthesis and Translation System*: This is the evidence synthesis, programme development, evaluation and programme refinement work that, alongside primary research, is the core business of What Works Centres.

2. *Implementing interventions – the Delivery System*: This is the work of identifying priority needs, reviewing options, selecting, implementing and sustaining them, undertaken by frontline agencies (schools, youth agencies, police forces, health services, social workers, and so on). Effective implementation relies on their general capacity (how well they function as teams and organisations) as well as their innovation-specific capacity (training, skills, resources, operating processes that support implementation of the innovation).

3. *Supporting the work – the Support System*: The Support System needs to provide both innovation specific capacity-building support (training, coaching, technical assistance, and so on) and general capacity-building to develop the infrastructure, leadership, culture and skills of the Delivery System. The agencies and organisations involved vary between sectors and include government and non-governmental agencies such as sector improvement, inspection and regulatory bodies, as well as purveyors' organisations which represent and support a specific programme and intermediary organisations supporting multiple programmes (Franks and Bory, 2015; Proctor et al, 2019).

The ISF also highlights the need for alignment, communication and collaboration between these three systems as early as possible: involving practitioners from the delivery system and support agencies in developing interventions and refining them for scale-up is important. The ISF also describes the wider context of policy, funding and climate (for example, expectations and norms) within which this work takes place, and which constrains or expands the scope for implementation at scale. None of these are static, and scaling up involves a constant dance of mutual adaptation and re-alignment between innovation, service system and wider system (Chambers et al, 2013).

In practice, the infrastructure to support scale-up is weak in many areas, reflecting the fact that the focus of investment has been on evidence generation, and not on the marketing, distribution and support systems needed to take evidence into practice at scale: 'We have produced effective products through research, but we have not invested in customer-centred marketing and distribution systems to bring these products to public health organisations when, where, and how they are needed' (Kreuter and Bernhardt, 2008, p 2123).

Kreuter and Bernhardt draw a compelling comparison between the car industry and the public health system, which applies just as well to any other human service system. In the car industry there is an expectation that new (more efficient, faster, more aesthetically appealing) models will be developed every year, and consumer demand is stimulated by mainstream and specialist media. A marketing and distribution system gets cars into showrooms, with sales agents knowledgeable about them, able to point out their key features and to help customers choose what is right for them. Key features of the car – engine size, number of doors, colour, convertible or not – are tailored to the customer. Financing is available through loan and lease arrangements. Customers drive away with a manual, online information and knowing where to get follow-up support. Service stations and garages have spare parts and specialist knowledge for repair and maintenance. MOT testing is adapted to include new functionality, such as hybrid and electric.

The parallel infrastructure in the human service system is fragile and patchy. There is a growing number of inventories or databases of effective programmes, but achieving a parallel with the car industry would mean a sustained intention among organisational leaders and practitioners to keep renewing their services to implement 'what works'. It would mean intermediary organisations working directly with services to help them to choose and adopt the right effective practices for them and their service users, and programmes that come with options and support for adaptation. It would mean access to ongoing support for implementation and sustainment, and access to funding for regular and sustained improvement. Elements of each of these exist but there are gaps, and they need to be developed, aligned and purposefully engaged in support of scale-up. This goes far beyond producing inventories of effective programmes, and means building demand for better programmes and services, investing in and working with the delivery and support systems, and mobilising systems and resources actively in support of scale-up. The case we make in this chapter is that this needs to be a part of the work of What Works Centres, and the chapter sets out what this involves.

Begin by defining the end vision

Supporting scale-up needs to begin by clarifying the end vision – what scale-up will actually look like. What level of scale is the ambition, in terms of geographic area and population reach? What will this look like in practice? Developing the programme to be ready for this end vision is part of the work involved, and the part that tends to receive most attention from What Works Centres, programme developers and researchers. But it is arguably the least difficult part of the work required.

In practice, few developers or originator organisations are in a position to deliver at scale. Delivery at scale is often not well aligned with organisational and incentive structures for originators. Academia rewards academic research rather than working with organisations and systems on the ground; a health trust's ambitions for a new mental health service will likely have geographical boundaries; a not-for-profit may find it difficult to accommodate disproportionate growth in one aspect of its offer when it also provides other programmes and services. Although structures and incentives can be changed (for example, the growing focus on impact and industry collaboration in academia), they often act as barriers to scale-up, and in practice few developers or originator organisations have the capacity to deliver at population-level scale. This means that scaling up will generally involve 'hitching a ride' on the public service system and the infrastructure of policy, regulation, funding, improvement, workforce development, and so on that supports it (Bradach and Grindle, 2014). As Patrick

T. McCarthy, then president of the Annie E. Casey Foundation in the US has said: 'The road to scale runs through public systems' (McCarthy, 2014).

An early consideration is therefore which of a range of end visions and overall delivery models is appropriate for any individual intervention. Gugelev and Stern (2015) describe this as the 'endgame', which they define as the specific role the programme developer intends to play in the scale-up vision. Drawing on their work and other framings (for example, Cooley et al, 2016), we categorise six 'endgame' options, set out in Figure 13.1, ranging from the developer or originator organisation delivering directly at scale, to handing the innovation over to a third party, to the innovation being available as an open source, with the amount of control retained dwindling across this spectrum.

Which of these is the optimal strategy for an innovation will turn on a number of considerations, and may change over time as the wider system evolves:

- The form and characteristics of the innovation itself: More complex and not easily standardised innovations will generally require an endgame where the originator organisation retains more control.
- How familiar the approach is and how consistent it is with norms, cultures and expectations: a more unfamiliar innovation or one that requires reshaping cultures and norms is also likely to need more originator control.
- The capacity of the originating organisation: its ability to provide intensive support at scale, and the degree to which this is already part of its core activities. If this capacity is lacking and can't be built, direct delivery or centrally managed replication will be challenging.
- The existence of potential partners and intermediary or support agencies able to support implementation at scale, and alignment with their work and interests: if these do not exist, direct delivery and centrally managed replication may be necessary.
- How universal the needs addressed by the innovation are: government adoption is more feasible if an innovation is of wide relevance and less likely for niche concerns.

Figure 13.1: Options for the endgame

Direct delivery	The developer delivers at scale, for example providing a service or distributing equipment or technology. This might require organisational expansion, restructuring, or spinning the delivery team out as an affiliated or autonomous organisation.	More control
Partnerships and collaborations	Delivery by a (usually small) group of organisations, operating as a formal partnership or an informal network, with distributed responsibilities for different aspects of the innovation and its delivery.	
Centrally managed replication	The originator organisation equips other organisations to deliver the innovation, for example training a network of trainers, certifying or licensing providers, or operating a social franchise model. They provide centralised services such as programme materials and resources, training, quality assurance and monitoring, and may also promote the programme and coordinate learning networks.	
Commercial or other third-party adoption	The innovation is taken on by a commercial organisation (or not-for-profit), which acquires the legal right to intellectual property and takes over responsibility for its maintenance and distribution.	
Government adoption	The innovation is adopted by government and integrated through policy, funding, regulation, professional support etc.	
Open source	The innovation is simply made available for anyone to take up as a methodology, approach or set of practices. The originating organisation may provide resources or guidance, promote and advocate for it, share learning etc, but places no constraints around its use.	Less control

Source: Drawing on Gugelev and Stern (2015) and Cooley et al (2016)

- The costs and potential sources of funding, whether directly from intended users or from other sources, and the financial and market viability of the innovation: these will particularly affect the scope for commercial or other third-party adoption.

Developers and originator organisations often progress for several years without a clear endgame in mind. What Works Centres should stimulate assessment of options, and start engaging right from the start with the organisations or stakeholders who will be essential to the targeted endgames to mobilise them in support.

Strategies and activities involved in scaling up

Although scaling up is sometimes described as a series of sequences or phases, in practice the work involved, and the learning and insights, develop organically. There is a growing body of evidence about what is required for effective implementation (see, for example, Damschroder et al, 2009; Powell et al, 2015), but much less empirical evidence on which strategies are effective for scaling up (Charif et al, 2017; Milat et al, 2020), and the specifics and intensity of work needed. We also know little about whether strength in one area can compensate for gaps or weaknesses in others. Overall, the available theory as well as synthesis of early scaling evidence point to the following areas as being important:

- *The 'what' of scale-up, or the innovation itself:* Implementation science points to the need for an innovation that has high usability (Lyon et al, 2021), credibility, relative advantage, low complexity, is adaptable and well designed (Damschroder et al, 2009), and is acceptable to practitioners and service users, appropriate, feasible and can be implemented as intended (Proctor et al, 2011). Key component parts need to be present, including clear target population and intended outcomes, theory of change, specific practices, core and adaptable elements or required elements and permitted adaptations, and infrastructure for quality assurance, monitoring and ongoing support.
- *Evidence to justify and support scale-up:* including evidence about need; effectiveness; operational, implementation and

infrastructure requirements; barriers and facilitators and the implementation strategies to address them; costs and cost-effectiveness. Evidence about effectiveness needs to reflect real-world conditions. It is common to see a 'voltage drop' or fall-off in effectiveness when optimal test conditions are replaced by real-world realities, so testing in the conditions that will pertain at scale is important (List, 2022).

- *Assessment of scalability*: aspects of the programme and evidence are generally actively (if not comprehensively) developed in the period leading up to scale-up, but an element usually missing is a scalability assessment. More work is needed to develop and test frameworks for assessing scalability but important early work (for example, Milat, 2020; Proctor et al, 2021) suggests the following need to be included:
  - level of demand for the innovation among service-users;
  - who will adopt or 'do' at scale, their locations and number;
  - what influences adoption choices;
  - any adaptations needed to the innovation to make it scalable: innovations often have to be simplified to be scalable as the direct control of the developer diminishes;
  - the size of the potential market, competitors and scale of demand;
  - who is the funder or payer at scale, what funding sources and resources are available, and influences on funding decisions: one of the challenges in scaling up in human service systems is that the 'do-er' and the 'payer' at scale are often not the same (Gugelev and Stern, 2015);
  - the capacity and readiness of the individuals and organisations involved to take on the implementation, and the resources required to support this;
  - how the innovation will be marketed and distributed to funders and end-users and the costs involved;
  - the alignment of the innovation with the wider system (policy, regulation, legislation, other service systems);
  - key stakeholders, influencers, opinion leaders and potential partners and how they can be engaged and mobilised.
- *Fostering organisational readiness*: strategies are likely to be needed to develop the capacity and readiness of intended adopter organisations, both innovation-specific and general

(Wandersman et al, 2008). Organisational readiness for change is a complex and contested concept (Weiner et al, 2020a) but is likely to involve attending to issues such as (Damschroder et al, 2009; Chambers et al, 2013; Weiner et al, 2020b):

- staffing, structure and business models;
- information systems;
- organisational culture and climate;
- training and supervisions systems;
- the readiness of practitioners and managers for change and leadership engagement;
- available resources (such as time, space and training);
- access to knowledge and information about the innovation and how it works.
- *Fostering a supportive wider system and securing commitments*: strategies will be needed to align with and mobilise potential facilitators within the wider system, and to either adapt the innovation or influence wider systems characteristics such as policy, regulations, systems architecture, alignment between systems, policy and funding (Chambers et al, 2013).

Reviewing efforts to scale up evidence-based interventions (EBIs) in five US public service systems, Fagan et al (2019) conclude that, across systems, the degree to which public policies required, recommended or provided funding for EBIs was key, and that attention needed to be paid to six key factors: developer and funder capacity for scale; public awareness of and support for EBIs; community engagement and capacity; public system leadership and support for EBIs; a skilled EBI workforce; and EBI data monitoring and evaluation capacity (see Figure 13.2).

Even in this summarised form, this may seem an overwhelming volume of work to undertake. There is no ducking the fact that scaling up is a huge task – evidenced by the fact that most EBIs do not scale. Scaling up also involves an element of opportunism and is not a linear and predictable process: only around half of scaled-up public health interventions examined in a recent review passed through both efficacy and real-world trials (Indig et al, 2018; Koorts et al, 2021). The positive message here is that scaling up does not require every factor to be addressed and every resource to be in place. However, it does call for approaches that are highly

Figure 13.2: Ecological model identifying the factors that affect evidence-based interventions scale-up in five public systems

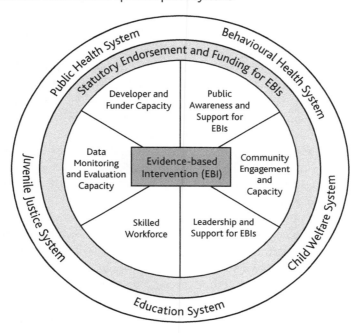

Source: Fagan et al (2019)

adaptive and agile, and that are cognisant of the personal and organisational attitudes, worldviews, agendas and goals of wider system stakeholders. And it definitely calls for more investment and more attention from What Works Centres.

What does this mean for the work of What Works Centres?

Not all of this work, of course, can or should be the direct responsibility of What Works Centres. We see the core roles of What Works Centres in scale-up as being to help build the evidence needed to justify scale-up; to support the development of programmes with the necessary features and components; to stimulate, undertake or commission scalability assessments;

and to catalyse and support decisions about the endgame and pathways to scale. From there, What Works Centres need to identify, convene and orchestrate – but not provide all of – the resources and activity needed to build organisational and systems readiness, and ensure that the engagement and commitment of the wide range of partners and stakeholders central to scale are secured, responsibilities assigned, shared plans made and progress monitored. Scaling up requires different skills to the evidence synthesis and evaluation activity that is the primary work of most What Works Centres, and it requires funding and infrastructure that What Works Centres do not have and will not be able to develop fully themselves. What Works Centres need to develop new capacity for supporting scale-up, but part of that capacity is mobilising others.

Our conversations and work with colleagues from the What Works Centres highlighted activity to support scale-up, including building implementation evaluations into trials; working directly with the delivery system to support the take-up of individual programmes; commissioning specialist support for implementation and scale-up; and mobilising existing implementation support capacity within the delivery or support systems. In addition they are working to build demand for and autonomous use of evidence to stimulate take-up at scale, and they advocate for change within the support system.

How this work is organised varies, and the strategies used by What Works Centres reflect their mission and scope as well as their scale and resources. For example, What Works for Children Social Care's Practice Team works with social work teams to support their adoption of programmes. The Education Endowment Foundation's Research Schools Network supports innovation, adoption and autonomous evidence cultures (Gu et al, 2020, 2021). The Youth Endowment Fund's mission implies scaling across a much wider range of practice settings (youth agencies, police, youth offending services, social work, health services, schools, and so on), and since it is unfeasible to reach them comprehensively, policy and other systems-wide levers are targeted to support scale-up. The College of Policing uses the operational guidance and standards part of its remit to embed proven approaches in mainstream policing practice.

Whatever the precise mechanisms, supporting scale-up to reach socially significant levels of change will require more resources and capacity within and outside What Works Centres. Each will need to assess the right balance between building their own capacity, commissioning additional specialist support, mobilising and strengthening the existing support system and building new scale-up infrastructure. The focus of work will therefore vary, but it is likely to call on an expanded set of skills within What Works Centres. Metz et al (2021) call out the following as core values and competencies for supporting implementation, which are likely to be relevant to supporting implementation at scale:

- Core principles and values: empathy, curiosity, commitment, working methodically, transdisciplinarity.
- Co-creation competencies: co-learning, brokering, addressing power differentials, co-design, tailoring support.
- Ongoing improvement competencies: assessing need and context, applying and integrating implementation science approaches, conducting improvement cycles.
- Sustaining change competencies: growing and sustaining relationships, building capacity, cultivating leadership, facilitation.

Competencies for working in complex adaptive systems will also be highly relevant, including applying systems analysis and theory, modelling, recognising self-organisation, planning for unpredictability, encouraging sense-making and using data for adaptive learning, developing adaptive capabilities, and harnessing conflict productively (Paina and Peters, 2012; Greenhalgh and Papoutsi, 2019). Entrepreneurship and market and investment dynamics are also highly relevant to scale-up, and as this expertise is not generally located in research communities this calls for new collaborations (Proctor et al, 2021).

Conclusion

Scaling up has thus far been an under-resourced and under-attended to area of work for What Works Centres, which have focused thus far on evidence synthesis and evaluation to build evidence. Scale-up needs to be given much more focus over the next ten years and onward. 'Hope is not a strategy for reaching scale' (Cooley et al, 2016: 3). It requires researchers to move beyond traditional, and perhaps comfortable, areas of focus and to tussle with challenging realities. Engaging in this work is essential for What Works Centres to fulfil their promise. All the work of What Works Centres involves tensions between the requirements of rigorous evidence and real-world priorities. When it comes to scaling up, the real world has to win!

References

Bradach, J. and Grindle, A. (2014) Emerging pathways to transformative scale. *Stanford Social Innovation Review*, Spring 2014: 7–11.

Chambers, D., Glasgow, R. and Stange, K. (2013) The dynamic sustainability framework: Addressing the paradox of sustainment and ongoing change. *Implementation Science*, 8(1): 1–11.

Charif, A.B, Zomahoun, H.T.V., LeBlanc, A., Langlois, L., Wolfenden, L., Lin Yoong, S., Williams, C.M. et al (2017) Effective strategies for scaling up evidence-based practices in primary care: A systematic review. *Implementation Science*, 12(1): 1–13.

Cooley, L., Kohl, R. and Ved, R. (2016) *Scaling up: From vision to large-scale change. A management framework for practitioners*, third edition. Management Systems International.

Damschroder, L.J., Aron, D.C., Keith, R.E., Kirsh, S.R., Alexander, J.A. and Lowery J.C. (2009) Fostering implementation of health services research findings into practice: A consolidated framework for advancing implementation science. *Implementation Science*, 4(1): 1–15.

Eccles, M.P. and Mittman, B.S. (2006) Welcome to implementation science. *Implementation Science*, 1(1).

ExpandNet/World Health Organization (2010) *Nine steps for developing a scaling-up strategy*. World Health Organization.

Fagan, A., Bumbarger, B.K., Barth, R.P., Bradshaw, C.P., Rhoades Cooper, B. Supplee, L.H. and Klein Walker, D. (2019) Scaling up evidence-based interventions in US public systems to prevent behavioral health problems: Challenges and opportunities. *Prevention Science*, 20: 1147–1168.

Franks, R. and Bory, C. (2015) Who supports the successful implementation and sustainability of evidence-based practices? Defining and understanding the roles of intermediary and purveyor organizations. *New Directions for Child and Adolescent Development*, 149: 41–56.

Green, L.W., Ottoson, J.M., García, C. and Hiatt, R.A. (2009) Diffusion theory and knowledge dissemination, utilization, and integration in public health. *Annual Review of Public Health*, 30: 151–174.

Greenhalgh, T. and Papoutsi, C. (2019) Spreading and scaling up innovation and improvement. *BMJ*, 365: I2068.

Gu, Q., Rea, S., Seymour, K., Smethem, L., Bryant, B., Armstrong, P., Ahn, M. et al (2020) *The research schools network: Supporting schools to develop evidence-informed practice*. Education Endowment Foundation.

Gu, Q., Seymour, K., Rea, S., Knight, R., Ahn, M., Sammons, P., Kamershwara, K.K. and Hodgen, J. (2021) *The research schools programme in opportunity areas: Investigating the impact of research schools in promoting better outcomes in schools*. Education Endowment Foundation.

Gugelev, A. and Stern, A. (2015) What's your endgame? *Stanford Social Innovation Review*, Winter: 41–47.

Indig, D., Lee, K., Grunseit, A., Milat, A. and Bauman, A. (2018) Pathways for scaling up public health interventions. *BMC Public Health*, 18(1): 1–11.

Koorts, H., Cassar, C., Salmon, J., Lawrence, M., Salmon, P. and Dorling, H. (2021) Mechanisms of scaling up: Combining a realist perspective and systems analysis to understand successfully scaled intervention. *International Journal of Behavioral Nutrition and Physical Activity*, 18(1): 1–16.

Kreuter, M.W. and Bernhardt, J.M. (2008) Reframing the dissemination challenge: A marketing and distribution perspective. *American Journal of Public Health*, 99(12): 2123–2137.

List, J.A. (2022) *The voltage effect*. Penguin Random House.

Lyon, A.R., Pullman, M.D., Jacobson, J., Osterhage, K., Al Achkar, M., Renn, B.N. Munson, S.A. and Areán, P.A. (2021) Assessing the usability of complex psychosocial interventions: The Intervention Usability Scale. *Implementation Research & Practice*, 2: 1–9.

McCarthy, P.T. (2014) The road to scale runs through public systems. *Stanford Social Innovation Review*, Spring: 12–13.

McLean, R. and Gargani, J. (2019) *Scaling impact: Innovation for the public good*. Routledge.

Metz, A., Albers, B., Burke, K., Bartley, L., Louison, L., Ward, C. and Farley, A. (2021) Implementation practice in human service systems: Understanding the principles and competencies of professionals who support implementation. *Human Service Organizations: Management, Leadership & Governance*, 45(3): 238–259.

Milat, A., Lee, K., Conte, K., Grunseit, A., Wolfenden, L., van Nassau, F., Orr, N., Sreeram, P. and Bauman, A. (2020) Intervention scalability assessment tool: A decision support tool for health policy makers and implementers. *Health Research Policy and Systems*, 18: 1.

Nores, M. and Fernandez, C. (2018) Building capacity in health and education systems to delivery interventions that strengthen early child development. *Annals of the New York Academy of Science*, 1419: 57–73.

Paina, L. and Peters, D.H. (2012) Understanding pathways for scaling up health services through the lens of complex adaptive systems. *Health Policy and Planning*, 27: 365–373.

Powell, B.J., Waltz, T.J., Chinman, M.J., Damschroder, L.J., Smith, J.L., Matthieu, M.M., Proctor, E.K. and Kirchner, J.E. (2015) A refined compilation of implementation strategies: Results from the Expert Recommendations for Implementing Change (ERIC) project. *Implementation Science*, 10(1): 1–14.

Proctor, E.K., Silmere, H., Raghavan, R., Hovmand, P., Aarons, G.A., Bunger, A.C. et al (2011) Outcomes for implementation research: Conceptual distinctions, measurement challenges, and research agenda. *Administration and Policy in Mental Health and Mental Health Services Research*, 38(2): 65–76.

Proctor, E., Hooley, C., Morse, A., McCrary, S., Kim, H. and Kohl, P.L. (2019) Intermediary/purveyor organizations for evidence-based interventions in the US child mental health: Characteristics and implementation strategies. *Implementation Science*, 14: article 3.

Proctor, E.K., Toker, E., Tabak, R., McKay, V.R., Hooley, C. and Evanoff, B. (2021) Market viability: A neglected concept in implementation science. *Implementation Science*, 16: article 98.

Wandersman, A., Duffy, J., Flaspohler, P., Noonan, R., Lubell, K., Stillman, L., Blachman, M. et al (2008) Bridging the gap between prevention research and practice: The interactive systems framework for dissemination and implementation. *American Journal of Community Psychology*, 41: 171–181.

Weiner, B.J., Clary, A.S., Klaman, S.L., Turner, K. and Alishahi-Tabriz, A. (2020a) Organizational readiness for change: What we know, what we think we know, and what we need to know. In B. Albers, A. Shlonsky and R. Mildon (eds) *Implementation science 3.0*. Springer.

Weiner, B.J., Mettert, K.D., Dorsey, C.N., Nolen, E.A., Stanick, C., Powell, B.J.H. and Lewis, C.C. (2020b) Measuring readiness for implementation: A systematic review of measures' psychometric and pragmatic properties. *Implementation Research & Practice*, 1: 1–29.

14

Measuring what matters

Nancy Hey

Introduction

The What Works Centres as a whole make use of a wide variety of data to understand the world and the impact that policy or other interventions can have on it. However, in the majority of cases, this leaves 'what works' research, evaluations and synthesis focused on things that are easy to measure, or indeed, which are already measured through administrative datasets. For example, grades achieved, days spent in care, number of crimes in a particular area. This approach is rational and sensible, especially given constrained resources. Primary data collection – measuring something that is not already captured in administrative datasets – can double the cost of an evaluation.[1]

This creates a trade-off for centres: do they measure what's easy, and miss out on the nuances of participant experiences, or do they measure what really matters, but find themselves able to run fewer studies overall? Most centres choose the former, and it is easy to see why. However, this runs the risk of missing out on important factors. If an intervention in education improves grades in maths through hot-housing (an intensive learning episode), but leaves students with low morale and wellbeing, it could damage their relationship with learning for the rest of their life. Is this intervention really a success? Successive governments have made a priority of adult learning, reflecting in part the failure of the mainstream education system. This work is made harder by the disaffection with learning felt by many adults – suggesting that a short-term boost to grades for some may have a longer, and more negative, impact for others (Hume et al, 2018). It is incumbent on the What Works Network to try and measure these longer-term, and more nuanced, outcomes.

Although the British government took steps to measure wellbeing as a national statistic, its lack of administrative records on the same means that wellbeing is too often a 'soft' or qualitative measure collected as an afterthought in what works type research. In this chapter we argue for a more holistic approach to administrative data collection, and for the What Works Network to be more ambitious in its data collection in the future.

Measuring what matters

The aim of government and of civil society is to improve the wellbeing of the whole population. Are they making the difference they hope? How do we know? If we have learned anything from other fields, it is that unless we rigorously measure outcomes, and robustly ascertain the causal impact of our policies, many – perhaps even most – efforts will fall short.

In 2011 the UK became the first nation to measure subjective wellbeing as part of its national statistics. A large-scale consultation of 60,000 people led to the creation of a series of wellbeing metrics encompassing different aspects of people's lived experience, and most prominently, the four 'wellbeing questions' (see Table 14.1) that are routinely collected at large scale.

The aim of these metrics, and the dashboards they feed into, is to move us closer to 'full' national accounts that account for the economic, social and environmental welfare of nations. The creators of national accounts and measures of gross domestic product did not intend that their metrics be the only measure of success. Gross domestic product, like life expectancy, has been a hugely successful proxy, and helpful in efforts that have seen massively improving lives of most citizens in the developed world in the 20th century. However there are established challenges to the metric that, while useful, is silent on the quality and purpose of that growth, at macro level on risk and environmental sustainability, and at an individual level, on our human relationships and sense of purpose and value in life (Stiglitz, 2009). Improving national accounts to take account of these other important factors is one step in the right direction, but so too must be creating and standardising measures of wellbeing, and making them available and useful at a local level. At present, a local government knows much more about people's satisfaction with their bin collections, than they do about their satisfaction with their lives. This 'hidden' wealth is often what makes life worth living, and so we ignore it at our peril (Halpern, 2010).

What is success and how do we know

The frameworks developed by government and researchers aim to provide a straightforward and clear structure for the understanding of subjective wellbeing. Unlike grades, or even motivation, there is not a revealed behavioural measure that can be used to assess wellbeing, and so the goal was to develop a short survey in which people could report their own wellbeing.

The UK's most commonly used survey contains four questions, each attempting to measure a different element of people's *subjective* wellbeing (that is, their impression of their own happiness or wellbeing, rather than a proxy like income, or some external sense of how 'happy' they ought to be) – as is shown in Table 14.1. As well as being brief, this framework aimed for the first time to harmonise measures of wellbeing across a wide

Table 14.1: Four-item wellbeing survey

Concept	Measure	Question
		On a scale of 0 to 10, where 0 is 'not at all' and 10 is 'completely'
Evaluative or cognitive	Life satisfaction	Overall, how satisfied are you with your life nowadays?
Eudaimonia	Purpose	Overall, to what extent do you feel that the things that you do in your life are worthwhile?
Positive affect	Happiness	Overall, how happy did you feel yesterday?
Negative affect	Anxiety	Overall, how anxious did you feel yesterday?

variety of contexts – making it possible to make apples-to-apples comparisons across different groups, settings and periods of time.

These measures, while not covering all aspects of our psychological wellbeing, are short enough to be used almost everywhere. Longer measures of mental wellbeing – the short Warwick Edinburgh Mental Wellbeing Scale (Stewart-Brown and Janmohamed, 2008) – are used in the wellbeing frameworks in Wales and Scotland and across the health and civil society sectors. Statisticians recommend using the four personal subjective wellbeing measures where space is limited. If even four questions are too many (for example, when a large number of metrics are being collected from a sample group), the single life satisfaction question ('Overall, how satisfied are you with your life nowadays?') can be used as a common currency. This latter is used as the basis for the use of wellbeing measures in HM Treasury appraisal methodology and is used as an economic indicator for example in the 2021 Budget presented to parliament by the Chancellor of the Exchequer (the UK government's chief financial minister).

These four questions are in the main Annual Population Survey – the largest household survey in the UK run by the Office for National Statistics, a wide range of other surveys from food to crime to community and sport, and in the many longitudinal and cohort studies, such as the millennium cohort study, children of the 1990s (also known as the Avon Longitudinal Study of Parents and Children) and the COVID Social Mobility and Opportunities study. This breadth is useful as well as impressive, but, due to its focus on household data, tends to undercount students, people living in residential care settings (either as adults or children), and, of course, the homeless.

Some have also challenged the use of these questions as very socially and culturally specific, although research conducted by Harvard and the Global Wellbeing initiative seems to suggest that these questions hold up better than might be expected across different cultures (Lambert et al, 2020).

Despite all the successes to date, there is a real need to increase the use of these questions to allow us to get a better and more diverse picture of the wellbeing of people in different circumstances. The What Works Centre for Wellbeing worked with the Office for National Statistics to develop a guide for adding the questions to surveys, which is important because there are well established order and mode effects that need to be controlled for but it is also possible to use very simple accessible versions of the questions. There are still questions for researchers about how the questions are understood across different cultures and generations, but there are tested questions available in both Urdu and Sylheti. The questions are increasingly added to other data collection, such as the Civil Service People Survey, which has used the four questions with over 400,000 UK civil servants since 2011. The Organisation for Economic Co-operation and Development also has a multi-measure 'wellbeing' framework called the Better Life Index and recommends the four personal subjective wellbeing measures for use around the world.

This is important because these metrics make up a shared evidence base and database for policy making, advice, analysis and evaluation. It allows for the possibility of developing theories as to what influences wellbeing for the better, and the starting point for efforts to understand the impact of different factors on wellbeing. This infrastructure is shared across nations through the Organisation for Economic Co-operation and Development, across government departments and nations in the UK by the Office for National Statistics, in Wales through the Wellbeing of Future Generations Act (a law that requires public bodies in Wales to think about the long-term impact of their decisions), across all public services working in a local area, and in Scotland and Northern Ireland across all sectors in a local area through the community planning legislation.

Measuring children and young people's wellbeing

Measuring young people's wellbeing is as important as that of adults. As the example given previously shows, a lot of work that aims to improve young people's more cardinal outcomes – like their grades, or their involvement in criminal justice – might do so at the detriment of their wellbeing. In addition to being an important task, capturing child wellbeing is a different task to measuring the same phenomenon among adults.

The same national statistics that capture wellbeing in general also include measures of wellbeing for those who are under 18. These are collected, and paid for, by the charity the Children's' Society in their Good Childhood Report. The statistics are robust, well tested, widely used and have allowed tracking of trends over time (spoiler: the kids are not doing so great), but it's a necessarily small sample of just over 2,000 young people aged 10–17 (The Children's Society, 2021).

The wellbeing of our young people is our nation's future wellbeing and from the longitudinal studies (WWCW, 2020) we know that:

1. Emotional health is as important as physical health, if not more so, to adult life satisfaction at age 34.
2. Schools can and do affect emotional health both positively and negatively.
3. The impact that individual teachers have on a child's wellbeing can be seen on later wellbeing from age ten – in primary school.
4. Low life satisfaction at 14 is predictive of higher incidence of mental health problems, self-harm and suicide in the high risk period of late teens and early 20s. (The Children's Society, 2021)

The importance of child wellbeing, not just at the time, but for their future outcomes means that there is a strong case for national measurement of subjective wellbeing in schools and colleges every term from Key Stage 3 (the three years of schooling between ages 11 and 14 for schools in England and Wales) linked to the national pupil database. This is very possible. There are increasing numbers of schools, academy chains and researchers monitoring wellbeing in school settings including 206 Greater Manchester secondary schools in the BeeWell project[2] and there are a range of providers who could plausibly collect this data en masse. The Netherlands, United Arab Emirates and South Australia have already demonstrated this is possible and useful to do over time. This would allow us to understand and improve wellbeing with the rigour we rightly give to other measures of children's outcomes such as literacy and numeracy. This data could be used by the Department for Education, Office for Standards in Education,

Children's Services and Skills (a government inspection body better known as Ofsted), or even parents, as well as in appraisal of policy options for schools in line with the HM Treasury Green Book – the government guidance on how to appraise policies, programmes and projects – for consideration in government spending decisions.

There is still ongoing research for example by Nuffield Foundation and others on how we accurately assess wellbeing of very young children too, for example Schoon et al (2010). This is hugely important – for example decisions in the family court, including taking children into care, are taken 'in the best interests of the child' but there is little by way of research to inform judgements on what can be lifelong decisions.

Evaluation

Subjective wellbeing metrics have been used in policy and the charity and non-governmental organisation sector evaluations since 2011, with a marked increase since 2018. The What Works Centre for Wellbeing have supported this activity with our measurement guide (WWCW, 2022). Alongside this, we have partnered with the charity Pro Bono Economics to produce our 'Plugging the gaps' guide (Franklin, 2020), to help civil society organisations which may not have already collected wellbeing data to make use of other metrics that are more readily available. Evaluating impacts of an intervention on wellbeing shares some challenges with other impact evaluations, as well as some of its own. The main obstacles we have identified are:

- *Effort and timing*: it can be hard to get the activity funded and delivered, let alone evaluated.
- *Competition* for priority in effort to get adoption, resulting in a proliferation of niche measures that aren't comparable.
- *Remaking* rather than building on existing measures. This is common in fields where small organisations are either unaware of existing metrics, or believe that their circumstances are unique, necessitating a bespoke metric.
- *Measure validity*: whether or not the measures meet certain statistical standards that demonstrate that they are measuring

a phenomenon consistently, and that different measures are measuring different things.

- *Use of findings*: not knowing how to interpret evaluation findings about wellbeing and hence how to act on them.
- *Primary interest* where funders are interested only in the 'main' outcome for their sector – for example grades in education – and not the broader, more holistic measure of wellbeing.
- *Unsystematic use*, for example, asking the questions only once.
- *Not liking the answer*, that is, stopping using them if they get 'worse' even if this was likely a normal path. For example, patients undergoing chemotherapy for cancer may experience a decline in wellbeing in the short and medium term, because the treatment is painful and has substantial side effects. However, they would likely have experienced a drop in wellbeing anyway due to the effects of the cancer.
- *Awkwardness*: frontline workers and even researchers may be reluctant to ask participants questions that they find awkward or socially challenging.

Concerns about asking personal emotional questions are common and normal. For frontline workers, especially those who know that the people they are working with and helping are likely to be unhappy (for example, terminally ill patients, or families undergoing a children's social care assessment), asking these questions may seem insensitive or even silly. Some of the phrasing of validated survey questions can also feel a little unnatural – for example 'Overall, how satisfied are you with your life nowadays?'.

To support researchers and practitioners, the What Works Centre for Wellbeing has produced the following guidance:

> Asking these questions may make some people uncomfortable. Loneliness can be a difficult subject for people to talk about, and also carries a stigma in our society. This is the case both for the people asking the question (who may be volunteers or people leading activities) and for those being asked. However, when researchers tested these questions, people were generally not upset by being asked, and people of all

ages felt that loneliness was an important topic to talk about and measure.

Staff and volunteers should be prepared and supported in having these conversations with people. If you're asking these questions of people who may be at particular risk of feeling lonely (such as those living alone, with health conditions, carers or unemployed people) you should make sure that you prepare to provide them with support or signpost to external support services if needed. You should also make sure they understand that answering the questions will not result in them being excluded from your project or activity. (WWCW, 2019)

It is important for anyone involved in administering a survey question to understand why that question is included and that it is important for it to be asked consistently – in the same way and for all participants. If this is not understood, the validity of the whole evaluation can be compromised by variable wording of the questions, or failing to capture the measures for some people – creating a form of survivorship bias – the error of concentrating on people that completed the endline survey and overlooking those that did not.

What next for subjective wellbeing and towards administrative data to support trials

The aim of What Works Centres is to fill policy-relevant gaps in evidence through increasingly robust evaluations using comparable metrics, often through partnership working – such as What Works Wellbeing's partnership with the UK civil service's human resources departments. We have seen increasing use of subjective wellbeing and related measures in impact evaluations, especially from 2018 onwards. The quality of the evidence is mixed, with some excellent studies, and others which for a variety of reasons fall short of providing reliable evidence due to study design or data limitations – which is expected for growing fields.

At What Works Wellbeing, we have worked to spearhead methodological development to increase the quantity and quality of research on harder-to-study activity. Our evidence gaps highlight the shortage of evidence in general, and areas where it is particularly weak – helping to focus attention where it is most needed. In particular, we hope to see fewer poor quality randomised controlled trials conducted of interventions that needed more 'pre-clinical' studies – to test the water with a smaller evaluation to see if we are ready to go to a full-blown trial – for example, interventions that aim to tackle loneliness. On the other hand, we also expect to see less repetition of less robust evaluations – for example, people conducting repeated feasibility studies (that check if an intervention is appropriate for further testing) and never proceeding to impact evaluations, for example around the use of mindfulness for students.

In order to continue to see things moving forward, we argue that there are three steps that would make a substantial difference:

1. Creating wellbeing data labs – storing the array of wellbeing data that already exists, and making benchmarking easier. These labs could ultimately hold data from across a wide range of sources and sectors and hence support creation of synthetic control groups[3] and eventual linking to administrative data.
2. Systematic measurement of wellbeing in schools – allowing wellbeing to be easily used as an outcome measure or moderator in education evaluations.
3. Direct funding for wellbeing measurement analysis and methodological development, creating a central resource to support the measurement and methodology of wellbeing research. This model could be similar to the trials units in some universities which specialise in the methods of randomised controlled trials, rather than on a particular domain of medicine.

It can be hard to make the case for evaluations and trials, especially in sectors where getting funding for the intervention or programme itself can be a long and arduous process, and an 'expensive' evaluation might seem not a good use of resources. When evaluations are funded, it is easy to discard or diminish them in the face of more urgent challenges to day-to-day delivery. Using readily available data that is collected independently of the project – for example systematic wellbeing surveys in schools, would make trials easier, quicker and, importantly, cheaper. We have already seen this effect in education research, where England's National Pupil Database has dramatically lowered the price and burden of evaluation.

One of the biggest barriers to progress is that there is no 'Ministry for Wellbeing', nor a department that takes the lead on wellbeing – despite wellbeing being the ultimate goal of much of public and civil society action. This means that policy often deals with wellbeing and relationships badly, despite these being desperately important to people's lives, to the resilience of our communities and the efficiency of our economy. These facts conspire to ensure that research on these areas is always at the edges of departments' spending priorities. This is both a general problem, and one that is specific to our situation as a What Works Centre. Instead of a government department dedicated to funding us, we are dependent on funding from a mixture of sources.

Conclusion

There has been major progress on measuring the things that make life worth living over the last 50 years and especially in the UK in the last 15 years. These are aspects of life where we all intuitively have a view and there can be a lot of policy noise as a result – witness regular newspaper debates over whether young people ('Millennial and Gen-Z'ers'), should give up one source of wellbeing (Netflix and avocados), in order to (slightly) increase their chances of having another (owning a house). This noise is usually an indicator of not enough clear evidence. It is both theoretically and practically possible to either build subjective wellbeing and related quality of life measures into administrative data available to researchers, or to put more useful values on proxies that are collected – by doing this, we could help end some of the debates about what is best for people's wellbeing and design interventions that have the biggest impact. I would much rather we argue about how best to improve the quality of lives based on better shared evidence. This would much enrich our public debate and strengthen our communities and nation as well as meaningfully improving lives.

Notes

[1] Approximate analysis of successful evaluator bids by two evaluators to the Education Endowment Foundation, and successful evaluator bids to What Works for Children's Social Care.

[2] https://gmbeewell.org/school/participating-schools/

[3] A statistical method used to evaluate the effect of an intervention in comparative case studies.

References

Children's Society, The (2021) *The good childhood report 2021*. The Children's Society. www.childrenssociety.org.uk/information/professionals/resources/good-childhood-report-2021

Forgeard, M.J., Jayawickreme, E., Kern, M.L. and Seligman, M.E. (2011) Doing the right thing: Measuring wellbeing for public policy. *International Journal of Wellbeing*, 1(1): 79–106.

Franklin, J. (2020) *Plugging the gaps: New cost-effectiveness guidance for charities*. What Works Centre for Wellbeing.

Halpern, D. (2010) *The hidden wealth of nations*. Polity.

Hume, S., O'Reilly, F., Groot, B., Chande, R., Sanders, M., Hollingsworth, A. et al (2018) *Improving engagement and attainment in maths and English courses: Insights from behavioural research*. Research and project report, Department for Education.

Lambert, L., Lomas, T., van de Weijer, M.P., Passmore, H.A., Joshanloo, M., Harter, J. et al (2020) Towards a greater global understanding of wellbeing: A proposal for a more inclusive measure. *International Journal of Wellbeing*, 10(2): 1–18.

Schoon, I., Cheng, H. and Jones, E. (2010) Resilience in children's development. In S. Dex and H. Joshi (eds) *Children of the 21st century*. Policy Press, pp 235–248.

Stewart-Brown, S. and Janmohamed, K. (2008) *Warwick-Edinburgh mental well-being scale*. User guide. Version 1(10.1037). www.mentalhealthpromotion.net/resources/user-guide.pdf

Stiglitz, J.E. (2009) GDP fetishism. *The Economists' Voice*, 6(8).

WWCW (What Works Centre for Wellbeing) (2019) *A brief guide to measuring loneliness*. What Works Centre for Wellbeing. https://whatworkswellbeing.org/resources/brief-guide-to-measuring-loneliness/

WWCW (What Works Centre for Wellbeing) (2020) *The origins of happiness*. What Works Centre for Wellbeing. https://whatworkswellbeing.org/wp-content/uploads/2020/06/www-briefing-origins4.2.pdf

WWCW (What Works Centre for Wellbeing) (2022) *Measuring your wellbeing impact*. What Works Centre for Wellbeing. https://measure.whatworkswellbeing.org/

15

Bringing it all together: the future of evidence synthesis

David Gough and Sandy Oliver

What Works Centres and other similar organisations, which we'll call 'knowledge brokerage intermediaries', are concerned with research evidence that can be useful to people making decisions, when 'useful' means being relevant to the problem being faced, offering reliable findings and being available *before* decisions are made. Turning to a single study is not enough. An individual study may have flaws or vagaries that, by design or chance, result in misleading findings, or it may be conducted in a setting that differs so much from the decision being faced it is barely relevant. These difficulties can be overcome, at least in part, by relying on collections of studies addressing the same or a similar issue. These are systematic reviews of research, or research syntheses.

What Works Centres all support decision makers by taking on the task of identifying relevant studies and checking their quality before pooling and summarising their findings to conclude what is known from existing studies. They make this work publicly available as systematic reviews for any decision makers to access. Typically, What Works Centres address questions about the effects of intervening in people's lives, for instance with education or social care policies or practices, to find out *what works*. They gather studies addressing causal questions, mainly controlled trials and particularly randomised controlled trials, and quasi-experimental studies that construct fair comparisons of different policies or practices through statistical means. However, the types of studies available to the different centres vary. Far more randomised controlled trials address questions about what works in medicine than in other fields, such as homelessness or wellbeing. Consequently, What Works Centres need different methods to find studies, appraise their quality or synthesise their findings. Indeed, in newly emerging research areas, where high-quality studies addressing what works questions are really sparse, important prior steps are finding out about the nature and the scale of the problem, before asking what interventions for tackling the problem are well designed, feasible and acceptable. When evidence about what works is plentiful, and policy decisions are made, the next step is learning from existing research what challenges may be faced when implementing policy, and how they can be overcome. Thus, these steps in the policy process ask different questions of research which, again, need different methods to find and learn from existing studies (Lavis, 2009).

Bearing in mind that useful evidence for different areas of health and social policy may come from studies addressing different questions with different methods, this chapter explains first how producing reviews with rigour involves matching the choice of questions to the methods for appraising the quality and synthesising the findings of research. Second, it considers how tackling simpler or smaller questions or streamlining processes can produce reviews rapidly, albeit with less learning or less rigour. Alternative approaches for producing reviews rapidly involve increasing effort with larger teams, or increasing efficiency with better knowledge infrastructure or automated processes. Third, it advocates working closely with decision makers to enhance the relevance of reviews to the problems they face. Lastly, it considers the What Works Centres as a network and the opportunities networks bring for developing new ideas, sharing them widely and embedding them in structures and procedures (Strasser et al, 2019, 2020).

The ideas offered here draw on 30 years of work at the Evidence for Policy and Practice Information and Co-ordinating Centre

(EPPI-Centre), some done with What Works Centres, and some with other partners or independently, but all of it informing decision makers in the public sector in the UK or internationally. There are over 100 systematic reviews authored by EPPI-Centre staff, and even more systematic reviews where EPPI-Centre staff gave methodological guidance in the fields of education and development studies. Additional learning has come specifically from our analysis of the aims, methods and contexts of the What Works Centres (Gough et al, 2018, 2021; Gough, 2021), more generally from advances we have made with synthesis methods by taking this approach from medicine to health more broadly, and to other social policy sectors (Gough et al, 2017), and insights about networks come from working with partners across the global south in PEERSS.[1]

Producing evidence with rigour: shared principles and diverse methods

Historically, synthesis was conducted inside the brain of individual academic experts. So, if you were an expert on Statins, you might be expected to know all of the main studies of their effects, and be able to combine them and summarise them. This 'walking synthesis' approach has three main flaws. First, the sheer volume of research on an individual topic is often (and increasingly) too large for any one person to assess; second, research may cut across different academic fields, meaning that one expert may miss an important part of the picture;[2] and finally, individual scholars are likely to exhibit biases, for example towards their own studies.

For all these reasons, since the 1980s in medicine, and later in other academic disciplines, more formal systematic methods have been increasingly used to clarify what is known from a body of research before making practice or policy decisions. Finding and analysing existing studies is itself a piece of research and, therefore, to be considered rigorous, requires a research process with formal methods clearly reported. Systematic reviews, in which a body of evidence is identified, assessed, categorised and synthesised (with or without statistical analyses) follow similar stages even though some details may differ (see Table 15.1).

Table 15.1: Common stages of systematic reviews

1. *Review question*: identifying the research question being addressed.
2. *Conceptual framework*: clarifying the perspectives (ideological and theoretical assumptions and priorities) and other details of the question in order to be able to operationalise it for the review.
3. *Inclusion criteria*: defining what type of studies would answer the review question.
4. *Search strategy and screening*: identifying the studies meeting the inclusion criteria.
5. *Coding*: recording relevant data from the included studies.
6. *Mapping*: describing the included studies.
7. *Quality and relevance appraisal*: appraising the relevance and trustworthiness of the data from the studies.
8. *Synthesis*: using the appraised evidence to answer the review question.

Stages and diversity in the review process

The first step of research synthesis involves formulating a clear research question, including clear definitions for all its important concepts. The research question and conceptual framework direct the search for studies and how they are analysed. Information science methods identify relevant studies, whether they are published formally, informally or not at all, by systematically searching bibliographic databases or the websites of key organisations for reports and contacting experts in the field. Having found the studies that match the research question they are matched to the conceptual framework to 'map' the literature by, for example, finding all papers which attempt to answer the question 'What is the impact of family group meetings on the likelihood of entering care?' This mapping can be useful by signposting studies to anyone interested in the field, and for identifying obvious gaps in the existing evidence. What Works Centres, for example the Youth Endowment Fund and the Centre for Homelessness Impact, share these maps via their websites.

Having found studies addressing the review question, next comes assessing their quality, pooling their findings and, finally, assessing the quality of the evidence overall. How this is done depends on the review question and the studies available.

Reviews asking 'what works?' combine the findings from similar studies to judge how often policies, programmes or practices have been shown effective, and in different circumstances. They *aggregate* the findings of these studies to draw their conclusions on more data. They also explore differences between them to ask whether the effects differ with different groups of people, or variations in interventions or contexts. They judge the quality of the studies by inspecting their methods for factors that might bias the findings, for instance, checking that everyone who entered a study also provided data at the end so that the findings take account of everyone involved, not only those fully engaged or more easily traced. Done well, these reviews adhere to standards for identifying all the relevant studies (not only those with higher profiles because their findings are exciting rather than disappointing) and for analysing the available data carefully with well-designed data templates completed by two analysts.

Reviews for understanding a problem or *how* an intervention works ask more open questions, and answer them by drawing on reviews that look at an issue from different angles. They *configure* the findings from different studies to create a more complete picture than is possible from one alone. Done well, these reviews adhere to standards for identifying all the relevant concepts and how well these are rooted in the data.

These two approaches illustrate a major distinction in research methods: the extent to which data involves either exploring data to arrange and develop new concepts (*configuring* data) or using predefined concepts to measure the extent of a phenomena or to test a hypothesis (*aggregating* data). This distinction is usually a question of degree and studies often do both. Thinking in terms of configuring and aggregating data is much broader than statistical meta-analyses that are more commonly recognised as systematic reviews.

An example of a configuring primary research study would be the examination of a social situation, for example social workers' interviews with their clients. Such a study might use ethnographic methods that are exploratory, iterative and flexible in examining the dynamics at play in such a situation. A systematic review asking the same questions would include such ethnographic primary studies and the method of review would be likely to also use an iterative strategy to configure the concepts identified across the primary studies to provide a new meta-level conceptual analysis (Nordesjö et al, 2021).

At the other end of the continuum is a study testing the effectiveness of some service or intervention, such as different ways of undertaking social work interviews. Such a study might use pre-set methods to experimentally test the hypothesis that a particular approach to undertaking social work interviews is more effective than others. The study is trying to measure or add up (aggregate) data on the outcomes of the interviews. A systematic review asking the same questions would include such experimental studies to provide a new meta-level empirical analysis.

Combining approaches to reviewing

What Works Centres focus particularly on aggregative analyses testing the effectiveness of social interventions. Nevertheless, centres are aware that understanding the effectiveness of interventions relies on also understanding the processes through which outcomes emerge. This is sometimes done through 'implementation and process' evaluations conducted as part of randomised controlled trials. Reviewing studies of effects and studies of implementation together provides a better theoretical understanding of phenomena, and of the relationship between context and effectiveness.

This combination of approaches was taken by an EPPI-Centre review commissioned to inform the National Institute for Health and Care Excellence (NICE) community engagement guidance (NICE, 2016). Three distinct components found that: (a) greater community engagement led to larger changes in behaviour (Brunton et al, 2015a); (b) greater engagement across design, delivery and evaluation came with two-way communication, collective decision making, and training for community members to deliver the intervention (Brunton et al, 2015b); and (c) interventions with online facilitators were used more often in studies with positive effects (Stokes et al, 2015).

Another form of theory driven review is 'realist' synthesis, which uses an iterative strategy for testing the stages of the causal chain

(Pawson et al, 2005), combining both configuring and aggregative approaches. An example of realist synthesis is the testing of the idea that banning smoking in a car where children are present would reduce risks of smoking related conditions to children (Wong et al, 2013). The first component of the review unpacked the causal chain in the theory. This chain included physical effects and health risks of passive smoking in a confined space, the extent to which a law like this would be complied with (and if it was enforceable), and possible unintended consequences like an increase in smoking in the home. The second component of the review sought the evidence for all of the stages of the causal chain, but this was done through an exploratory, detective-like approach.

Producing evidence rapidly: coordinated effort and efficiency

While decision makers appreciate reliable reviews underpinned by rigorous methods, when facing urgent decisions they also appreciate rapid delivery. What Works Centres have responded with rapid reviews that adopted a range of strategies to accelerate delivery. Whichever strategies are employed (and several are described here), the label 'rapid review' needs to be accompanied by a clear report of how a speedy delivery has been achieved and what impact this may have on the comprehensiveness and the rigour of the review (Tricco et al, 2015).

Rapid reviews with more focused effort

Reviews are quicker when they address conceptually easier questions, where some of the thinking is already done, so there is prior consensus of how to conceptualise issues, for example agreement on what precisely an intervention entails, or on how and when outcomes can be measured. Such consensus among experts in the field may make it easier and quicker to identify, code, appraise and synthesise the results of primary studies. However, in social policy, unlike medicine, fairly few areas have reached this consensus. This argues for including field experts alongside stakeholders in shaping reviews.

Reviews are quicker when they ask narrower questions and answer them in less depth. Unfortunately such reviews sometimes provide too little evidence to be useful for decision making.

Reviews are quicker when effort focuses on speed more than rigour. For example, search strategies may be quicker if they draw on fewer sources, apply fewer search terms or only capture studies that are easier to find. Assessing study quality may be quicker if a reviewer works alone, or applies fewer criteria. For this it is important to know what 'short cuts' have been undertaken and the impact on the trustworthiness and relevance of the evidence claims being made by the review.

Reviews are quicker when done by larger, well-coordinated teams. This should enable no loss of breadth and depth but also no saving in costs and may be difficult to achieve in practice unless there is a large, highly skilled team available to respond at short notice.

Rapid reviews with greater efficiency

Reviews can also be conducted more quickly when working with literatures that have received earlier attention, and after developing knowledge infrastructure for maintaining coded studies (Wilson et al, 2021). Work is quicker when studies have already been collated in specialist databases, when reviews are available in review libraries and can be updated or re-analysed, or when a field of studies has been systematically described previously. Starting with existing reviews or coded studies reduces the time required to identify studies and may also reduce time spent coding and analysing them.

Individual reviews can be accelerated by automating some of the processes, such as identifying studies and repeating search strategies automatically at regular intervals. Electronic search strategies are over-inclusive. Inspecting all the titles and abstracts they catch is tedious and time-consuming. Better is to train software algorithms to prioritise those studies most likely to be relevant, check those and, when fewer and fewer studies are judged relevant, discard the rest. Although some relevant studies may be missed, the alternatives are reviewers introducing inaccuracies as they become tired and bored, or spending too much time identifying studies and too little analysing what is found.

Automation allows rapid searching of the Internet for academic publications. These regular automated searches, followed by automatically sorting and categorising studies, underpin the EPPI-Centre's living maps of COVID-19 research (Shemilt et al, 2022).[3] These living maps enable researchers and users of research to keep abreast of fast developing fields. Two years into the pandemic they mapped over 130,000 reports, including 1,417 of social science systematic reviews. The same principle of regular automated searches applies for living systematic reviews, where they can be kept up to date with a re-analysis on finding a new study that might change the findings of the existing review (Elliott et al, 2014).

Automation also helps with the process of reviewing. An initial impression of the field can be gained from automatically clustering studies. For more rigorous analysis, several What Works Centres use EPPI-Reviewer (Thomas et al, 2020), software developed by the EPPI-Centre for managing studies through the review process, including coding, analysis (whether statistical or thematic) and reporting, included studies and the whole review. Software can also assist with the visualisation of results as in EPPI-Mapper software.[4]

These approaches to increasing efficiency all rely on searchable evidence resources, often publicly available and together creating a global knowledge infrastructure. For instance, the Centre for Homeless Impact curates and makes publicly available evidence maps of effectiveness research (White et al, 2020) and implementation studies (White and Narayana, 2021).[5] Using the same systems across evidence products offers additional efficiencies. These include developing system-specific skills, reducing duplication of coding of studies included in different reviews, developing common coding and evidence standards, and being able to have an overarching database of studies and reviews to ease management and development of work. A successful example of this is the NICE community engagement review mentioned earlier in this chapter, where the details of studies accrued from years of reviewing public health interventions were searched for engagement terms that were often missing from titles and abstracts and thus could not be found by searching bibliographic databases.

Producing evidence with relevance

Decision makers appreciate reliable and timely evidence, but unless evidence is relevant to their concerns, they will tend to ignore it (Oliver and Cairney, 2019). What Works Centres address this challenge by engaging potential evidence users in producing reviews and guidance (Gough et al, 2018). NICE has well-developed processes for stakeholders to drive and comment on guidance during its development. Three What Works Centres, for Scotland, Wales and Crime Reduction, all adopt co-production models when conducting systematic reviews.

There has been little formal analysis of ways that reviewers and decision makers can build a mutual understanding and agreement on policy-relevant questions and the kind of evidence needed to answer them (Langer et al, 2016). In our experience at the EPPI-Centre, and from interviewing systematic reviewers and policy makers, we see policy-relevant systematic reviews emerging when producers and potential users of reviews engage with each other, listening carefully, particularly to what is unfamiliar, and challenge each other to co-construct review questions and then answer them with methods chosen to suit both the questions and the breadth and depth of the literature available (Oliver et al, 2018). Moreover, our own work with systematic reviews addressing developing economies suggests that involving potential users in shaping systematic reviews makes them more relevant to policy problems, and encourages clearer communication of policy implications leading to greater use in policy decisions (Oliver et al, 2020).

What next for the What Works Network?

The What Works Centres have made impressive developments in embedding evidence into policy systems using publicly available toolkits. They could go further with developing evidence synthesis as a transformative social innovation (Strasser et al, 2019, 2020), sharing across the network novel methods that have been developed in different centres, and taking advantage of their impressive portfolio of systematic reviews by conducting research on research to improve synthesis methods.

So far, their focus has been predominantly on research about the *effects* of interventions. New opportunities include making sense of literatures where effectiveness studies are lacking, such as research about local economic growth. The Centre for Homelessness Impact, as already mentioned, and others such as the Youth Endowment Fund and Youth Futures Foundation, have made a start by mapping process studies as well as effectiveness studies, to highlight where studies are available for synthesis, and where gaps indicate a need for primary research. This approach can be expanded to learn from literatures that can inform intervention design – studies about problems and potential solutions to construct theories of change that are prerequisites to effectiveness studies – mapping the breadth and the depth of research available. These innovations with evidence-gap maps and reviewing different types of research are ripe for sharing across the network, as are ideas about co-production and information technology for knowledge management.

Co-production of systematic reviews, already adopted by some What Works Centres, is not just an idea to be shared, but an idea to be explored more deeply. Another idea deserving more attention is how to reliably translate review findings from where studies were conducted to the contexts where decisions are being made. This is important not only for making the best use possible of studies from North America – where the vast majority of research is published – but also for making use of research findings thoughtfully across the UK, with all its diversity of populations and settings. Advances are being made, and What Works Centres could offer newly developed tools alongside access to rigorous evidence.

Some What Works Centres are already adopting co-production methods to prepare systematic reviews. They are ideally placed, with their databases of systematic reviews, to investigate whether the findings of systematic reviews prepared in this way are more readily used to inform policy decisions.

Looking to the future, harnessing the power of the What Works Network has the potential to advance both the policy-relevance and wider application of systematic reviews.

Notes

[1] Partnership for Evidence and Equity in Responsive Social Systems (PEERSS), https://peerss.org/

[2] In social policy an example of this might be bodywork video cameras for the police. This one intervention has been studies by criminologists, economists, psychologists and public administration scholars, each with their own questions, methods and academic journals.

[3] EPPI-Centre, COVID-19: A living systematic map of the evidence, http://eppi.ioe.ac.uk/cms/Projects/DepartmentofHealthandSocialCare/Published reviews/COVID-19Livingsystematicmapoftheevidence/tabid/3765/Default.aspx. EPPI-Centre, Living map of systematic reviews of social sciences research evidence on COVID-19, https://eppi.ioe.ac.uk/cms/Default.aspx?tabid=3806

[4] EPPI-Mapper, https://eppi.ioe.ac.uk/cms/Default.aspx?tabid=3790

[5] Centre for Homeless Impact, Evidence and gap maps, www.homelessnessimpact.org/evidence-and-gap-maps

References

Brunton, G., Caird, J., Stokes, G., Stansfield, C., Kneale, D., Richardson, M. and Thomas, J. (2015a) *Review 1: Community engagement for health via coalitions, collaborations and partnerships: A systematic review.* EPPI-Centre, Social Science Research Unit, UCL Institute of Education, University College London.

Brunton, G., Caird, J., Kneale, D., Thomas, J. and Richardson, M. (2015b) *Review 2: Community engagement for health via coalitions, collaborations and partnerships: A systematic review and meta-analysis.* London: EPPI-Centre, Social Science Research Unit, UCL Institute of Education, University College London.

Elliott, J.H., Turner, T., Clavisi, O., Thomas, J., Higgins, J.P.T., Mavergames, C. et al (2014) Living systematic reviews: An emerging opportunity to narrow the evidence-practice gap. *PLoS Med*, 11(2): e1001603.

Gough, D. (2021) Appraising evidence claims. *Review of Research in Education*, 45(1): 1–26.

Gough, D., Oliver, S. and Thomas, J. (2017) *Introduction to systematic reviews*, 2nd edition. London: Sage.

Gough, D., Maidment, C. and Sharples, J. (2018) *UK What Works Centres: Aims, methods and contexts.* EPPI-Centre, Social Science Research Unit, UCL Institute of Education, University College London. https://eppi.ioe.ac.uk/cms/Default.aspx?tabid=3731

Gough, D., Maidment, C. and Sharples, J. (2021) Enabling knowledge brokerage intermediaries to be evidence-informed. *Evidence & Policy* (published online ahead of print 2021). https:// bristoluniversitypressdigital.com/view/journals/evp/aop/arti cle-10.1332-174426421X16353477842207/article-10.1332-174426421X16353477842207.xml

Langer, L., Tripney, J. and Gough, D. (2016) *The science of using science: Researching the use of research evidence in decision-making.* EPPI-Centre, Social Science Research Unit, UCL Institute of Education, University College London.

Lavis, J.N. (2009) How can we support the use of systematic reviews in policymaking? *PLoS Med*, 6(11): e1000141.

NICE (National Institute for Health and Care Excellence) (2016) *Community engagement: Improving health and wellbeing and reducing health inequalities.* NICE Guideline No 44. www.nice.org.uk/ guidance/ng44

Nordesjö, K., Scaramuzzino, G. and Ulmestig, R. (2021) The social worker–client relationship in the digital era: A configurative literature review. *European Journal of Social Work*: 1–13.

Oliver, K. and Cairney, P. (2019) The dos and don'ts of influencing policy: A systematic review of advice to academics. *Palgrave Communications*, 5: article 21. https://doi.org/10.1057/s41 599-019-0232-y

Oliver, S., Bangpan, M. and Dickson, K. (2018) Producing policy relevant systematic reviews: Navigating the policy-research interface. *Evidence & Policy*, 14(2): 197–220.

Oliver, S., Anand, K. and Bangpan, M. (2020) *Investigating the impact of systematic reviews funded by DFID.* EPPI-Centre, Social Science Research Unit, UCL Institute of Education.

Shemilt, I., Gough, D., Thomas, J., Stansfield, C., Bangpan, M., Brunton, J. et al (2022) *Living map of systematic reviews of social sciences research evidence on COVID-19.* EPPI–Centre, UCL Social Research Institute, University College London.

Stokes, G., Richardson, M., Brunton, G., Khatwa, M. and Thomas, J. (2015) *Review 3: Community engagement for health via coalitions, collaborations and partnerships (on-line social media and social networks): A systematic review and meta-analysis.* EPPI-Centre, Social Science Research Unit, UCL Institute of Education, University College London.

Strasser, T., de Kraker, J. and Kemp, R. (2019) Developing the transformative capacity of social innovation through learning: A conceptual framework and research agenda for the roles of network leadership. *Sustainability*, 11(5): 1304. https://doi.org/10.3390/su11051304

Strasser, T., de Kraker, J. and Kemp, R. (2020) Three dimensions of transformative impact and capacity: A conceptual framework applied in social innovation practice. *Sustainability*, 12(11): 4742.

Thomas, J., Graziosi, S., Brunton, J., Ghouze, Z., O'Driscoll, P. and Bond, M. (2020) *EPPI-Reviewer: Advanced software for systematic reviews, maps and evidence synthesis.* EPPI-Centre Software. UCL Social Research Institute.

Tricco, A.C., Antony, J., Zarin, W., Strifler, L., Ghassemi, M., Ivory, J. et al (2015) A scoping review of rapid review methods. *BMC Med*, 13: 224.

White, H. and Narayana, M. (2021) *Why interventions to improve the welfare of people experiencing homelessness or at risk work or not: An updated evidence and gap map.* Centre for Homeless Impact.

White, H., Saran, A., Verma, A. and Verma, K. (2020) *The effectiveness of interventions to improve the welfare of those experiencing and at risk of homelessness: An updated evidence and gap map.* Centre for Homeless Impact.

Wilson, M.G., Oliver, S., Melendez-Torres, G.J., Lavis, J., Waddell, K. and Dickson, K. (2021) Paper 3: Selecting rapid review methods for complex questions related to health policy and system issues. *Systematic Reviews*, 10: article 286.

Wong, G., Greenhalgh, T. and Westhorp, G., Buckingham, J. and Pawson, R. (2013) RAMESES publication standards: Realist syntheses. *BMC Medicine*, 11: 21.

16

Frontiers in equality

Ella Whelan and Michael Sanders

There has been a wide acceptance in recent years of the importance of equality. Legislation in the UK and many other places make discrimination on grounds of race, gender identify, sexual orientation and disability illegal. The Government Equalities Office, established in 2007, has responsibility for achieving equality, and advises the rest of government on this – particularly regarding gender equality.

Tackling inequality is, to a certain extent, baked into the What Works Network. The Education Endowment Foundation (EEF), for example, is explicitly focused on reducing the attainment gap in education between rich and poor (as defined by eligibility for free school meals). The Transforming Access and Student Outcomes in Higher Education centre indicates from its name a desire to broaden both attendance and attainment in higher education. Given that there are substantial attendance gaps across racial, disability and poverty lines, there is an explicit focus on inequality. For other centres, the focus on inequality is more tacit, but is clearly a part of their missions. What Works for Children's Social Care, for example, aims to improve health, education and criminal justice outcomes for young people with a social worker. Although this group is not one of those identified by many interested in inequality, it contains many who are. Because every child with a disability is classed as a 'child in need'; because of the correlation between poverty and being in foster or residential care; because of the correlation between race and state involvement in family life – each of these makes it more likely that young people with a social worker are members of other groups on which equality campaigns focus. The same can be said of centres focused on local economic growth, reducing youth violence and increasing employment.

Despite this implicit and explicit focus across the network, there has been relatively less work that focuses particularly on equality in and of itself. In most research projects, the outcome of interest is usually some absolute measure of performance – number of students passing their GCSEs, progressing to university or avoiding a particular illness. Although early trials funded by the EEF prioritised recruiting schools in areas of high deprivation (measured by the Income Deprivation Affecting Children Index[1]), the need to recruit large numbers of participants in order to find statistically meaningful results makes this an impossible prospect – particularly if large numbers of trials are to be conducted. Recruitment into trials is always a challenge (as we know from trials both at What Works for Children's Social Care, and having acted as an evaluator on a number of EEF projects[2]). As a result it is common to recruit as many schools as possible given the constraints of geography, delivery and budget, with explicit recruitment for diversity or disadvantage taking a back seat.

The magnitude of this practical and statistical challenge should not be underestimated, for a number of reasons. First, if the 'diverse' subsample is too small, the likelihood of both false positives (declaring an effect when there is none), and false negatives (declaring that there is no effect when there is one), rises (Simmons et al, 2011). Second, there is a trade-off faced in considering subsamples themselves, which is particularly prominent on matters of racial and ethnic diversity – bundling anyone from an ethnic minority into a category marked 'Black, Asian and Minority Ethnicity (BAME)', may be helpful from a statistical power perspective, but it treats people with diverse backgrounds, upbringings and cultures – perhaps even biologies – as a monolith. This aggregation is seen by many as offensive and oppressive per se, and its statistical merits may be overrated, if the differences between groups include differences in how much they are affected by a given treatment.

Third, taking results from an entire sample and assuming that any effects found will extrapolate to either out-of-sample-groups (that is, to people not inside the study) or within-sample-subgroups (that is, that average effects across the whole sample will be the same as average effects for any particular sub-group, like race, gender, or sexual identity or orientation) is risky, and hinges on potentially heroic assumptions about 'a rising tide lifting all boats'.

Finally, taking a 'whole sample' approach is not purely a methodological decision, but may shape the interventions that we choose to test (and/or those that are subjected to systematic review). If we are trying to ensure that everyone in, for example, a local area, is able to, or likely to, benefit from an intervention, this encourages a 'lowest common denominator' approach. That is, identifying interventions that are theorised to work for the broadest possible grouping – and not those for whom economic, social or cultural challenges might make supporting them arguably more important. In fact, we can potentially go even further. Although a minority of interventions might be focused on people with English as a Second or Additional Language, the vast majority might take it as a given that participants can speak and read in English. This is even more prescriptive than looking for a lowest common denominator, and resorts to majoritarian thinking in its place. Recent efforts to 'decolonise' curricula in universities and elsewhere give a hint of how damaging this might be – by appealing to the majority group (from which researchers themselves are disproportionately likely to be drawn),[3] we risk finding interventions that work *on average*, but exacerbate inequalities. These 'effective gap wideners' are perhaps the most potentially damaging consequence of the What Works movement. Although other criticisms of the What Works movement – for example that it is impossible to make causal claims about complex social phenomena, or that we select the wrong outcomes – can be chalked up to interdisciplinary differences in methodology and philosophy or too strong an adherence to the concrete and pragmatic, there is surely nobody who could seriously argue that widening existing inequalities is a good thing.

The central and in our minds most powerful flaw with the What Works movement and its methodologies is that it explicitly and implicitly privileges a particular set of viewpoints – typically

White, male, able bodied, cis-gendered and straight – over others. Our choice of outcome measures, analytical approaches and interventions can, with the best of intentions, reinforce the status quo.

The solution to this is not to despair. As with many problems, acceptance is the first step on the path to recovery. Many of us who advocate for 'evidence-based policy' and for the use of better causal understanding of policy and practice interventions do so because we believe that this approach is the best way to systematically improve outcomes. In accepting the weakness of the approach, it is important not to discard it. Instead, we must consider how we can be better.

Two types of question: gaps and animus

When we think about a 'what works' type research into inequality, there are two broad types of questions that we might be interested in. Which of these a particular project, trial, initiative or synthesis is interested in will lead to a series of implications that will be the focus of most of the rest of this chapter.

The first type of question we can think about as relating to *gaps*. These occur when one group with one characteristic (or a set of characteristics) experiences different levels of a particular outcome than their peers. This might be differences in grades, in rates of entering care, likelihood of committing a crime, or of developing a particular health or mental health issue. Often, researchers will be interested both in maximising (or minimising) a positive (or negative) outcome at sample or population level, *and* decreasing the gap in outcomes between more and less privileged participants.

The second type of question relates to *animus* (List, 2004). For these questions, we will be interested more in reducing the absolute amount of hostility, ill feeling or discrimination that is experienced, either by a particular group, or against groups that experience discrimination more generally. In these circumstances, we are more generally interested in only one question – how do we reduce the levels of animus experienced (Gneezy et al, 2012).

Of course, no typology of research questions is exhaustive, and these two categories are also not mutually exclusive. It is easy to think of research questions that incorporate elements of both types. Decolonising the curriculum – which aims to reduce gaps in attainment by reducing tacit discrimination, falls into both camps. Similarly, interventions like 'blinding' applications to remove details on a prospective employee's race, gender, age or educational background aim to reduce gaps in employment by reducing the impact of implicit bias. Nonetheless, we think this typology is useful in thinking about how we can find out what works to reduce inequality.

Gaps

Gaps exist across a number of lines of disadvantage, and in almost every outcome in which policy makers are interested. Race and poverty are strongly associated with outcomes in education, criminal justice, employment, homelessness and social care involvement.

It can be tempting to presume that a group that is disadvantaged on one outcome, or perhaps in general, will tend to experience disadvantage on all outcomes. The picture is, of course, more nuanced than this. This can be clearly seen in education, where some ethnic groups – like Chinese, tend to outperform their White peers, while others, like people of Black-Caribbean heritage, tend to get lower grades than their White peers.[4]

When conducting evaluations of interventions that aim to reduce gaps, we therefore need to be clear not only on the outcome measures of interest, but also on which group, or groups, for which we are seeking to explore the gaps in those outcomes. There is a stark trade-off between acknowledging and recognising the differences between groups that are disadvantaged across a common set of characteristics (for example, ethnic minorities of the various constituent identities under the lesbian, gay, bisexual, transgender, queer and other [LGBTQ+] umbrella), which pushes us towards more groups, and statistical practicality, which pushes in the other direction. The exact way the decision is made will be a matter for individual researchers, but a few rules of thumb should be considered, as discussed in the following subsections.

Mean difference

How different are outcomes for two groups you are thinking of aggregating? Do their outcomes resemble each other, or the majoritarian group, more closely?

Cultural, historical and theoretical difference

How do the groups differ in terms of their backgrounds and culture? For example, is there a cultural weight put on the pursuit of education? Are language barriers likely to exist for both groups? To what extent does it seem theoretically sound to expect a characteristic of business as usual — for example, the colonised curriculum — to affect both groups in the same way? Although all groups will of course have their own culture and experience, the extent to which these are similar will vary. For example, deaf participants have their own language and culture which is different to that of hearing people, in a way that may not be the same case for someone who must use a wheelchair; lesbian and gay people may have more in common with each other than trans-women and trans-men, and so on.

Study design

There is always a statistical cost from conducting more analysis, and in splitting a sample into more and smaller groups. However, the extent to which this is problematic varies a lot depending on the design of the study itself. In cluster randomised controlled trials, an entire group is randomised together — for example, when randomisation takes place at the level of the school, or hospital, rather than at the individual level. Where this is the case, the experiment will have less statistical power per observation than an individually randomised study, because of the tendency for outcomes within a cluster (school, hospital, geography), to be correlated with each other even in the absence of the intervention. When trying to ensure that studies are 'well powered' with clustered randomisation, we focus on the number of clusters more than the number of participants per cluster. We can estimate this crudely, by taking two samples of the same size — 2,000 participants each, divided evenly between a control and treatment group. These studies differ, however, in their structure – one has ten clusters of 100 participants each, and the other has 100 clusters of ten participants each. The first study loses more power through clustering – in fact, you'd need to increase its sample size by 5.7 times (keeping the cluster sizes the same and increasing the number of clusters) to have the same amount of power as the second study. As we can see, clustering is bad for power. However, when looking at equality, this same fact works in our favour. Because there are small returns to additional observations within a cluster, there are also small losses from fewer observations within a cluster. Hence if a cluster randomised controlled trial is well powered overall, it is much more likely to be well powered for sub-group analysis, even if the sub-group is in a minority.

Oversampling

Having made a decision to investigate gaps, which outcomes and which groups you are interested in, there are still things which can be done to increase the rigour of the study. The first is oversampling members of the disadvantaged group we are interested in. This might mean either choosing to recruit in areas where the group is more prevalent, as is possible for some ethnic minorities (and was undertaken regarding lower household incomes as a focus of early EEF trials), or aiming to over-recruit participants from a particular group into the study, as may be more desirable if the group of interest is people with a disability or LGBTQ+ people – although we are not aware of this happening in practice to date. As well as oversampling for quantitative, impact evaluation, we should also consider over-recruiting people from this group for any qualitative, implementation and process evaluations as well, to ensure that any differences in effects (good or bad), can be understood and used to inform future research.

Manipulation checks

When considering impact evaluations to reduce gaps in substantive outcomes, we need to recognise that this may not be practical or affordable. Research funders are often reluctant to fund high-quality impact evaluations as it is, and are even less likely to be willing to fund one on a scale that recruits sufficient numbers of a disadvantaged group in order to test impacts as rigorously as we would like. Even if we were to be able to secure funding on this scale, it would still be appropriate to question the wisdom in this scale of research. Here, two factors argue against us. First – the act of scaling the intervention to this extent might reduce the effect itself. Al-Ubaydli et al (2021) find that interventions lose as much as two-thirds of their effectiveness when scaled. For an intervention that has been proven to work at a smaller scale, this loss of effectiveness may be a price worth paying to reach more people, and after all, the effect remains positive. However, if we 'skip-to-scale' in our impact evaluations, we may spuriously fail to detect an effect, dooming a potentially impactful intervention. The second factor is that studies do not exist in a vacuum. Running a study three times the size costs (about) three times as much. This means we face an opportunity cost of three normal-sized studies for each giant study we run. Putting all of our experimental eggs into one basket is a risky strategy. Lortie-Forgues and Inglis (2019) find that many of the EEF's trials, which focus on hard measures of attainment, are not 'informative' because of their size and study design.[5] We can borrow their proposal that measuring intermediate outcome measures could improve studies. In this case, they give the example of a study that tests the impact of giving students free eye tests and (if needed) glasses. They argue that the evaluation is likely to be minimally informative if looking at changes to attainment, but more likely to be informative about the impact on whether children have glasses. This might seem obvious but it gives a sense of whether the intervention is affecting an outcome on the path to effectiveness. Putting it differently, if this intervention didn't lead to people getting glasses, it is difficult to see how it could be effective at increasing attainment down the line. When thinking about equality, we could look for similar measures. An intervention which aims to raise grades may do so by increasing school attendance. We may not be powered to see changes for a sub-group in the (hard to move) measure of grades, but might be better able to look at changes in (easier to move) attendance. If attendance doesn't move, we can conclude that the intervention probably doesn't work for a sub-group, and move on to other promising interventions.

Animus

Studies looking at reducing animus, or animus-generated inequalities, will often have a different focus than those looking to reduce gaps. We can think about an animus study looking at one of three samples: discriminators, discriminated and events.

In a sample of discriminators, the study will look at the broader population of people who might demonstrate a discriminating belief or behaviour. For example, in Broockman and Kalla (2016), participants are members of the public who may (or may not), hold homophobic or transphobic attitudes. These are the people on whom the intervention will be tested, aiming to reduce the incidence of these attitudes. As such, we have either N observations, where each observation, n, is a potential discriminator, or N x T observations, where T is a time series.

In a sample of the discriminated, our study looks more similar to those investigating gaps. Our sample looks at people who might be discriminated against or otherwise experience animus-based inequality. Our outcome measure would hence be whether each participant experiences the form of animus under consideration during the time period of the study. This approach is challenging, as interventions to reduce animus are likely to be delivered to discriminators, not the discriminated. The lack of a one-to-one concordance between a treated person and a person experiencing an outcome means that cleanly identifying causality will be hard – either because someone's treatment/control status is unclear, or because it is probabilistic – because the discriminated individual could have come across multiple discriminators, of which some proportion are treated. Delivering interventions at a geographical or other cluster level might ameliorate this lack of concordance, but is unlikely to reduce it entirely. Where we have probabilistic treatment assignment, our evaluation becomes in practice an instrumental variables problem, with the loss of power that this entails. We should be cautious about using samples of the discriminated in equalities studies.

Our final sample is of events.[6] Here, we're aiming to strip a particular set of outcomes from its human participants (this might be helpful when trying to convince partners to run experiments). In this case, an event might be an interview for a specific job in a firm. CV audit studies, pioneered by Bertrand and Mullainathan (2004), test discrimination in a neat (if logically burdensome) way. In the study (Bertrand and Mullainathan, 2004), researchers submit fictional applications for a large number of jobs. These applications are identical in all important ways, except for the name of the fictional application – which is either a typical 'White' name, like Emily, or a typical 'Black' name, like Lakisha. Researchers then monitor to see how many of these CVs elicit an interview. Other studies might take the job advert itself as an 'event', which can be applied to, or not, by some unknown number of real participants. Research carried out by the Behavioural Insights Team's Gender and Behavioural Insights programme does this, by varying the wording of the adverts to foreground workplace flexibility with a view to attracting a more diverse range of applicants. We cannot know how many people saw each advert, or their characteristics, so participant level propensity-to-apply data would lack a denominator. Instead, we can treat the advert as an event, with the number and type of applicants to each being the outcome measure.

Differences in approach

We have outlined two types of 'what works' study with the explicit goal of reducing inequality. Although there is naturally a lot of overlap between these (reducing employment gaps by tackling discrimination, reducing educational attainment gaps by curriculum reform, and so on), the distinction leads to both philosophical and practical implications.

Philosophically, the distinction reminds us that animus is only a part of the story of inequality. Even if every ounce of ill-will and bias were to be purged from people's minds tomorrow and for all eternity, inequalities would likely persist in a number of domains. Centuries of previous disadvantage, both overt and covert, have left deep scars. If Black families are more likely to live in poverty, or in areas without as much access to work; if the children of poor families continue to be born to parents who are less educated, or have less access to learning resources the home; if those who have been discriminated against maintain an understandable wariness of the those in power, it would still take time, investment and effort to achieve equality. Removing animus is a necessary condition for equality, but not a sufficient one.

Practically, the role of existing entities differs depending on the type of questions to be answered. It makes little sense to have a 'What Works Centre for Reducing Gaps in Educational Attainment Along Racial Lines' while the EEF exists. Instead, each extant What Works Centre is responsible for understanding and alleviating inequality within its domain. For reducing discrimination, bias and the beliefs and behaviours of individuals or organisations – such as through contact studies like Kalla and Broockman (2020), this disaggregated approach is unlikely to work – there is not an obvious programme of work within existing centres to answer these questions.

Conclusion

These implications lead us to a conclusion about how best the What Works movement can tackle issues of inequality. First, existing centres should acknowledge their role in reducing inequality, even where it is not their core mission. If centres do this, it licenses researchers and others to think about these questions, and avoids the issue that inequality is always 'someone else's problem'. If you hold the largest database of trial results in a particular domain, either in terms of raw data or systematic reviews, there is nobody better to facilitate the use of those data. Second, centres should put (some of) their money where their mouths are, to encourage more studies which focus on equality at least in part. This means funding oversampling, and analysis of outcome gaps, particularly in clustered trials where the power implications are less severe. It could be argued that this analysis is atheoretical, however, the basis of sound theory is empirical observations of the world – and if we do not know about differential effects and where they occur, how can we form a theory about *why* they occur and, most importantly, how to fix gaps. Third, it is clear that every centre can benefit from the lived experience of those who experience inequality in all its forms, and that work programmes will benefit from expert advice.

It is also true that each centre is unlikely to be well enough resourced to build in-house teams in each area of inequality efficiently. As such, a central hub of experts on tackling inequality, from both a practical, theoretical and methodological standpoint, could and should be convened, to support the work that individual centres do, and to drive them to do more. Given the differential sizes of existing centres, either additional funding from central government, or contributions according to centres' sizes, might be appropriate. Finally, this central hub could focus its own research agenda on interventions working with public, private and third sector organisations that aim to tackle inequality caused by animus, and animus itself.

Notes

[1] www.gov.uk/government/statistics/english-indices-of-deprivation-2019
[2] https://educationendowmentfoundation.org.uk/projects-and-evaluation/projects/maths-for-life; https://educationendowmentfoundation.org.uk/projects-and-evaluation/projects/community-apprentice; https://educationendowmentfoundation.org.uk/public/files/Projects/Visible_Classroom_SAP.pdf
[3] https://blogs.lse.ac.uk/equityDiversityInclusion/2014/08/black-academia-in-britain/
[4] www.ethnicity-facts-figures.service.gov.uk/education-skills-and-training/11-to-16-years-old/a-to-c-in-english-and-maths-gcse-attainment-for-children-aged-14-to-16-key-stage-4/latest
[5] Informative here is used in its Bayesian sense – to what extent should the study lead us to update our priors if we do so according to Bayes's rule rather than informative in the lay sense.
[6] This should not be confused with an event study, a quasi-experimental approach to identify causality in time-series data.

References

Al-Ubaydli, O., Lee, M.S., List, J.A., Mackevicius, C.L. and Suskind, D. (2021) How can experiments play a greater role in public policy? Twelve proposals from an economic model of scaling. *Behavioural Public Policy*, 5(1): 2–49.

Bertrand, M. and Mullainathan, S. (2004) Are Emily and Greg more employable than Lakisha and Jamal? A field experiment on labor market discrimination. *American Economic Review*, 94(4): 991–1013.

Broockman, D. and Kalla, J. (2016) Durably reducing transphobia: A field experiment on door-to-door canvassing. *Science*, 352(6282): 220–224.

Gneezy, U., List, J. and Price, M.K. (2012) *Toward an understanding of why people discriminate: Evidence from a series of natural field experiments.* No w17855. National Bureau of Economic Research.

Kalla, J.L. and Broockman, D.E. (2020) Reducing exclusionary attitudes through interpersonal conversation: Evidence from three field experiments. *American Political Science Review*, 114(2): 410–425.

List, J.A. (2004) The nature and extent of discrimination in the marketplace: Evidence from the field. *The Quarterly Journal of Economics*, 119(1): 49–89.

Lortie-Forgues, H. and Inglis, M. (2019) Rigorous large-scale educational RCTs are often uninformative: Should we be concerned? *Educational Researcher*, 48(3): 158–166.

Simmons, J.P., Nelson, L.D. and Simonsohn, U. (2011) False-positive psychology: Undisclosed flexibility in data collection and analysis allows presenting anything as significant. *Psychological Science*, 22(11): 1359–1366.

17

Evidence at the grassroots

Ben Linton

Moving policing towards a more evidence-based future seems to me the single most effective mechanism for police reform and improvement. That sounds like a bold claim, but the reason it is so powerful and compelling is the scope to change the mindset towards a scientific and professional approach to balance the perhaps excessive focus on individual experience and craft in policing before the evidence-based policing (EBP) movement started to have an impact. Moving us towards a style of leadership that values certainty of impact and more scientific methods is at the heart of EBP and the wider public sector adoption of evidence-based practice.

By way of an introduction, I am a Metropolitan Police Officer and have been for 15 years. It doesn't feel like 15 years ago that I first put a warrant card in my pocket and sincerely declared that I would discharge all my duties to the best of my knowledge and skill, but more importantly, I don't think I could even guess at what those skills might end up being. I've picked up many of the more 'usual' skills along the way, but for me the most transformative and useful skills were sparked at a presentation given by one of the great leaders of EBP, Alex Murray, in about 2010. Alex is now a Commander in the Metropolitan Police Service (the Met), and at the time of the presentation was a Chief Inspector in West Midlands Police and had just formed the Society of Evidence Based Policing (SEBP).

With a slide deck covering a wealth of different pieces of evidence, Alex concluded with a stark suggestion. He had given us knowledge about how to be more evidence based, how to test more effectively and learn more about our impact – so how could we fulfil our policing oath if we didn't start to make use of what he had told us? He pointed out the fundamentally unethical behaviour of failing to use the best evaluation methods to understand the impact of policing and justify how we spend enormous sums of public money. Could we really say that we were discharging our duties to the best of our knowledge if we failed to use the knowledge that we could more scientifically test our impact?

I joined the SEBP, became its London coordinator, and set about thinking how I could push policing in London towards an evidence-based future, focused on what works in policing, using the best available evidence. My hope here is to set out some of the successes and challenges to help others seeking to push the same change and improvement elsewhere.

Crucial to research is the engagement of the frontline practitioners who need to put into action the change that is either being tested, or has been tested and is now the new business-as-usual. For many years, however, I struggled to understand how EBP would be of interest to an operational constable driving a response car around South London, or investigating dozens of crimes allocated to them. What does talk of 'being more evidence based' and using randomised controlled trials, ethnographic research or randomised vignette studies actually mean to a police officer whose day job is responding to 999 calls? I couldn't conceptualise how to get those people excited about research given their seeming lack of opportunity to alter their policing tactics at the scale required to be experimental.

In persuading colleagues of the benefits of EBP, I have generally focused my efforts on people higher up the rank structure, given their ability to move resources, change policies and refocus priorities in a way that could be evaluated, especially considering the number of officers needed to achieve statistically valid tests. Those people are still crucially important, but I want to explore how we've engaged frontline response officers. Those frontline officers are of course the people who are the most visible face of policing, have the most challenging and varied roles, and sometimes feel that they get asked to do whatever nobody else thinks is 'in their remit'! They are also the future of policing, given that the vast majority of our future senior officers start at the constable level and rise through the ranks. Disengage them from the idea of police science and research in their first few years and we're storing up problems for a generation or more. And, of course, policing is inherently a human endeavour – even the most EBP behaviours aren't very useful if frontline officers can't be convinced to actually do them.

Drawing parallels between the medical profession and policing seems to be a useful mechanism to change thinking, with the corticosteroid randomisation after significant head injury (CRASH) research into the use of steroids for head injuries being a great example of the requirement to evaluate even those treatments we are sure work. This research is superbly summarised in 'Test, Learn, Adapt', a paper I regularly send to colleagues asking about randomised controlled trials. For decades, severe head injury in adults was treated with steroid injections. Steroids were believed to reduce brain swelling, and so reduce brain injuries. However, this was never rigorously tested and, when suggested, the randomised trial was controversial with critics suggesting it was removing a valid treatment for purely 'academic' purposes. The results, published in 2005, found that those receiving steroid injections suffered higher death rates, showing that this treatment had in fact been killing people. The trial was stopped early to prevent further deaths and clinical practice changed. Of particular note, though, is the observation: 'Despite this recommendation, a survey of US trauma centres, done 5 years after dissemination of the guidelines, found that about 50% routinely gave steroids to patients with severe traumatic brain injury.' When I explain this research to police colleagues, I always follow it with the questions: 'How many things do we do in policing that are assumed to be positive, but might actually be causing harm? How many police tactics have this level of evidence so that we can know if they are actually beneficial?'

The National Institute for Health Research sets out mechanisms to embed a research culture from which we can draw strong parallels to policing. Our frontline officers may be best thought about as those who ensure the research is done right, rather than directing it. That focus implies a wholly different set of motivations and persuasions to employ to ensure that taking part in research becomes an accepted and valued part of day-to-day policing. This may not be without considerable challenges of course. The extraordinary Restorative Justice Conference (RJC) experiments highlight some of the challenges.

A RJC is a planned and scheduled face-to-face conference in which a trained facilitator 'brings together offenders, their victims, and their respective kin and communities, in order to decide what the offender should do to repair the harm that a crime has caused'. They are in addition to any criminal justice sanction and were evaluated in the Met in 2004 and 2005 via a randomised controlled trial. The evaluation sought to understand the impact of RJCs on the trauma and stress experienced by victims as well as on the reoffending of suspects. They showed a modest but highly cost-effective reduction in repeat offending, with substantial benefits for victims including measurably reducing their levels of post-traumatic stress symptoms.

A key question for the research design was at what stage should the randomisation be conducted. The decision was made that randomisation should take place at the point at which the victim and the offender had both agreed to take part in the RJC. Methodologically this was of course correct, so that the treatment and control groups were made up of the most similar types of people possible. The issue for implementation was the disappointment to be managed when, after officers had arranged the conferences and persuaded the victims and offenders to take part, having to explain that the case had been randomly assigned to not progress.

Managing this was possible because the team of officers was very small and a great deal of time had been spent explaining why this was so necessary. Human buy-in, and statistical validity, had to work hand-in-hand, and I cannot emphasise enough the need to gain that buy-in. This has been challenging in the current evaluation of Knife Crime Prevention Orders (KCPOs) taking place in the Met. KCPOs are court orders intended to prevent people from carrying knives in London. Orders can be applied for by any officer in the Met, and our ability to gain buy-in for the randomisation process specifically for this evaluation has been limited by that large number of potential applicants. As such, the conversation has to be had when an officer has applied for a KCPO through the project team and been told 'this application is suitable but has been randomly selected for the control group so no KCPO application can be made'. As one frontline officer commented, it feels as if operational decisions are made on the basis of 'computer says no'! As experimentation becomes more embedded in policing, we will need to increase the understanding of these issues to prevent push-back from those who, through no fault of their own, haven't been exposed to the mechanisms of experimentation in the same way as most in the medical professions are. The solutions to this probably include embedding EBP in initial recruit training and through designated local leaders championing these experimental approaches (many of whom are alumni of the Cambridge Master of Studies in Applied Criminology).

EBP sits within the Met's corporate structure as an element of Organisational Learning. This incredibly broad area covers everything from giving officers the skills to conduct rapid operational debriefs, through the organisational responses to inquests, to harnessing and encouraging local innovation and problem-solving as well as what we in the SEBP think of as EBP, namely the use, production and communication of the best available evidence. EBP has progressed enormously in the Met, and one of the drivers of this has been the Organisational Learning support to the informal and entrepreneurial network of interested people who meet regularly as a Research and Evidence Based Policing Group. As well as officers and staff members, the group has representatives from the College of Policing (of which the What Works Centre for Crime Reduction is a part – see Chapter 4, this volume) as well as academic partners, and seeks to encourage interest in these areas at all levels of the organisation. A key element of this has been setting a level playing field, where the hierarchy of the organisation is minimised, and the value of evidence pushed above the opinions of individuals, regardless of their ranks. The simple mechanism of ensuring that people are referred to by their first names rather than their ranks has had a huge impact on the engagement of different groups, and the quality of the discussions had within the group, avoiding what is often referred to as 'Highest Paid Person's Opinion (HIPPO)' thinking. This challenge will exist in most organisations, but in one as hierarchical as a police service, it can be particularly pronounced. Having served in a number of high risk operational roles, the single best way to ensure higher quality decision making among groups of people, in my opinion, is to lose the rank references. If I was commissioner for a day ...

Within all the narrative about becoming more evidence-based, there is a bit of an elephant in the room, and that is the quality of the evidence. It is enormously encouraging that 'What is the evidence base?' is a much more common discussion within the Met, but there is a danger that poor evidence can be used to justify decision making, giving the decision only a thin veneer of evidence-based justification. Not all evidence is equal. The SEBP promotes the use, production and communication of the best available evidence, and sometimes no evidence – or very poor evidence – is all that exists, and this produces two issues – relying on weak evidence, and doing research that is not of the highest standard we can achieve. The science writer and former physician Ben Goldacre and others have written widely on bad evidence, and the challenge of promoting the suitable weighting of research dependent on its strength is a challenge for society in general, as well as the Met. The dangers of the small-scale survey that reports a population level finding are not, sadly, restricted to policing. However, the Met has taken a significant step towards ensuring that research conducted by or in collaboration with us is done to high ethical standards, by forming the first UK committee dedicated to policing research ethics – the Met Research Ethics Committee (MetREC).

Research ethics committees are generally thought of as having two primary functions: safeguarding research participants, and balancing the risks of research against the potential benefits, as summarised on the Met's website:

> MetREC should ensure that policies, considerations, standards and safeguards are applied appropriately and for the purpose of safeguarding the rights, dignity, welfare and safety of people participating in research.

It should ensure that any risks involved in conducting and participating in research are appropriate and proportionate to the potential benefit of the research.

Prior to the formation of MetREC, ethical considerations for research were a matter for the university (or other research organisation) with which the Met partnered when conducting the research. This posed two issues – first, the consistency and rigour of ethical review across multiple universities, but perhaps more significantly, the process for ethical review when the Met conducts research independently of a university.

To highlight the first issue, the committee has considered two research protocols that included interviewing children suspected of involvement in crime. The question posed by the committee was when the researcher would pass information to the police, disclosed to the researcher. One response was only in the cases of 'serious, preventable, future harm' while the other researchers stated that 'all information about criminality' would be passed to the police, as it was not felt to be right for the researcher to have to assess a threshold test. Both these positions were backed by well-articulated ethical standpoints, but highlight the inconsistency of approach – this now allows the Met to consider this issue more generally and propose a more general approach which the MetREC can expect researchers to adhere to, within reasonable limits.

The balance of risk versus reward is a significant consideration for the committee, and indeed the wider Met. High risk research, perhaps into inherently risky areas of policing areas such as domestic abuse policing or high risk offender management should only be conducted if the research is capable of answering the question posed – and where the methodology is appropriate to the risk. Especially when delivering research as an randomised controlled trial, there has to be an ethical justification for having a control group who receive policing as normal, and hence miss out on the new, potentially more effective, intervention. This is easily justified if the methodology will answer the question – we have a general ethical requirement to understand the impact of policing. However, if the power calculations and analytical strategy are insufficiently documented and developed, it is not possible to ascertain if this benefit could be realised through the research. To put it another way, if the Met were to think that changing policy regarding arrest in certain domestic abuse situations was beneficial for victims, then there is an ethical requirement to evaluate that properly. However, an underpowered randomised controlled trial with insufficient numbers of cases to demonstrate the expected effect would not answer the question, so does not justify the potentially beneficial 'treatment' being withheld from the control group. In these cases, an underpowered study is both more likely to conclude that the intervention works when it doesn't, and that it doesn't work when it does. It is also a waste of resources to undertake such research. MetREC is the mechanism for the Met to ensure that these considerations are robustly, and independently, considered. It also demonstrates to those inside and outside the Met that scientific evaluation of operations is important, and that quality of research is more important than quantity.

Persuading senior leaders that EBP is the way forward has taken a combination of the structural and process type approaches considered already, as well as a more transformational and persuasive approach, balancing the benefit to the individuals against the benefit to our communities. By benefit to the individual, I don't mean to suggest that policing is about personal gain, and in my experience, police officers are exceptionally driven by their vocation and values, and seek little personal gain from their careers. Rather it is about individuals not being disadvantaged through the desire to be evidence-based, compared to those who have not seen the light. To illustrate this, I give an anecdote about evaluating the impact of automatic number plate recognition (ANPR) cameras on crime, reported to me many years ago by someone whose identity is lost to memory. He had submitted a report detailing that his deployment of ANPR cameras had resulted in a staggering reduction in crime – over 80 per cent reduction across the whole borough during the operation. I rang him up to understand how we could replicate this staggering impact more widely, and asked how he ascertained the reduction. His response was that he had looked at the crime levels in the corresponding week a year previously, and seen that the lowest crime day in the week of the operation this year was 80 per cent lower than the highest crime day in the week a year ago. He genuinely didn't understand that this analysis couldn't allow him to conclude that his operation had resulted in staggering crime reductions until I explained it further. At that point, he sounded rather crushed – 'Did my operation have any impact at all then?' being his question. I had taken him from someone who could proudly tell his peers and promotion board members that he had reduced crime substantially, to someone who hoped that he had an effect. To take it a stage further, would those interviewing him for promotion (perhaps with the same understanding of evaluating impact as him) be more impressed with the 80 per cent reduction or the 'I hope it achieved something'?

This is at the core of my point about individual benefit – really well evidenced measures of impact are far smaller than those which are often cited in the Met. An experiment reported in 2020 (Wood et al, 2020) found that giving officers in Chicago training in procedural justice principles reduced complaints made against them by 10 per cent and officer use of force by 6.4 per cent over two year. The training

> emphasised the importance of voice, neutrality, respect, and trustworthiness in policing actions. Officers were encouraged to provide opportunities for civilians to state and explain their case before making a decision, apply consistent and explicable rules-based decision-making, treat civilians with dignity and respect their status as community members, and demonstrate willingness to act in the interests of the community and with responsiveness to civilians' concerns.

This experiment showing a reduction between control and treatment of 10 per cent is considered a big impact by EBP practitioners. However, for those used to claiming big impacts (like our ANPR friend), 10 per cent seems a small impact. It has taken me a long time to get the Chicago experiment acted upon in the Met, precisely because the impact is perceived as low by those who are used to providing reductions of 40 per cent plus to senior officers and promotion boards, based on less rigorous evaluation. Interestingly, the traction with the Chicago experiment came from a group of practitioners who had recognised that procedural justice was important, and were then slightly disappointed by the potential impact when shown the Chicago results. This overstating of impact is often not intentionally dishonest, but rather is a lack of knowledge driven by an enormous desire to make people in London safer, and to have a big impact. These are honourable intentions, and the landing of evidence-based practice has to carefully augment these desires, not ride roughshod over previous measures of impact.

Two mechanisms I have created inside the Met have helped with this understanding of reasonable evaluation – the Research and Evidence Based Policing group discussed earlier, and the Universities at the Met seminars. These seminars ran monthly until COVID-19 hit us, and researchers from a range of universities very generously presented research findings to captivated audiences at New Scotland Yard. The presentation of research findings, from operational delivery inside police forces, was transformational in the understanding of audience members about how this work is actually better thought of as really good performance management, rather than 'purely academic' research. Presentations included predicting and preventing knife injuries, ethnographic research into the policing of the Notting Hill Carnival, the impact of diversion schemes in custody, legitimacy and support for policing in London and many more. I'm enormously grateful to all the speakers for spearheading this 'invasion of the police' by academics and I look forward to restarting the series when possible – sign up to www.sebp.police.uk if you want to be updated.

18

Conclusion

Jonathan Breckon and Michael Sanders

Introduction

Over the last few hundred pages, this book has tried to offer a whistle-stop tour of the What Works agenda – how it came to be, what it has achieved to date, where it has struggled and where it can – and must – go in the future.

We do not intend to rehash the various points made throughout the book in our own words in our summation. Instead, we focus on two things: our tips for starting a new What Works Centre, based on what has been learned both from our own experience and from that of the authors of the book's chapters; and our recommendations for those leading the network to see it thrive into the future.

Top tips for new centres

So, you've decided to launch a new What Works Centre – now what?

Carts and horses

Your centre is probably starting in a unique position – so you won't want to copy exactly what one of the other centres has done wholesale. Nonetheless, you need to know what that unique position *is*, and work out what needs to be done first.

If you're lucky enough to be leading a financially solvent centre, then you have options about where to begin – with your engagement with policy makers or practitioners – with generating new evidence – with synthesising what is already known. And (especially if you're a solvent centre), you'll have no shortage of people telling you *which option* is most important – usually the one that they specialise in.

Building a relationship with your stakeholders and your sector is important, but isn't a good idea if you have no evidence to show them. Building up an appetite for high-quality evidence, only to let people know that it's half a decade away, is unlikely to win you many fans. Equally, if there's no primary research – like randomised controlled trials and quasi-experimental designs – in your area, commissioning a large number of systematic reviews will only tell you that there's no primary research in your area – which you probably already knew. However, if there are a large number of randomised controlled trials already in your area – as is the case, for example, for parenting programmes – then synthesis followed by rapid communication could be exactly the right thing to do.

Standards of evidence and rigour

What Works Centres are unusual and their place in the evidence ecosystem – not part of government, not part of a university (mostly) and focused, for the most part, on questions of impact – is something to be guarded. There can be a temptation, particularly in areas with sparse existing research, to lower our standards, or to disproportionately concern ourselves with questions other than 'what works'. There are other questions that are important, and the methodological pluralism of the What Works Network is, by and large, a good thing – but we can't lose track of the fact that finding out 'what works' is our core agenda. For us, finding out that something is implemented well, or received well, or anything else, is of secondary importance. To put it bluntly, if an intervention didn't work, then it doesn't really matter to us if people liked it. If an intervention wasn't implemented well during the trial, leading to the conclusion that it didn't work – why should we have any confidence that it would be implemented well *outside* of the trial?

Similarly, we must be fairly strict on our standards of evidence. Small, qualitative studies are valuable, pre–post evaluations can tell us something about what's happening – but they can't give us causality, at least not reliably – and so we shouldn't either pretend that they do, or sit quietly when others make similar claims. We cannot stand up for good evidence only when it is comfortable.

Be relentlessly practical

Just because we need to hold people to a high standard of evidence, doesn't mean we can't be practically minded. Most centres' stakeholders – whether they're government officials or frontline social workers – are comfortable with ambiguity, and surprisingly accepting (in our experience) of caveats around results – as long as the caveats aren't the only thing they're going to get from us.

We need to think when we're communicating our results about what the audience needs to take away. If there's no effect of a promising but expensive intervention, say this – if the evidence is overwhelmingly positive, say that. If, as is more common, the evidence is mixed, put forward a balanced but clear view – what would you do if you were in the decision-maker's chair, and you needed to make a choice about whether to scale up this, or something else?

This focus on practicality needs to start *way* before we're talking about our findings, but at the very inception of the project. We need to ask ourselves 'Who will this be useful for, and what decision(s) will it help them to make?' – if the answer is unclear, we should walk away from a project. This can be hard – many people working in centres came up through an academic career path where the questions might be 'Does this interest me?' or 'Will this publish well?'. A successful What Works Centre needs to put these questions aside. Our interests are not important, and the views of reviewers at journals that officials and practitioners can't access and wouldn't read even if they could can be safely disregarded.

Listen – and think

On the other hand, the views of the people you're working with, and trying to help, should play a central role in your decision making. When working at What Works for Children's Social Care, the insight that we got from young people, from parents and foster carers, from social workers up and down the country – and from senior leaders in local and national government – were invaluable in setting our research agenda, leading to greater focus on young people's mental health, and on the risk of homelessness for young people with a social worker – as well as the national policy agenda round reducing the number of young people entering care. By listening, the work we did was made more impactful.

Listening isn't enough, however – you also have to think. You need to recognise the value of each group's opinions, but recognise that they come from a particular perspective. Collecting and assembling multiple views is the only way to get a clear picture of the landscape. Even with this being done, there is still thinking to do. People interacting with services, practitioners and officials all have their lives to live and their jobs to do – and so do you. There is huge amounts of positive support from students, parents and teachers for the idea of lowering class sizes (for other policy areas substitute 'caseloads', 'bobbies on the beat', and so on). Your job isn't, therefore, to divert the full resources of your centre towards that one idea which emerges as a consensus from everyone you speak to. Most leaders would love smaller class sizes but achieving it *is* hard, even with massive national attention on teacher recruitment and retention. The benefits are also (based on the best evidence), fairly modest relative to the cost. You need to think about what can be evaluated (and how), and what will get traction with people with the power to make the change.

Everyone needs to do their own jobs – and as someone running a What Works Centre, yours is to produce and promote the best possible, most impactful evidence possible, given the cards you've been dealt. Good luck to you.

Recommendations for the future

The previous section has described our 'top tips' for setting up a new What Works Centre, putting the onus on potential funders and the founding team of new centres. We now turn to those stewarding the existing network – and championing the cause of 'what works' across government.

Data

We opened our introduction with a quote from the Nobel Laureate Richard Thaler – '[W]e cannot do evidence based policy without evidence'. We would add to this that 'We cannot do evidence without data'. What Works Centres are able to be most successful when it is easy to measure the outcomes they care about. The Education Endowment Foundation's biggest asset may not be their endowment, but in fact the sheer volume of education data that exists in England, and the fact that it is accessible to researchers. Not all Education Endowment Foundation trials use administrative data, of course – many use standardised, or even quite bespoke tests, targeting a particular outcome, or a particular age group of young people where national level data don't exist (for example for younger children) – but where administrative data can be used, it can dramatically reduce the cost of running trials, and provide policy makers with an outcome that they understand and are interested in.

The UK government has supported, either internally or externally, a number of similar datasets – the hospital episode statistics dataset, information on general-practitioner-level prescribing of individual drugs; the Ministry of Justice's DataLab to give a few examples – but more could be done first to collect more meaningful data as standard – for example on measures of wellbeing or other issues of quality of life – and second, to make that data accessible, if not publicly, then to researchers conducting trials. Given that trials require consent from their participants, there is nothing to stop adding permission to access relevant datasets to this process – if only we know what the datasets are, and what we need to do to access them.

A strategic approach to new centres

The What Works Centres have largely come into existence independently of each other (with the exception of the first tranche of centres established after the National Institute for Clinical Evidence and the Education Endowment Foundation), often in response to a minister's agenda. As such, the topography of the What Works Network makes for curious observation.

There are centres for higher and mainstream education, but not for further education – something that the Social Mobility Commission, among others, have recommended be rectified, and despite further education settings catering to a disproportionately less fortunate cohort of students, including those from poorer families, those with experience of social care, and adult learners.

There is a centre for crime reduction, which does not have sufficient budget to fund many large-scale trials, and a centre for reducing serious youth violence (a subset of all crime), with a substantial endowment. Even among the affluent centres, the specific sizes of endowments are out of kilter with the size of the challenge faced – all children will go through education, and the vast majority will want jobs. Serious violence, while awful, is nowhere near this ubiquitous.

What is done is done. Instead of re-arbitrating the past, the government and other funders have the opportunity to consider new centres strategically. While reluctant to create another framework, one that we have found useful in prioritising projects within a single What Works Centre might be usefully applied here to the meta question. This approach encourages us to focus on the 'three Ms';

- Many – how many people are affected by a policy area?
- Misery – when people experience negative outcomes (or fail to experience positive ones) how bad is it?
- Money – how much do government and others spend on this?

There are some policy areas where all three Ms apply – we might think about climate change, for example – but we needn't meet all three to consider an area worth building an evidence base. The promise of early intervention is that by intervening fairly broadly, and early, we can prevent a lot of misery and cost to a relatively small number of people. Similarly, youth violence does not affect a huge number of people, but every time a child loses their life prematurely, it is an unspeakable tragedy. Any approach to developing new centres should focus on a triangulation of the three Ms.

Initiatives – not centres

The spread of the What Works movement across many policy domains is undoubtedly (to our minds at least) a positive thing for the world. However, it does not necessarily follow that every issue should have a What Works Centre of its own, even if it meets one or more of the three Ms.

Consider, for example, one of the greatest social issues of our time, and the topic of one of the chapters of this book – inequality. Inequality is an issue which causes a lot of misery to a lot of people, and its economic consequences are as profound as its social ones. Nonetheless, inequality is also, as has been described, a many-headed beast. Any 'What Works Centre for Equality', would quite naturally focus on education, employment and health. If focusing on racial inequality, it might focus more on policing; if gender, on economic growth; and if sexual and gender identities, on mental health or homelessness. Inequality is a problem that exists for all What Works Centres, in the policy areas where we try to effect change; in the research we conduct and commission, and in the makeup of our own organisations.

We might also think about a different kind of policy area – Levelling Up. As we write this in October of 2022, the Levelling Up Agenda has been a major part of the UK government's economic plan under now former Prime Minister Boris Johnson. This agenda is focused particularly around increasing economic opportunity and growth in what are known as 'red wall' seats, claimed by the Conservative Party from the Labour Party at the 2019 general election. Much energy has been spent in the last two years in trying to drive this agenda forward. However, in the first weeks of a new administration under Prime Minister Liz Truss, it seems to have been downrated in favour of a very different growth agenda focused more on tax cuts and less on investment in reducing regional inequalities. While the department that bears its name still exists, it seems likely to have much of a future – just as George Osborne's 'Northern Powerhouse' did not survive the transition to the Conservative government of Theresa May – a handover of power within the same party and maintaining the same MPs. We might similarly think of David Cameron's 'Big Society' agenda, which was a substantial interest of the Cabinet

Office for several years but is now rarely spoken about. This is not to say that these issues are not important, but we must recognise that they are at least somewhat transitory, at least in terms of the terminology used.

These two areas – inequality and transitory policy agendas – are very different – but we'd propose that they have a common solution in the What Works movement – Initiatives. A 'What Works Initiative' could be established as a partnership between existing centres and partners with expertise in the specific domain. For example, multiple What Works Centres could work together on the challenge of inequality, each seconding staff from their core centres to work on the initiative for duration of its funding, while also drawing in experts on the various facets of inequality. This initiative would need its own funding, but this could be time-limited, and/or on a core costs basis only – the initiative would then use its coexistence with relevant What Works Centres, government officials and sector bodies to increase the focus – and research resource – going on in their area. For something transitory like Levelling Up, an initiative could be funded for the duration of a Spending Review period, or even the length of a parliament, drawing together expertise – in this case perhaps from the What Works Centre for Local Economic Growth, Youth Futures Foundation, and Education Endowment Foundation – as well as experts from Local Enterprise Partnerships, or others to ensure relevance to the specific areas that 'Levelling Up' is focused on – which might be very different from other similar initiatives.

Collaboration

Our final recommendation is a plea for more cooperation between What Works Centres. We take the point that 'collaboration for collaboration's sake' is not desirable, and may even be counterproductive. There is little space for collaboration between the Early Intervention Foundation and the Centre for Ageing Better.

However, collaboration between centres is both sensible from a financial point of view (how many different trials or systematic reviews including Triple P or multi-systemic therapy do we need?), and increasingly reflects the way that professionals at the frontline are expected to behave – especially when working with young people.

If a child is experiencing criminal exploitation, a multi-agency team, including teachers, police, social workers and others will be deployed to try and support the child and their parents/carers to support them. Successive reviews have encouraged greater collaboration between services at a local level, and many local areas have embarked on this by themselves. A dream future for those of us whose dreams revolve mostly around the use of evidence would see a police officer, a social worker, a teacher, a nurse, a youth worker and other professionals gathered around a table working out how best to support a child and their family. All of them would have a series of evidence-based interventions at their fingertips, rigorously tested and ready to deploy. This world cannot work if each profession speaks about evidence in a different language. Yet, this is the future we risk creating. How is an intervention that increases attainment by two months' progress in maths, to be compared to one that reduces entry to care by one percentage point? How many College of Policing strength circles is worth an Education Endowment Foundation padlock?

Trials that look at multiple outcomes, shared by different What Works Centres, run an obvious statistical challenge to the principle of statistical parsimony which is a core methodological tenet for many trialists. But only looking at one facet of an individual's life, and treating them as though the rest of their context is a mere abstraction to be randomised away, poses its own ethical as well as practical challenges. A shared set of evidence standards might be confusing, and risks the independence of individual centres by holding them in thrall to some central rulebook.

These problems are not trivial, and they will not be easy to overcome. But there is much value in overcoming them – and without doing so, it is unclear whether the promise of evidence-based policy making can ever be achieved. Collaboration not just on individual projects or funding rounds (although the increase in both of these is encouraging), but at the root and branch of the work of What Works Centres – from inception to dissemination – is the only way it will be realised. And, to echo our introduction once again, we must choose to do these things not because they are easy, but because they are hard.

Index

References to figures appear in *italic* type; those in **bold** type refer to tables.